EDINBURGH

THE MINI ROUGH GUIDE

KT-443-574

There are more than one hundred and fifty
Rough Guide travel, phrasebook and music titles,
covering destinations from Amsterdam to Zimbabwe,
languages from Czech to Thai, and musics from
World to Opera and Jazz

Forthcoming titles include

Croatia • Cuba • Las Vegas
Rome • Switzerland

Rough Guides on the Internet

www.roughguides.com

Rough Guide Credits

Text editor: Ruth Blackmore
Series editor: Mark Ellingham
Proofreading: Russell Walton
Typesetting: Helen Ostick, Link Hall
Cartography: Maxine Repath

Publishing Information

This second edition published March 2000 by
Rough Guides Ltd, 62–70 Shorts Gardens, London WC2H 9AB

Distributed by the Penguin Group:
Penguin Books Ltd, 27 Wrights Lane, London W8 5TZ
Penguin Books USA Inc., 375 Hudson Street, New York 10014, USA
Penguin Books Australia Ltd, 487 Maroondah Highway,
PO Box 257, Ringwood, Victoria 3134, Australia
Penguin Books Canada Ltd, 10 Alcorn Avenue,
Toronto, Ontario, Canada M4V 1E4
Penguin Books (NZ) Ltd, 182–190 Wairau Road,
Auckland 10, New Zealand

Typeset in Bembo and Helvetica to an original design by Henry Iles.
Printed in Spain by Graphy Cems.

ISBN 1-85828-505-4

The publishers and authors have done their best to
ensure the accuracy and currency of all the information
in *The Rough Guide to Edinburgh*. However, they can
accept no responsibility for any loss, injury or
inconvenience sustained by any traveller as a result of
information or advice contained in the guide.

EDINBURGH

THE MINI ROUGH GUIDE

by Donald Reid

with additional research by Julian Ward,
Gordon MacLachlan and Ellie Buchanan

We set out to do something different when the first Rough Guide was published in 1982. Mark Ellingham, just out of university, was travelling in Greece. He brought along the popular guides of the day, but found they were all lacking in some way. They were either strong on ruins and museums but went on for pages without mentioning a beach or taverna. Or they were so conscious of the need to save money that they lost sight of Greece's cultural and historical significance. Also, none of the books told him anything about Greece's contemporary life – its politics, its culture, its people, and how they lived.

So with no job in prospect, Mark decided to write his own guidebook, one which aimed to provide practical information that was second to none, detailing the best beaches and the hottest clubs and restaurants, while also giving hard-hitting accounts of every sight, both famous and obscure, and providing up-to-the-minute information on contemporary culture. It was a guide that encouraged independent travellers to find the best of Greece, and was a great success, getting shortlisted for the Thomas Cook travel guide award, and encouraging Mark, along with three friends, to expand the series.

The Rough Guide list grew rapidly and the letters flooded in, indicating a much broader readership than had been anticipated, but one which uniformly appreciated the Rough Guide mix of practical detail and humour, irreverence and enthusiasm. Things haven't changed. The same four friends who began the series are still the caretakers of the Rough Guide mission today: to provide the most reliable, up-to-date and entertaining information to independent-minded travellers of all ages, on all budgets.

We now publish more than 150 titles and have offices in London and New York. The travel guides are written and researched by a dedicated team of more than 100 authors, based in Britain, Europe, the USA and Australia. We have also created a unique series of phrasebooks to accompany the travel series, along with an acclaimed series of music guides, and a best-selling pocket guide to the Internet and World Wide Web. We also publish comprehensive travel information on our Web site: **www.roughguides.com**

The Author

Donald Reid was born and brought up in Glasgow, studied law at Edinburgh University and left the country soon afterwards to avoid the threat of an office. Having worked on an island in the Caribbean and as a trawler fisherman in Australia, he floated into Cape Town on the eve of the South African elections in 1993 and took a notion to hang around, working on books, magazines and newspapers in Southern Africa for the next three years. He returned to Scotland and now lives in Edinburgh working as a freelance writer and editor. He is co-author of the Rough Guides to South Africa, Scotland and The Scottish Highlands and Islands.

Acknowledgements

The author would like to thank all those who smoothed the way with information, assistance, opinions, good leads, meals, coffees, ideas and enthusiasm, including Jenni Steele and Edinburgh & Lothians Tourist Board, Neil Campbell, Peter Collingridge, the National Trust for Scotland and Historic Scotland, as well as Mo and all my friends who have helped me through it. Thanks also to Ellie, Rob, Paul and Helena for their contributions, all involved at Rough Guides for their support, and Ruth, for her patience and efforts in bringing the book together.

Help Us Update

We've gone to a lot of effort to ensure that this second edition of *The Rough Guide to Edinburgh* is as up-to-date and accurate as possible. However, if you feel there are places we've underrated or overpraised, or find we've missed something good or covered something which has now gone, then please write: suggestions, comments or corrections are much appreciated.

We'll credit all contributions, and send a copy of the next edition (or any other Rough Guide if you prefer) for the best letters. Please mark letters: "Rough Guide Edinburgh Update" and send to:

Rough Guides, 62–70 Shorts Gardens, London WC2H 9AB, or
Rough Guides, 375 Hudson St, New York, NY 10014.

Or send email to: mail@roughguides.co.uk
Online updates about this book can be found on
Rough Guides' Web site (see p.iv)

Readers' letters and emails

Thanks to all the readers who have taken the time to write in or email us with comments and suggestions:

Alan Thwaite, Carole Gray & Jane Thompson, Alice Lear, Richard D. Lysons, Louise Fournier and Roger Simard, Claire Stolk, Peter Richards, David Crerar & Julia Lawn, Lynne Kopac, Carolyn Ellenberger, Susan Bartlett Weber, G. Tite, David Wood, Amanda Wood, Morris Paton, Geoff Wilmott, Lisa Stewart.

CONTENTS

Introduction

Perched on a series of extinct volcanoes and rocky crags which rise from the generally flat landscape of the Lothians, **Edinburgh** enjoys a natural setting unrivalled by any other major European city. One native author of genius, Robert Louis Stevenson, declared that "No situation could be more commanding for the head of a kingdom; none better chosen for noble prospects".

At the heart of the city lie the **Old Town** and **New Town**, both inscribed on UNESCO's World Heritage List. The former, perched on the ridge leading down from the majestic cliff-girt Castle, is tightly packed, brooding and still predominantly medieval; the latter, with its Georgian terraces and Grecian architecture, is a planning masterpiece of the Age of Enlightenment, when Edinburgh took the lead in many fields of intellectual endeavour. Between them they contain most of the main sights, as well as a large section of the city's business and shopping sector. Over the last hundred and fifty years Edinburgh has expanded considerably from its historic core, but it isn't a very built-up city and boasts a marvellous range of parks and green spaces, as well as a seemingly inexhaustible supply of surprising and dramatic vistas.

The return of the **Scottish Parliament** to Edinburgh in 1999, after Scotland was ruled for nearly three hundred years from London, has lent renewed vigour to the city's political, business and cultural scene. While Edinburgh never lost the style, appearance and trappings of a capital city, with its concentration of museums, galleries, historic buildings and national institutions, for many its self-importance rang hollow. Now, however, the city is taking the opportunity to prove itself a dynamic, influential and thoroughly modern European capital. The recent opening of an important new **National Museum** and various ambitious tourist attractions has also contributed to the upturn in the vitality and spirit of the city.

One event that has been in rude health for many years is the remarkable **Edinburgh Festival**, the world's largest arts festival, held each August, when every conceivable performance space, from large concert halls to tiny pubs, are roped into use for a bewildering array of drama, comedy, music, film and performance. Around a million visitors flock to the city for the Festival, generating a carnival atmosphere which is absent – save for the boisterous celebrations centred on Hogmanay – for the remaining eleven months of the calendar. Nonetheless, Edinburgh maintains a vibrant **cultural life** throughout the year, with a wide variety of theatre, live music and literary and artistic events. Among the city's many galleries, the National Gallery of Scotland boasts as choice a collection of Old Masters as can be found anywhere; its offshoot, the Scottish National Gallery of Modern Art, has Britain's oldest specialist collection of twentieth-century painting and sculpture.

The city also has a superb range of **restaurants** offering most leading international cuisines, as well as a thriving café culture. Its distinctive *howffs* (pubs), allied to its brewing and distilling traditions, have given it the status of a great **drinking** city, and the presence of three universities, plus several colleges, means that there is a youthful presence for most of the year – a welcome corrective to the stuffiness which is often regarded as Edinburgh's Achilles heel.

Edinburgh's climate and when to visit

Edinburgh's **climate** is typically British, with damp, cold conditions threatening on all but rare days of sparkling summer sunshine. Situated on the east coast of Scotland, Edinburgh suffers less rainfall than western parts of the country, but is prone to blustery and often bitter winds blowing in off the North Sea. Another local phenomenon is the *haar* or sea mist, which is wont to roll in from the Firth of Forth and envelop the city after a few warm days in summer. The coldest months are January and February, when the highest daily temperature averages at 6°C (42°F) and overnight frosts are common. July is the warmest month, reaching an average high of 18°C (65°F), although late spring (May) and early autumn (September) are often good times to visit for welcome spells of bright weather and less of

	°F Average daily		°C Average daily		Rainfall Average monthly	
	MAX	MIN	MAX	MIN	IN	MM
Jan	42	34	6	1	2.2	57
Feb	43	34	6	1	1.5	39
March	46	36	8	2	1.5	39
April	51	39	11	4	1.5	39
May	56	43	14	6	2.1	54
June	62	49	17	9	1.9	47
July	65	52	18	11	3.3	83
Aug	64	52	18	11	3.0	77
Sept	60	49	16	9	2.2	57
Oct	54	44	12	7	2.6	65
Nov	48	39	9	4	2.4	62
Dec	44	36	7	2	2.2	57

the tourist scrum which marks the Royal Mile in high season. With the Festival in full swing, August is a great time to visit the city, but be prepared for large crowds, scarce accommodation and busy restaurants.

THE GUIDE

Introducing the city

Spread out over seven hills and stretching towards the Firth of Forth in the north and the Lothians in the south, **Edinburgh** occupies a large area relative to its population, which numbers less than half a million. Most of the city's sights and attractions, however, are concentrated in the centre and are easily explored on foot, though be prepared for punishing inclines and steep flights of stairs.

From whichever direction you enter the city centre, it is undeniably **Edinburgh Castle** on its crag which draws the eye. Still a working castle with a garrison of soldiers and a gun fired daily at 1pm, it is the home of two of Scotland's most potent symbols of nationhood, the Honours of Scotland (crown jewels), and the Stone of Destiny. From the Castle, Scotland's most famous street, the **Royal Mile**, runs west to east through the heart of the medieval **Old Town** past the Assembly Hall, the temporary home of the newly re-established **Scottish Parliament**, and medieval **St Giles**, the nearest there is to a principal church in the Scots Kirk's rigorously egalitarian framework. Running off the main street are numerous cobbled wynds (narrow lanes) and tightly packed closes associated with Edinburgh's underworld lore, in particular the schizophrenic Deacon Brodie, the inspiration for Robert Louis Stevenson's *Dr Jekyll & Mr Hyde*, and the body snatchers Burke and Hare.

The Royal Mile ends at the **Palace of Holyroodhouse**, which maintains its historic function as the monarch's Scottish residence. Immediately opposite the palace sprawls a large building site, the location of the **new Scottish Parliament**, due to be completed in 2002. South of the Royal Mile, the district is less medieval in character, but retains some impressive individual buildings, including the **Old College** of the University, a late masterpiece of Robert Adam; the splendid Venetian-style *palazzo* that houses the **Royal Museum of Scotland**; and the spectacular new **National Museum of Scotland** next door, a fusion of vernacular and modern styles in honey-coloured sandstone.

Immediately to the north of Edinburgh's Old Town and divided from it by Princes Street Gardens, lies the **New Town**. Running parallel to the Royal Mile, the New Town's main thoroughfare, **Princes Street**, offers wonderful views of the Old Town skyline, while unexpected vistas of the Firth of Forth open out from the elevated streets to the north. There are many magnificent Neoclassical set pieces here, notably Adam's **Register House** and **Charlotte Square**, the various Grecian edifices atop **Calton Hill**, and William Henry Playfair's **Royal Scottish Academy** and **National Gallery of Scotland**. The last of these houses a very impressive collection of European masterpieces, and has two engaging outstations elsewhere in the New Town in the **Scottish National Portrait Gallery** and the **Scottish National Gallery of Modern Art**, Britain's oldest specialist collection of twentieth-century painting and sculpture.

To the northwest of the New Town lies the most happening suburb of the city, **Leith**, the historic port of Edinburgh, where, in recent years, old warehouses have been converted into yuppie flats and a lively restaurant scene has emerged. Permanently docked in Leith and open to the public is the former **Royal Yacht Britannia**, while another grande dame of Scotland's engineering heritage, the **Forth Rail Bridge** across the Firth of Forth, is a spectacular sight best viewed from the water or by walking across the parallel road bridge from **South Queensferry**, another of Edinburgh's suburbs.

A tantalizing sample of the wild beauty of Scotland's scenery can be had in **Holyrood Park**, an extensive area of open countryside just beyond Holyrood Palace in the very heart of the city, dominated by the highest and most impressive of Edinburgh's volcanoes, **Arthur's Seat**. Very different in character are the manicured **Royal Botanic Garden**, to the north of the New Town, and **Edinburgh Zoo**, set on a hillside in the western part of the city.

ARRIVAL

Edinburgh International Airport (℗0131/333 1000) is at Turnhouse, seven miles west of the city centre, close to the start of the M8 motorway to Glasgow. Regular shuttle buses connect to Waverley Station in the town centre: both Guide Friday's Airbus Express (£3.60) and LRT's Airline service (£3) leave every 15–20 minutes throughout the day and take just under half an hour to get into town. Taxis charge around £14 for the same journey.

Waverley Station (timetable and fare enquiries ℗0345/484950), right in the centre of town at the eastern end of Princes Street, is the terminus for all mainline **trains**. All lines west and north are also served by Haymarket Station at the junction of Dalry Road and Haymarket Terrace in the west end of the city.

The main intercity **bus terminal** is located on St Andrew Square, a few minutes' walk from Waverley Station. One of the major local bus companies, First Edinburgh, has a shop at the southeastern corner of the station (Mon–Fri

ARRIVAL

8.40am–5pm, Sat 9am–5pm; ☎0131/557 5061), where timetables are kept and tickets sold for a number of the local bus operators, as well as for Citylink and National Express intercity buses.

INFORMATION AND MAPS

Edinburgh's main **tourist office** is at the top of Princes Mall, on Princes Street near the northern entrance to the station (July Mon–Fri 9am–6pm, Sat 9am–5.30pm, Sun 9.30am–5pm; Aug Mon–Fri 9am–7pm, Sat 9am–6pm, Sun 9am–5pm; rest of year Mon–Fri 9am–5.30pm, Sat 9am–4.30pm, Sun 9.30am–2.30pm; ☎0131/473 3800). There's also a much smaller **branch** at the airport (daily: April–Oct 6.30am–10.30pm; Nov–March 7.30am–9.30pm). As well as providing an accommodation reservation service and currency exchange, they also stock various publications, including the excellent fortnightly **listings** magazine, *The List*, which costs £1.95 and provides coverage of the arts in Edinburgh and Glasgow, as well as comprehensive listings of forthcoming events. For more backpacker-related information head to the **Haggis Office** at 60 High St (daily 9am–6pm; ☎0131/557 9393). Although they'll try and sell their minibus tours of Scotland to you, they're a good source of general information about the backpacker scene in Scotland, and you can book both SYHA and independent hostels in Edinburgh from here. The best **maps** of the wider city are Bartholomew's *Streetfinder Colour Atlas* or fold-out *Colour Map* (both £2.99).

TRANSPORT

The best way to get around Edinburgh's compact centre is on foot. Getting around by **car** or **bus** is notoriously problematic: traffic jams are commonplace and finding a parking place is difficult. If you're travelling between the centre and the suburbs, a bus is your best bet, though one or two suburbs to the east and northwest are served by suburban train lines. **Taxis** are common and useful when you're in a hurry or later at night, while a **bike** can be a handy way of getting around, though the prevalence of hills and cobbled streets means that the ride isn't always smooth.

Buses

Edinburgh is well served by **buses**, although even locals get confused by the number of companies offering competing services along similar routes. Lothian Regional Transport (LRT) provides the most comprehensive service and its maroon buses are easily recognizable; all buses referred to in the text are run by them unless otherwise stated. You can buy your ticket on board; the most common fare is 70p – be sure to have the correct change. A good investment, especially if you're staying a long way out or want to explore the suburbs, is the £10.50 pass allowing a week's unlimited travel on LRT buses (passport photo needed). You can also buy an LRT day-pass for £2.40 (£4.20 including the airport service). Timetables and **passes** for LRT services are available from most newsagents and at the ticket centres on Waverley Bridge (May–Oct Mon–Sat 8am–7pm, Sun 9am–4.30pm; Nov–April Mon–Fri 9am–4.30pm; ✆0131/554 4494) or 27 Hanover St (Mon–Sat 8.30am–6.00pm).

The green buses run by Eastern Scottish/First Bus, and the green and yellow buses of Lowland Scottish/First Bus, link the capital with outlying towns and villages. Most services depart from and terminate at the St Andrew Square bus station. For longer journeys contact the National

Express booking office in the St Andrew Square bus station: for journeys within Scotland, ring ℗0990/505050, for cross-border travel, ring ℗0990/808080. National Express tickets are also sold at the First Edinburgh shop (see p.5), in the bus station.

Sightseeing tours

Of the guided tours available, the best are Guide Friday (℗0131/556 2244) **bus tours**. Their open-top buses depart from Waverley Bridge and cruise through the city streets, allowing you to get on and off at leisure. Tickets cost around £7.50.

Various companies offer guided **walking tours** of the city by day and night. Robin's Tours (℗0131/225 6593) run a Grand Tour which takes in both the Old and New Towns, departing at 10am each day from the tourist information centre. Mercat Tours (℗0131/225 6591), which leave from beside the Mercat Cross on High Street, lead groups along the Royal Mile at regular intervals throughout the day, while their evening "Ghost and Ghoul" tours (daily: April–Sept 7pm & 8pm; Oct–March 8pm), conducted by a costumed guide, visit some of the city's haunted nooks and crannies. A more entertaining and light-hearted version of the ghost tour is run by Witchery Tours (daily 7–10pm; booking essential ℗0131/225 6745) from outside the *Witchery Restaurant* at 352 Castlehill, Royal Mile. If you want something a bit more down to earth you might join one of Geowalks' guided hikes up Arthur's Seat, led by a qualified geologist (℗0131/228 2410).

For a bird's-eye view of the city, Forth Helicopter Services, Edinburgh Airport (℗0131/339 8877), runs spectacular **aerial sightseeing trips** of the city for £29 per person (10min), or £45 including the Forth Bridges (15min).

Taxis

The city has plenty of **taxi** ranks, especially around Waverley Bridge, and it's also relatively easy to hail a black cab on the street. Fares are around £2.50 for the first mile and £1.50 for each mile thereafter. The phone numbers of the main local cab companies are: Capital Castle Cabs (℗0131/228 2555), Central Radio Taxis (℗0131/229 2468) and City Cabs (℗0131/228 1211).

Cars

It is emphatically *not* a good idea to take a **car** into central Edinburgh: despite the presence of several multistorey car parks, looking for somewhere to park usually involves long, fruitless searches. Traffic calming measures have been introduced in several key areas – Princes Street is now one-way for cars and Charlotte Square has adopted a complicated traffic-flow system – and there is a growing network of green-painted bus lanes called "Greenways", which must be left clear during rush hours. Most ticket and parking-meter regulations operate from 9am to 6.30pm Monday to Friday, and from 9am to 1.30pm on Saturday.

Bicycles

Thanks to a good network of cycle paths, Edinburgh is a reasonably cycle-friendly city – although hilly. The local cycling action group, Spokes (℗ 0131/313 2114) publishes an excellent cycle map of the city, which can be picked up at most cycle shops. **Bicycles** are available for rent from Central Cycles, 13 Lochrin Place (℗ 0131/228 6333), or Scottish Cycle Safaris, 29 Blackfriars St (℗ 0131/556 5560), which stocks everything from old boneshakers to state-of-the-art mountain bikes, along with accessories such as panniers and child seats.

TAXIS, CARS, BICYCLES

Edinburgh Castle

The imposing bulk of **Edinburgh Castle** dominates the skyline of the entire city from atop its volcanic crag. With formidable sheer rockfaces on three sides, it requires no great imaginative feat to comprehend the strategic importance that underpinned the Castle's, and hence Edinburgh's, pre-eminence within Scotland. Would-be attackers, like modern tourists, were forced to approach the Castle from the crag to the east, along which the Royal Mile runs down to Holyrood.

The Castle's disparate styles reflect its many changes in usage, as well as advances in military architecture: the oldest surviving part, **St Margaret's Chapel**, is from the twelfth century, while the most recent additions date back to the 1920s. Nothing remains from its period as a seat of the Scottish court in the reign of Malcolm III (the king who overthrew Macbeth in 1057) and there are only very few traces of the fortifications built during the Castle's most turbulent period, the Wars of Independence. Indeed, having been lost to, and subsequently recaptured from, the English on several occasions, the defences were dismantled by the Scots themselves in 1313, and only rebuilt in 1356, when the return of King David II from captivity in England introduced a modicum of political stability. Thereafter, the fortress gradually developed into Scotland's premier castle,

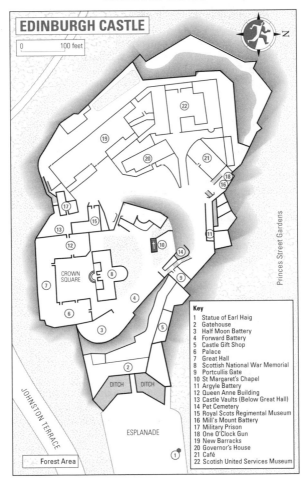

EDINBURGH CASTLE

0   100 feet

N

Princes Street Gardens

CROWN SQUARE

DITCH   DITCH

JOHNSTON TERRACE

ESPLANADE

Forest Area

Key
1. Statue of Earl Haig
2. Gatehouse
3. Half Moon Battery
4. Forward Battery
5. Castle Gift Shop
6. Palace
7. Great Hall
8. Scottish National War Memorial
9. Portcullis Gate
10. St Margaret's Chapel
11. Argyle Battery
12. Queen Anne Building
13. Castle Vaults (Below Great Hall)
14. Pet Cemetery
15. Royal Scots Regimental Museum
16. Mill's Mount Battery
17. Military Prison
18. One O'Clock Gun
19. New Barracks
20. Governor's House
21. Café
22. Scottish United Services Museum

with the dual function of fortress and royal palace. It last saw action in 1745, when the Young Pretender's forces, fresh from their victory at Prestonpans, made a half-hearted attempt to storm it. Subsequently, advances in weapon technology diminished the Castle's importance, but under the influence of the Romantic movement it came to be seen as a great national monument. A grandiose "improvement" scheme, which would have transformed the Castle into a bloated nineteenth-century vision of the Middle Ages, was considered, but only a few elements of the scheme, such as the present Gatehouse, were actually built.

Today, the Castle still houses an important garrison, used by the Scottish regiments in the British Army, and in addition to the well-turned out guards on duty at the Castle entrance you'll often see officers and soldiers going about their daily business within the Castle walls.

Edinburgh Castle is open daily: April–Oct 9.30am–6pm; Nov–March 9.30am–5pm; £6.50.

You might like to join one of the somewhat overheated **guided tours**, with their talk of war, boiling oil and the roar of the cannon. There are also **audio guides**, available from a booth just inside the gatehouse. Both the guided tours and audio guides are included in the entrance price.

The Esplanade

The Castle is entered via the **Esplanade**, a parade ground laid out in the eighteenth century and enclosed a hundred years later by ornamental walls, the southern one of which commands fine views of the Pentland Hills. This is the setting for the city's most shameless and spectacular demonstration of tourist kitsch, the Edinburgh Military Tattoo, held each evening during the Festival (see p.267). An unfortunate side effect of this is that the skyline is disfigured for virtually the entire summer by the grandstands needed to accommodate the spectators.

In the northeast corner of the esplanade are two reminders of unhappy times. An Art Nouveau **drinking fountain** on the wall of the Weaving Centre shows witches' heads entwined by a snake and marks the spot where around three hundred women deemed to be witches were burned at the stake between 1479 and 1722. Nearby, an equestrian statue of **Field Marshal Earl Haig** recalls the controversial Edinburgh-born commander of the British forces in World War I, whose trench warfare strategy of sending men "over the top" led to previously unimaginable casualties.

The lower defences

The **Gatehouse** to the Castle is a Romantic-style addition from the 1880s, complete with the last drawbridge ever built in Scotland. It was later adorned with appropriately heroic-looking statues of Sir William Wallace and Robert the Bruce.

Continuing uphill, you pass through the **Portcullis Gate**, a handsome Renaissance gateway, marred by the nineteenth-century addition of an upper storey, known as the **Argyle Tower**, complete with anachronistic arrow slits. The tower was named after Archibald, ninth Earl of Argyll, said to have been imprisoned in a room above the Portcullis Gate prior to his execution in 1685.

The road takes you on to the six-gun **Argyle Battery**, built in the eighteenth century by Major General Wade, whose network of military roads and bridges still forms an essential part of the transport infrastructure of the Highlands. Further west on **Mill's Mount Battery**, a well-known Edinburgh ritual takes place – the daily firing of the

THE LOWER DEFENCES

One O'clock Gun. Originally designed for the benefit of ships in the Firth of Forth, it's now used as a time signal by city-centre workers. Both batteries offer wonderful panoramic views over Princes Street and the New Town to the coastal towns and hills of Fife across the Forth.

A steep and tortuous road takes you up to the **Governor's House**, a 1740s mansion whose harled masonry and crow-stepped gables are archetypal features of vernacular Scottish architecture. It now serves as the officers' mess for members of the garrison, while the governor himself lives in the northern side wing. Behind, stands the largest single construction in the Castle complex, the **New Barracks**, built in the 1790s in an austere Neoclassical style. From here the road snakes round towards the enclosed citadel at the uppermost point of Castle Rock, entered via **Foog's Gate**.

St Margaret's Chapel

Standing at the eastern end of the citadel, twelfth-century **St Margaret's Chapel** is the oldest surviving building in the Castle, and probably in Edinburgh itself. Although once believed to have been built by the saint herself, and mooted as the site of her death in 1093, the chapel's architectural style suggests that it dates from about thirty years later, and was thus probably built by King David I as a memorial to his mother. Used as a powder magazine for three hundred years, this tiny Norman church was eventually rededicated in 1934, after sympathetic restoration. Externally, it is plain and austere, but the interior preserves an elaborate zigzag archway dividing the nave from the sanctuary.

The battlements in front of the chapel offer the best of all the Castle's panoramic views and are interrupted by the **Lang Stairs**, which provide an alternative means of access from the Argyle Battery via the side of the Portcullis Gate.

Just below the battlements there's a small and immaculately maintained **cemetery**, the last resting place of the soldiers' pets. Continuing eastwards, you skirt the top of the Foreward and **Half Moon Batteries**. The latter stands on the site of David's Tower, which was the setting for the infamous **Black Dinner** in 1440, when the keeper of the Castle, Sir William Crichton, effectively the guardian of the 9-year-old King James II, son of the murdered James I, arranged for a potential rival, the Earl of Douglas, and his younger brother to attend a meal in the tower. After a huge banquet, the visitors were presented with a bull's head – a sign of condemnation to death. They were accused of treason and summarily executed in the Castle courtyard.

Crown Square

Immediately behind Half-Moon Battery is the 108-foot **Castle Well**, which you pass on the way into **Crown Square**, the highest, most secure and most important section of the entire Castle complex. The buildings around the square include the Royal Palace and banqueting hall used by James IV and his granddaughter, Mary, Queen of Scots. The former is now the secure home of the Honours of Scotland – Scotland's Crown Jewels.

The Palace

The **Palace**, a surprisingly unassuming edifice built round an octagonal stair turret, is on the eastern side of Crown Square. Begun in the 1430s, the palace owes its present Renaissance appearance to King James IV, though it was remodelled for Mary, Queen of Scots and her consort Henry, Lord Darnley, whose entwined initials (MAH), together with the date 1566, can be seen above one of the doorways. In the nineteenth century, the turret was heightened to bear the Castle's main flagpole. Inside, one of the

CROWN SQUARE

The Stone of Destiny

Legend has it that the **Stone of Destiny** (also called the Stone of Scone) was "Jacob's Pillow", on which Jacob dreamed of the ladder of angels stretching from earth to heaven. Its real history is obscure, but it is known that it was moved from Ireland to Dunadd by missionaries, and thence to Dunstaffnage, from where Kenneth MacAlpine, king of the Dalriada Scots, brought it to the abbey at Scone in 838. There it remained for almost five hundred years and was used as a coronation throne on which all kings of Scotland were crowned.

In 1296, an over-eager Edward I stole what he believed to be the Stone and installed it at Westminster Abbey, where, apart from a brief interlude in 1950, when it was removed by Scottish nationalists and hidden in Arbroath, it remained for seven hundred years. In December 1996, after an elaborate ceremony-laden journey from London, the Stone was finally returned to Scotland, one of many doomed attempts by the Conservative government to convince the Scottish people that the Union was a jolly good thing. Much to the annoyance of the people of Perth and the curators of Scone Palace, and to the general indifference of the Scottish public, the Stone was placed in Edinburgh Castle.

However, speculation surrounds the authenticity of the Stone, for the original is said to have been intricately carved, while the one seen today is a plain block of sandstone. Many believe that the canny monks at Scone palmed this off on to the English king and that the real Stone of Destiny lies hidden in an underground chamber, its whereabouts a mystery to all but a chosen few.

most interesting rooms is the tiny panelled bedchamber at the extreme southeastern corner, where Mary gave birth to

James VI. Along with the rest of the palace, the room was remodelled for James's triumphant homecoming in 1617. This was to be the last time it served as a royal residence.

The northern section of the palace is given over to a detailed audiovisual presentation on the **Honours of Scotland**, the originals of which are housed in the Crown Room at the very end of the display. These magnificent crown jewels – the only pre-Restoration set in the United Kingdom – serve as one of the most potent images of Scotland's nationhood. They were last worn by Charles II when he was crowned king of Scotland in 1651. The event provoked the wrath of Oliver Cromwell, who attempted to have the jewels melted down. However, the jewels were smuggled out of the Castle and hidden in a rural church. They later served as symbols of the monarch at sittings of the Scottish Parliament before being locked away in a chest following the Union of 1707. For over a century they were out of sight and eventually presumed lost, before being rediscovered in 1818 as a result of a search initiated by Sir Walter Scott.

Of the three jewels comprising the Honours, the oldest is the **sceptre**, which bears statuettes of the Virgin and Child, St James and St Andrew, rounded off by a polished globe of rock crystal: it was given to James IV in 1494 by Pope Alexander VI, and refashioned by Scottish craftsmen for James V. Finer still is the **sword**, a swaggering Italian High Renaissance masterpiece by the silversmith Domenico da Sutri, presented to James IV by Pope Julius II. Both the hilt and the scabbard are engraved with Julius's personal emblem, showing the oak tree and its acorns, the symbols of the risen Christ, together with dolphins, symbols of the Church. The jewel-encrusted **crown**, made for James V by the Scottish goldsmith James Mosman, incorporates the gold circlet worn by Robert the Bruce and is surmounted by an enamelled orb and cross. The glass case containing

CROWN SQUARE

the Honours has recently been rearranged to create space for a new addition, the **Stone of Destiny** (see box on p.16).

The Great Hall and Scottish United Services Museum

The south side of Crown Square is occupied by the **Great Hall**, built during the reign of James IV as a venue for banquets and other ceremonial occasions. Until 1639, the hall was the meeting place of the Scottish Parliament. Since then it has served variously as a barracks and a hospital. During this latter period, its hammerbeam roof – the earliest in the city – was hidden from view, but restored towards the end of the nineteenth century, when the hall was decked out in the full-blown Romantic manner.

On the west side of the square, the eighteenth-century Queen Anne Building houses part of the **Scottish United Services Museum**; the rest of the museum is housed in the late-nineteenth-century hospital beyond the Governor's House (see p.14). There are displays on each of the Scottish military regiments, plus the navy and air force. One of the more unusual exhibits includes a model of *The Great George*, a ship made by French prisoners incarcerated in the Castle during the eighteenth and early nineteenth centuries.

In 1755, the Castle church of St Mary on the north side of the square was replaced by a barracks, which in turn was skilfully converted into the quietly reverential **Scottish National War Memorial** in honour of the 150,000 Scots who fell in World War I.

The rest of the complex

From Crown Square, you can descend to the **Vaults**, a series of cavernous chambers erected by order of James IV to provide an even surface for the showpiece buildings above. They were later used as a prison for captured foreign nationals, who have bequeathed a rich legacy of graffiti, the most telling being the figure of "Lord Nord" (Lord North, prime minister during the American War of Independence), dangling from a gallows. One of the rooms houses the famous fifteenth-century siege gun, **Mons Meg**, which could fire a 500-pound stone nearly two miles. The gun was used in a number of sieges, but, because of its huge size, could only be transported three miles a day and was soon relegated to ceremonial status. In 1754, Mons Meg was taken to the Tower of London, where it stayed till Sir Walter Scott persuaded George IV to return it to Scotland on the occasion of his 1822 state visit.

Directly opposite the entrance to the vaults is the **Military Prison**, built in 1842, when the design and func-tion of jails was a major topic of public debate. Although generally used as a military prison, civilian offenders were also confined here during World War I, the most notable being the Marxist John Maclean, who was later to found the Workers' Republican Party. The cells, though designed for solitary confinement, are less forbidding than might be expected.

The Royal Mile

The **Royal Mile**, the name given to the road which travels down along the crest of the ridge linking the Castle with the Palace of Holyroodhouse, was described by Daniel Defoe in 1724, as "the largest, longest and finest street for Buildings and Number of Inhabitants, not in Bretain only, but in the World". Closely linked to centuries of Scottish history, the Royal Mile remains very much at the heart of Scotland's political life – the new Scottish parliament is based here, housed temporarily in the Assembly Hall, and due to move in 2002 to more permanent premises at the Holyrood end of the Royal Mile.

The mile-long cobbled street is divided into four separate sections – **Castlehill**, **Lawnmarket**, **High Street** and **Canongate**. Branching off from these at right angles is a series of tightly packed closes and steep lanes, entered via archways known as pends. After the construction of the New Town in the 1700s, the tenements on these closes degenerated into notorious slums, but the area has since been transformed, once again becoming a highly desirable place to live. Although somewhat marred by too many tacky tourist shops and the odd misjudged new development, it is still one of the most evocative parts of the city, and one that particularly rewards detailed exploration.

CASTLEHILL

Map 3, C8.

The narrow uppermost stretch of the Royal Mile is known as **Castlehill**. The first building on the northern side of the street as you leave the Castle Esplanade is the **Edinburgh Old Town Weaving Centre** (Mon–Sat 9am–5.30pm, Sun 10am–5pm), formerly the reservoir for the Old Town. Very much a commercial enterprise, the centre contains various large shops selling kilts, rugs and other tartan wares, while noisy looms rhythmically churn the stuff out on the floors below. You can see these up close and try your hand at weaving on a self-guided tour (£4), or dress up in ancient tartan dress and have your photo snapped (£7).

Behind the Weaving Centre rise up the red-and-white turrets of **Ramsay Gardens**, surely one of the most picturesque blocks of city-centre flats in the world. The oldest part is the octagonal Goose Pie House, home of the eighteenth-century poet Allan Ramsay, author of *The Gentle Shepherd* and father of the better-known portrait painter of the same name. During the Jacobite Rebellion of 1745, while Ramsay stayed safely away from the hurly-burly, it was used by Bonnie Prince Charlie's soldiers for shooting at the Castle sentries. The rest of the block dates from the 1890s and was the brainchild of Patrick Geddes, a pioneer of the modern town-planning movement, who created these desirable apartments in an attempt to bring back the middle classes to the main streets of the Old Town. Geddes' hope was to make "the dingy grey of our cities gain something of the pure azures and flash across its smoky wilderness the gleam of Renaissance hope". In later life, as his Scottish experiment floundered, he went off to pursue his ideals in Grenoble and India. Geddes' lasting legacy is the revival of the Old Town, and the student resi-

CASTLEHILL

dences he established at nearby Milne's Court are still in use today.

Back on Castlehill, opposite the Weaving Centre, the so-called **Cannonball House** takes its name from the cannonball embedded in its masonry, which according to legend was the result of a poorly targeted shot fired by the Castle garrison at Bonnie Prince Charlie's encampment at Holyrood. The truth, however, is far more prosaic: the ball simply marks the gravitation height of the city's first piped water supply. Alongside, the **Scotch Whisky Heritage Centre** (daily: June–Sept 9.30am–6pm; Oct–May 10am–5.30pm; tours £3.25 & £4.95) gives the lowdown on all aspects of Scotland's national beverage, featuring a gimmicky ride in a "barrel" through a series of uninspiring historical tableaux and a free dram (a measure) of whisky at the end. The longer tour also offers a detailed explanation of aspects of production and blending, although there's little on offer here which you won't find done rather better on a tour of a real distillery. The centre's shop, with its dozens of different brands, will give whisky novices an idea of the sheer range and diversity of the drink.

Across the street, the **Outlook Tower** (daily: April–Oct Mon–Fri 9.30am–6pm, Sat & Sun 10am–6pm; Nov–March 10am–5pm; £3.95) has been one of Edinburgh's top tourist attractions since 1853, when the original seventeenth-century tenement was equipped with a **camera obscura**. It makes a good introduction to the city: panoramic images are beamed on to a white table in the auditorium, accompanied by a running commentary. For the best views, visit at noon when there are fewer shadows. The viewing balcony is one of Edinburgh's best vantage points, and there are exhibitions on pinhole photography, holography, Victorian photographs of the city, and topographic paintings made between 1780 and 1860.

A few doors further on is the **Assembly Hall**, built in 1859 for the breakaway Free Church. Nowadays, however,

CASTLEHILL

it is where the annual General Assembly of the Church of Scotland usually meets, though since May 1999 it has been temporarily displaced by the Scottish Parliament, awaiting a more permanent home in Holyrood (see box on p.25). The Hall is nothing to look at from the Royal Mile side; at its northern entrance, however, on Mound Place, stand the twin towers which feature so prominently in the Old Town's skyline.

Before moving to its present site, the established church used to meet at the imposing black church building opposite. Its superb neo-Gothic detailing is by Augustus Pugin, co-architect of the Houses of Parliament in London, and its majestic spire is the highest in Edinburgh, easily recognizable from around the city. Formerly known as Tolbooth Kirk, the church was vacated by its Gaelic-speaking congregation in 1981 and converted in 1999 into a permanent home for the Edinburgh International Festival. Rechristened **The Hub** (daily 8am–late), the building now provides performance, rehearsal and exhibition space, and has a ticket office, where you can get tickets for the Edinburgh International Festival and some of the city's other festivals held throughout the year. Also on the ground floor, the bright-yellow *Hub Café* (daily 8am–11pm) sells drinks and snacks, with extra seating outside on a large terrace. Permanent works of art have been incorporated into the centre: lining the walls of the main stairwell, for example, are over two hundred delightful foot-high sculptures by Scottish sculptor Jill Watson, depicting Festival performers and audiences. Also worth checking out is the main hall upstairs, where the original neo-Gothic woodwork and high-vaulted ceiling is further enlivened with a fabulous wall hanging in Rastafarian colours. During August and early September, the hall becomes the venue for the **Festival Club** (daily 10am–2am; membership £5 per day, £25 per week), a

CASTLEHILL

highly-charged daily social gathering of the great and the good of the Festival scene.

LAWNMARKET

Map 3, D8.

Below the The Hub, the Royal Mile opens out into the much broader expanse of **Lawnmarket**, which was once the setting for a linen market, "lawn" being a corruption of "Laon", a town in France where the fabric was made. At its northern end is the entry to **Milne's Court**, whose excellently restored tenements now serve as student residences. Temporarily parked in the courtyard here is a rather incongruous-looking steel-and-glass construction – the public entrance to the Scottish Parliament's debating chamber in the Assembly Hall (open Mon–Fri 10am–noon & 2–4pm; free; see also box on Parliament opposite). Immediately beyond, **James Court** was one of Edinburgh's most fashionable addresses before the New Town was built, counting David Hume and James Boswell among its residents.

Back on Lawnmarket itself, **Gladstone's Land** (April–Oct Mon–Sat 10am–5pm, Sun 2–5pm; £3.20), a magnificent six-storey mansion, takes its name from the merchant Thomas Gledstane [sic], who in 1617 acquired a modest dwelling on the site, and transformed it into the building you see today. The Gledstane family are thought to have occupied the third floor, renting out the rest to merchants, in the style of tenement occupation still widespread in the city today. The arcaded ground floor, the only authentic example left of what was once a common feature of Royal Mile houses, has been restored to illustrate its early function as a shopping booth. Several other rooms have been kitted out in authentic period style to give an impression of the lifestyle of a well-to-do household of the late

The Scottish Parliament

In 1998, a referendum was held in which the Scottish people were given the chance to vote on whether they wanted their own parliament, separate from Westminster. Seventy-five percent of voters were in favour, and Scotland gained its first **national parliament** since the Treaty of Union between England and Scotland in 1707. Following the elections to the parliament the following year, a government was formed by a coalition between Labour and Liberal Democrat MSPs (Members of the Scottish Parliament), with the leader of the Labour group, **Donald Dewar**, as First Minister. The main opposition party is the Scottish National Party (SNP), led by Alex Salmond, which favours Scotland's complete independence from the UK. Made up of 129 MSPs, the devolved parliament governs most aspects of Scottish affairs, including education, health and transport, while Westminster retains control over matters such as foreign affairs, defence and macroeconomic policy.

While the Labour/Lib Dem administration is largely pursuing policies aligned to the Labour government in London, the parliament has the power to adopt legislation which diverges from the rest of the UK, and it is in these areas, including such sensitive issues as land reform, education and even fox hunting, that the parliament will prove its effectiveness.

Until 2002, the Parliament is meeting in the **Assembly Hall** of the Church of Scotland on the Lawnmarket, after which it will move to a permanent home at Holyrood (see p.46). You can watch the **debates** from the public gallery in the Assembly Hall when Parliament is in session – tickets are available on an ad hoc basis either from the desk at the public entrance in Milne's Court (see opposite) or from the Scottish Parliament **Visitor Centre** on the corner of George IV Bridge and High Street; they can also be booked by calling ©0131/348 5000 up to a week before the date you wish to attend.

seventeenth century; the Painted Chamber, with its decorated wooden ceiling and wall friezes, is particularly impressive. Elsewhere, underlining the importance of trade with continental Europe and beyond, the building has Dutch and Chinese porcelain and seventeenth-century Dutch paintings by Jacob Ruisdael and others. It's also possible to stay here (see p.165).

A few paces further on, steps lead down to Lady Stair's Close where you'll find **Lady Stair's House** (Mon–Sat 10am–5pm; also Sun 2–5pm during the Festival; free), named after the gorgeous and foul-mouthed eighteenth-century society figure on whose life Walter Scott based his story *My Aunt Margaret's Mirror*. Built in the 1620s, the house now contains a humdrum museum celebrating Scotland's literary trinity of Scott, Burns and Stevenson. It's a strange collection which hedges its bets with labels such as "said to be", "reputed to be" or even "similar to". There are assorted locks of hair, walking sticks and a few mementoes of Stevenson's stay in Samoa, plus some oddities such as an enamelled marble apple given by Robert Burns to his wife Jean Armour. Don't miss the painting, *Parliament Square and Public Characters of Edinburgh*, in the Burns Room, which gives a good idea of the layout of the area around St Giles in the eighteenth century. In the courtyard outside, called the **Makars' Court** after the Scots word for a "maker" of poetry or prose, look out for quotations by twelve of Scotland's most famous writers and poets inscribed on paving stones.

Riddle's Close, on the south side of Lawnmarket, leads to **Riddle's Court**, where you'll find **MacMorran's Close** and the home of the Baillie MacMorran, a wealthy merchant who was killed in 1595 while attempting to quell a school riot: local boys barricaded themselves into the High School and demanded a week's holiday, and when MacMorran came to sort them out he was shot through the head by William Sinclair, later to become Sir William Sinclair of Mey. Further down the street, **Brodie's Close** is named after the father of one of Edinburgh's most notorious characters, **Deacon William Brodie** (see box on below) pillar of society by day, burglar by night.

Deacon Brodie

On the surface, **William Brodie**, wit, town councillor, cabinetmaker and head of the Incorporation of Wrights and Masons, was an honourable member of late eighteenth-century society. However, like many of his contemporaries he was involved in a variety of more lowly activities, bestowing his custom on cock-fights and various drinking clubs, where he indulged in a constant round of bingeing, gambling and womanizing. In order to fund these activities, he always carried a piece of putty which he would use to take an impression of any keys left hanging up in houses that he visited. Armed with a copy of the keys cut by a local blacksmith, Brodie then robbed the houses. After the audacious robbery of the Excise Office in Chessel's Court, Canongate, which netted the dismal sum of £16, Brodie disappeared to Holland. One of his accomplices revealed his identity, Brodie was arrested and brought back to Edinburgh, where he was executed in 1788 on a gallows of his own making. Brodie remained blasé to the end, even writing an absurd will, which he ended with the dedication: "I recommend to all rogues, sharpers, thieves and gamblers, as well in high as in low stations, to take care of theirs by leaving of all wicked practices, and becoming good members of society."

Brodie has since provided the inspiration for many stories, most notably Robert Louis Stevenson's *Dr Jekyll and Mr Hyde*. Rather more unexpectedly, Muriel Spark's Jean Brodie is described as a direct descendant of the disreputable Deacon.

DEACON BRODIE

Lawnmarket ends where the Royal Mile reaches a cross-roads with George IV Bridge and Bank Street. On the latter stands the grand sandstone **Head Office of the Bank of Scotland**, whose Italianate domes and Corinthian pillars stand tall above the gardens. The Bank of Scotland was established in 1695 and is the oldest commercial bank in the UK still trading under its original name and statutes. In one of the more colourful episodes in its long history, in 1745 the bank had to shift over £80,000 in banknotes into the Castle to protect them from the army of Bonnie Prince Charlie – regarded, of course, as a threat to the state. The core of the building was designed by Robert Reid and Richard Crichton, pupils of Robert Adam, but its present appearance owes a great deal to David Bryce, who added domes, wings and quadrants in 1862. The banking hall offers a glimpse of the opulent interior and views out over Princes Street, while downstairs a small **museum** (June–Aug Mon–Fri 10am–4.45pm; free) displays an intriguing collection of scales, coins, primitive cheques and bank notes, including a selection of forgeries dating back to 1716.

PARLIAMENT SQUARE

Map 3, E9.
Immediately on your right after crossing George IV Bridge and Bank Street, is Parliament Square, dominated by the High Kirk of St Giles (see p.30) and by the continuous Neoclassical facades of the **Law Courts**. These were originally planned by Robert Adam, one of four brothers in a family of architects (their father William Adam designed Hopetoun House; see p.113), whose work helped give the New Town much of its grace and elegance. Because of a shortage of funds, Adam couldn't be kept on to complete the work, and the present exteriors were built to designs by

Robert Reid, the designer of the northern part of New Town, who faithfully quoted from Adam's architectural vocabulary, though without matching his flair. William Stark, a more flamboyant architect, designed the **Signet Library**, which occupies the west side of the square and has one of the most beautiful interiors in Edinburgh – its sumptuous colonnaded hall a perfect embodiment of the ideals of the Age of Reason. Unfortunately, it can only be seen by prior written application, except on very occasional open days (details available from the tourist office).

Facing the southern side of St Giles is **Parliament House**, built in the 1630s to house the Scottish Parliament, a role it maintained until the Union, when it passed into the hands of the legal fraternity. Following the Union in 1707, the building became the centre of the Scottish legal profession – still its function today. The entrance lobby will give you access to the impressive **main hall** (Mon–Fri 9am–5pm), the most notable feature of which is the extravagant hammerbeam roof and the delicately carved stone corbels from which it springs – in addition to some vicious grotesques, they include accurate depictions of several castles, including Edinburgh's. In the far corner, a small **exhibition** explains the history of the building and courts, but it's more fun simply to watch the everyday business, with solicitors and bewigged advocates in hushed conferrals, often following the time-honoured tradition of pacing up and down the main hall to prevent their conversation being overheard by anyone sitting on the benches around the walls. Most of the courtrooms have public galleries, and you can sit in on the hearings if you're interested – ask one of the attendants in the lobby to point you in the right direction.

Outside, in the square, rears a life-size **equestrian statue of King Charles II**, wearing the garb of a Roman emperor. Back on the High Street, set into the pavement beside a bloated memorial to the fifth Duke of Buccleuch, there's a brickwork pattern, known as the **Heart of Midlothian**. Immortalized in Scott's novel of the same name, it marks the site of a demolished Tolbooth; you may see passers-by spitting on it for luck. The **Mercat Cross**, at the eastern end of St Giles, was once the setting for public executions, as well as rather more joyous events, such as the return from France of Mary, Queen of Scots in 1561, when the spouts of the cross were said to have flowed with wine. Little of what remains today is original: the first cross collapsed in 1756, and was only rebuilt in 1885 with financial assistance from William Gladstone. The site is still occasionally used for the reading out of Royal proclamations, such as the dissolution of Parliament.

High Kirk of St Giles

Map 3, E8. April–Sept Mon–Fri 9am–7pm, Sat & Sun 9am–5pm; Oct–March Mon–Sat 9am–5pm, Sun 1–5pm; free.

There's been a church on the site of the **High Kirk of St Giles**, in the middle of Parliament Square, since the ninth century, and though there are surviving sections of a Norman church built in the early twelfth century, the basic structure of the church is a late fifteenth-century design. St Giles is almost invariably referred to as a cathedral, although it was only the seat of a bishop on two brief and unhappy occasions in the seventeenth century. It was from St Giles that John Knox (see box on p.37) launched and directed the Scottish Reformation. According to one of the city's best-known legends, the attempt in 1637 to introduce the English prayer book, and thus episcopal government, so incensed a humble stallholder named Jenny Geddes that she hurled her stool at the preacher, uttering the immortal words: "Out, out, does the false loon dare say Mass at my lugg [ear]?", thus prompting the rest of the congregation to chase the offending clergyman out of the building. A tablet

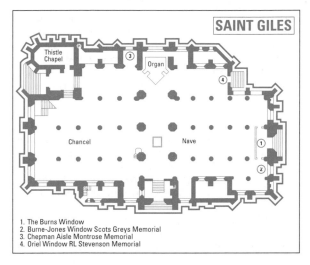

SAINT GILES

- Thistle Chapel
- Organ
- Chancel
- Nave

1. The Burns Window
2. Burne-Jones Window Scots Greys Memorial
3. Chepman Aisle Montrose Memorial
4. Oriel Window RL Stevenson Memorial

in the north aisle marks the spot from where Jenny let rip.

In the early nineteenth century, St Giles received a much-needed but unsympathetic restoration, covering most of the Gothic exterior with a smooth stone coating that gives it a certain Georgian dignity while sacrificing its medieval character almost completely. The only part not to receive this treatment is the late fifteenth-century tower, whose resplendent crown spire is formed by eight flying buttresses.

The **interior** has survived in much better shape. Especially notable are the four massive piers supporting the tower, which date back, at least in part, to the church's Norman predecessor. In the nineteenth century, St Giles was adorned with a whole series of funerary monuments in order to give it the character of a national pantheon on the lines of Westminster Abbey. Several Pre-Raphaelite stained-glass windows were also installed. The best of these, designed by Edward Burne-Jones and William Morris, showing Old Testament prophets and the Israelites crossing the River Jordan, can be seen on the facade wall of the **north aisle**. Alongside is the great **west window**, which was dedicated to Robbie Burns in 1985, causing enormous controversy – as a hardened drinker and womanizer, the national bard was far from being an upholder of accepted Presbyterian values. Look out also for an elegant bronze relief of Robert Louis Stevenson on the south side of the church by the American, Augustus St Gaudens. The original design had the author reclining on a bed smoking a cigarette; he now lies on a chaise longue, pen in hand. Opposite is a memorial to the **Marquis of Montrose**, leader of the forces of Charles I in Scotland, who was captured, executed and dismembered in 1650.

At the southeastern corner of the church, the **Thistle Chapel** was built by Sir Robert Lorimer in 1911 as the private chapel of the sixteen knights of the Most Noble Order of the Thistle. Self-consciously derivative of St George's Chapel in Windsor, it's an exquisite piece of craftsmanship, with an elaborate ribbed vault, huge drooping bosses and extravagantly ornate stalls.

HIGH STREET AND AROUND

Map 3, E8.

The third section of the Royal Mile proper is known as **High Street**, and occupies two blocks on either side of the intersection between North Bridge and South Bridge.

The first main building on the northern side of the High Street is the **High Court of Justiciary**, Scotland's highest criminal court, outside which stands a statue of the philosopher David Hume, one of Edinburgh's greatest sons, looking decidedly wan and chilly dressed in nothing but a Roman toga. A little further on, opposite the Mercat Cross,

Robert Louis Stevenson

Born in Edinburgh, **Robert Louis Stevenson** (1850–94) was a sickly child, his solitary childhood dominated by his governess, who told him tales from Calvinist folklore. In 1875, Stevenson abandoned a career in law and decided to channel his energies into literature.

While a student, Stevenson had made his mark as an essayist, and in his lifetime he published over 100 essays. Other early successes were two **travelogues**, *An Inland Voyage* and *Travels with a Donkey in the Cevennes*, kaleidoscopic jottings based on journeys in France in 1878–9. It was there that Stevenson met Fanny Osbourne, an American, who was estranged from her husband and had two children in tow. His voyage to join her in San Francisco formed the basis for his most important factual work, *The Amateur Emigrant*, a vivid firsthand account of the great nineteenth-century European migration to the United States.

Having married the now-divorced Fanny, Stevenson began an elusive search for an agreeable climate that took the couple to Switzerland, the French Riviera and the Scottish Highlands. It was around this time that he began writing **novels**, achieving immediate acclaim in 1881 for *Treasure Island*, a highly moralistic adventure yarn that began as an entertainment for his stepson. Published in 1886, his most famous **short story**, *Dr Jekyll and Mr Hyde*, was an allegory of Edinburgh's Old Town dual personality of prosperity and squalor, and an analysis of its Calvinistic preoccupations with guilt and damnation. The same year saw the publication of the historical romance, *Kidnapped*.

In 1887, Stevenson left Britain for good and eventually settled in Samoa. Scotland continued to be his main inspiration, however: he wrote *Catriona* as a sequel to *Kidnapped*, and was at work on two more novels with Scottish settings at the time of his sudden death from a brain haemorrhage in 1894. He was buried on the top of Mount Vaea overlooking the Pacific Ocean.

ROBERT LOUIS STEVENSON

the U-shaped **City Chambers** were designed by John Adam, brother of Robert, as the Royal Exchange. Local traders never warmed to the Exchange, however, preferring to remain outdoors on the street, so the town council established its headquarters there instead. Amazingly, the rear of the building has twelve storeys to accommodate the sharp drop onto Cockburn Street

Beneath the City Chambers lies **Mary King's Close**. Built in the early sixteenth century, it was closed off for many years after the devastation of the 1645 plague, before being entirely covered up by the chambers in 1753. During World War II, parts of the close were brought back into public use as an air-raid shelter, and today brief tours of this rather spooky "lost city" are run regularly throughout the day by Mercat Tours (see p.8) – meet outside the City Chambers. A little further down the High Street is **Anchor Close**, site of the printing works of William Smellie, who published the first ever edition of the *Encyclopædia Britannica* there in 1768.

At the junction of the south side of High Street and South Bridge stands the **Tron Kirk**, for many years the focal point for Hogmanay revellers, until today's organized events shifted the crowds to other parts of the city. Built in the 1630s to house the congregation evicted from St Giles when the latter became the seat of a bishop, the church has a less than happy history: the south aisle was removed in the late eighteenth century in order to make room for the South Bridge, and the original spire was destroyed in the Great Fire of 1824. The Tron remained in use as a church until 1952 and was then closed for forty years before reopening as the **Old Town Information Centre** (Easter–May Thurs–Mon 10am–1pm & 2–5pm, June–Sept daily 10am–7pm).

Excavations within the church have revealed sections of an old close, **Marlin's Wynd**. The cobbled steps and the traces of old foundations on the wynd, which formerly contained bookshops and markets, are highly evocative of Edinburgh's past, making this an essential stop on the Royal Mile. In the same building, the **Edinburgh Old Town Renewal Trust** presents a series of informative displays on the history of the Old Town.

Beyond the intersection of North Bridge and South Bridge, back on the northern side of High Street, nestles **Paisley Close**, above the entrance of which is a bust of a youth with the inscription "Heave awa' chaps, I'm no' dead yet", the words uttered in 1861 by a boy trapped by rubble following the collapse of a tenement in the close, and who was subsequently dug out by rescue workers.

In **Chalmer's Close**, just to the east, **Trinity Apse** serves as a poignant reminder of the fifteenth-century Holy Trinity Collegiate Church, formerly one of Edinburgh's most outstanding buildings, but demolished in 1848 to make way for an extension to Waverley train station. The stones were carefully numbered and stored on Calton Hill so that the church could be reassembled at a later date, but many were pilfered before sufficient funds became available, and only enough remained to reconstruct the apse on this site. This now houses a **Brass Rubbing Centre** (Mon–Sat 10am–5pm, also Sun 2–5pm during the Festival; free), where you can rub your own impressions from Pictish crosses and medieval brasses (from £1.20).

On the other side of the High Street, the **Museum of Childhood** (same opening hours as Brass Rubbing Centre; free), was founded by an eccentric local councillor who disliked children. Although he claimed that the museum was a serious social archive for adults, it has always attracted swarms of kids, who delight in the dolls' house, teddy bears, marionettes and other toys. The founder's quirky sense of humour comes over on some of the captions for exhibits and even more so in his unendearing wish to have a memorial window in honour of **King Herod** placed at the museum's entrance.

Opposite the museum is **Moubray House** (closed to the public), built around 1462. It provided lodging for **Daniel Defoe** who stayed in the capital as a propaganda agent for the English in 1706 prior to the Act of Union.

John Knox's House, on the "knuckle" of the High Street, adjoins the Netherbow Arts Centre, a busy theatre venue during the Festival. Throughout the rest of the year it hosts art and photography exhibitions and has a popular lunchtime café (see p.174).

John Knox's House

Map 3, G8. Mon–Sat 10am–4.30pm; £1.95.

Next door to Moubray House is the much-photographed **John Knox's House**, a three-storeyed building with distinctive wooden balconies projecting out into the High Street. With its outside stairway, biblical motto and sundial adorned with a statue of Moses, it gives a good impression of how the Royal Mile must have once looked. Thought to have been built around the beginning of the sixteenth century, it was partially destroyed by English soldiers in 1544, and has since been restored many times. Although Knox is thought to have stayed here between 1560 and 1572, the link may stem solely from a period at the end of the eighteenth century when the house was known as "Knox the Booksellers". What's known is that James Mosman, royal goldsmith to Mary, Queen of Scots, did reside in the house: the initials IM and MA (Mosman and his wife Mariota Arres) are still visible on the outer west wall of the building.

The rather bare **interior**, with its labyrinthine layout, typical of Old Town houses, contains a sparse **museum** displaying explanatory material on Knox's life and career, including early editions of works by him (such as the inimitably titled

John Knox

The Protestant reformer **John Knox** was born around 1510 in East Lothian. Ordained to the priesthood in 1540, Knox became a private tutor, in league with Scotland's first significant Protestant leader, **George Wishart**. After Wishart was burned at the stake for heresy in 1546, Knox became involved with the group who carried out the revenge murder of Cardinal David Beaton, subsequently taking over his castle in St Andrews. The following year, this was captured by the French; Knox was carted off to work as a galley slave and freed in 1548 by the English.

When the Catholic Mary Tudor acceded to the English throne in 1553, Knox fled to Geneva, where he was quickly won over to Calvin's radical version of Protestantism. It was here that he wrote his most infamous treatise, attacking the three Catholic women then ruling Scotland, England and France.

When Knox was allowed to return to Scotland in 1555, he took over as spiritual leader of the Reformation. He championed an alliance with Protestant Elizabeth I, which proved crucial to the establishment of Protestantism as the official religion of Scotland in 1560: the deployment of English troops against the French garrison in Edinburgh dealt a fatal blow to Franco–Spanish hopes of re-establishing Catholicism in both Scotland and England. Although the following year saw the accession of Catholic Mary, Queen of Scots, to the Scottish throne, apparently Knox was able to retain the upper hand in his high-profile disputes with her.

Before his death in 1572, Knox began mapping out the organization of the Scots Kirk, sweeping away all vestiges of episcopacy and giving laymen a more prominent role. He also proposed a nationwide education system, to be compulsory for the very young, and free for the poor. His final legacy was the posthumously published *History of the Reformation of Religion in the Realm of Scotland*, a justification of his life's work.

JOHN KNOX

Answer to a Great Number of Blasphemous Cavillations) and other notable contemporaries. In recognition of the building's connection with James Mosman, a mock-up of a goldsmith's workroom has been installed on the first floor. On the second floor, there are fireplaces with attractive, albeit somewhat haphazardly positioned, Dutch tiles, wood-panelled walls and painted ceilings, which together create a passable replica of a sixteenth-century town house.

CANONGATE

Map 3, H8.

For over 700 years from 1128, the district through which **Canongate** runs was a burgh in its own right, officially separate from the capital. Since the 1950s, much effort has been expended in restoring the area's many run-down buildings. Recent efforts have concentrated on the area abutting Holyrood, where the new Scottish Parliament building is being erected, along with various new hotels and offices.

On the northern side of the street, as you walk towards Holyrood, look out for two large tenements, **Shoemaker's Land** at no. 197 and **Bible Land** at nos. 183–7, both erected in the heyday of the Old Town by the Incorporation of Cordiners, one of Edinburgh's powerful guilds: the Cordiners' emblem of a crowned shoemaker's knife flanked by cherubs' heads appears above both buildings.

Near the top of Canongate, on the southern side, lies **Chessel's Court**, a mid-eighteenth-century development, with fanciful Rococo chimneys. It is best known as the location of the long-vanished Excise Office – the scene of the robbery that led to the eventual arrest and execution of Deacon Brodie (see box on p.27).

Dominated by a turreted steeple, the late sixteenth-century **Canongate Tolbooth**, a little further down the north side of the street, has served both as the headquarters of the burgh administration and as a prison, and now houses **The People's Story** (Mon–Sat 10am–5pm; also during the Festival Sun 2–5pm; free), a lively museum devoted to the everyday life and work of Edinburgh people down the centuries, with sounds and tableaux of various aspects of city life – including a typical Edinburgh pub. Next door, **Canongate Kirk** was built in the 1680s to house the congregation expelled from Holyrood Abbey (see p.45) when the latter was commandeered by James VII (James II in England) to serve as the chapel for the Order of the Thistle. It's a curiously archaic design, still Renaissance in outline, and built to a cruciform plan wholly at odds with the ideals and requirements of Protestant worship. Its churchyard, one of the city's most exclusive cemeteries, commands a superb view across to Calton Hill. Among those buried here are Adam Smith, father of the science of political economy, Mrs Agnes McLehose (better known as Robert Burns's "Clarinda") and Robert Fergusson, who died at the age of 24 and is regarded by some as Edinburgh's greatest poet; his headstone was donated and inscribed by Burns, a fervent admirer.

Directly opposite Canongate Kirk stands **Huntly House** (Mon–Sat 10am–5pm, also during the Festival Sun 2–5pm; free). The main building, which dates back to the late sixteenth century, was bought by the Incorporation of Hammermen in 1647 and converted into flats. It was restored in 1927, and since then it has served as a **museum of local history**. Exhibits include a quirky array of old shop signs, some dating back to the eighteenth century, as well as displays on indigenous industries such as glass, silver, pottery and clockmaking, and on the career of Earl Haig. Also on view is the original version of the National Covenant of 1638 (see box on p.58); modern science has failed to resolve whether or not some of the signatories signed with their own blood, as tradition has it.

CANONGATE

On the same side of the street, narrow Crichton's Close leads to the **Scottish Poetry Library** (Mon–Fri noon–6pm; during the Festival also Sat noon–4pm; free), a small island of modern architectural eloquence amid a sea of monstrous construction work and large-scale developments. The eastern side of the building is made from a section of an old city wall, while the rest is an attractive, thoroughly contemporary design using brick, wood, glass, Caithness stone and blue tiles. The library, which moved here in 1999 from older premises further up the Royal Mile, contains Scotland's most comprehensive collection of native poetry. Visitors are free to come and read the books, periodicals and leaflets, or listen to recordings of poetry in English, Scots and Gaelic. Occasional readings and events are organized throughout the year.

The lower section of the Royal Mile is currently undergoing a dramatic transformation, triggered by the decision to locate the new Scottish Parliament building at the very end of the street opposite the Palace of Holyroodhouse. Many large and mostly disused old warehouses and industrial sites are either being converted or knocked down in favour of new hotels and offices (for more details see p.46). However, most of the buildings of significant historical interest are being retained, among them several fine seventeenth-century mansions on the easternmost stretch of Canongate, including **Panmure House**, which was for a time the home of Adam Smith. At the very foot of the street, the entrance to the residential **Whitehorse Close** was once the site of the inn from where stagecoaches began the journey to London. It drips with all the most characteristic features of Scottish vernacular architecture: crow-stepped gables, dormer windows, overhanging upper storeys and curving outside stairways.

Holyrood and around

At the foot of the Canongate section of the Royal Mile lies **Holyrood**, Edinburgh's historic royal quarter, site of the seventeenth-century Palace of Holyroodhouse, where the monarch stays when visiting the city, and twelfth-century Holyrood Abbey. The area is undergoing something of a transformation, as the site immediately opposite the palace has been chosen as the location for the new **Scottish Parliament**, and work is underway on the building, due to be completed in 2002. Accompanying ranks of new hotels, offices and tourist attractions are also going up nearby.

Holyrood's origins go back to the twelfth century and are described in a fifteenth-century manuscript which is still kept in the palace: the story goes that King David I, son of Malcolm III and St Margaret, went out hunting one day and was suddenly confronted by a stag who threw him from his horse and seemed ready to gore him. In desperation, the king tried to protect himself by grasping its antlers, but instead found himself holding a crucifix, whereupon the animal ran off. In a dream that night, he heard a voice commanding him to "make a house for Canons devoted to the Cross"; he duly obeyed and founded an **abbey** in 1128, which he named Holyrood ("rood" being an alternative name for a cross). A more likely story, however, is that David, the most pious of all Scotland's monarchs, simply acquired a supposed relic of the True Cross and decided to build a suitable home for it.

During the reign of James II a wing was added to the abbey for the exclusive use of the court, its situation in a secluded valley making it far more agreeable to the royals than the draughty castle. The accommodation was transformed into a full-blown palace for James IV, which in turn was replaced by a much larger building called the **Palace of Holyroodhouse**, built for Charles II, although he never actually lived here. Indeed, it was something of a white elephant until Queen Victoria started making regular trips to her northern kingdom, a custom that has been maintained by her successors.

Just beyond the palace grounds lies the marvellous **Holyrood Park**, a large area of semi-wild parkland and peaceful lochs, dominated by **Arthur's Seat**, an extinct volcano, which affords stupendous views from its summit. Easily reached on foot through the park is the attractive village of **Duddingston**, home to a twelfth-century parish church and the house in which Bonnie Prince Charlie is reputed to have spent the night before the battle of Prestonpans.

THE PRECINCTS OF THE PALACE

Map 3, K8.

On the north side of **Abbey Strand**, which forms a sort of processional way linking Canongate with Holyrood, stands **Abbey Lairds**, a four-storey sixteenth-century mansion which once served as a home for aristocratic debtors and is now occupied by royal flunkies during the summer seat of the court.

Legend has it that Mary, Queen of Scots used to bathe in sweet white wine in the curious little turreted structure nearby known as **Queen Mary's Bath House**; it is more likely, however, that it was either a summer pavilion or a dovecote. Its architecture is mirrored in the **Croft an Righ**, a picturesque L-shaped house in a quiet, generally overlooked corner beside the eastern wall of the complex. The eastern edge of the palace grounds was formerly a debtor's sanctuary, known as St Anne's Yards, housing over a hundred residents in the early nineteenth century.

THE PALACE OF HOLYROODHOUSE

Map 5, B3. Daily: April–Oct 9.30am–5.15pm; Nov–March 9.30am–3.15pm; £5.50.

In its present form, the **Palace of Holyroodhouse** is largely a seventeenth-century creation. However, the tower house of the old palace was skilfully incorporated to form the northwestern block, with a virtual mirror image of it erected as a counterbalance at the other end. The three-storey **courtyard** is an early exercise in Palladian style, exhibiting a punctilious knowledge of the rules of classical architecture to create a sense of absolute harmony and unity.

....

Holyroodhouse is a working palace and the buildings are closed to the public at certain times for state functions, usually for a fortnight in the middle of May, and the first two weeks in July. At quiet times of the year (Nov–March), free guided tours are conducted by the palace's staff.

....

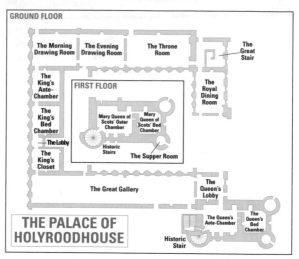

GROUND FLOOR

The Morning Drawing Room | The Evening Drawing Room | The Throne Room | The Great Stair

The King's Ante-Chamber

FIRST FLOOR

The Royal Dining Room

The King's Bed Chamber

Mary Queen of Scots' Outer Chamber | Mary Queen of Scots' Bed Chamber

The Lobby

Historic Stairs

The King's Closet

The Supper Room

The Great Gallery

The Queen's Lobby

THE PALACE OF HOLYROODHOUSE

The Queen's Ante-Chamber | The Queen's Bed Chamber

Historic Stair

Inside, the **State Apartments** are decked out with oak panelling, tapestries, portraits and decorative paintings, all overshadowed by magnificent white stucco **ceilings**. In the Morning Drawing Room portraits of Bonnie Prince Charlie and George IV, loser and winner, hang side by side. The most eye-catching chamber, however, is the **Great Gallery**, which takes up the entire first floor of the northern wing. During the 1745 sojourn of the Young Pretender this was the setting for a lively banquet, evoked in detail in Scott's novel *Waverley*, and it is still used for big ceremonial occasions. On the walls of the gallery hang 89 portraits commissioned from the seventeenth-century Dutch artist Jacob de Wit to illustrate the royal lineage of Scotland from its mythical origins in the fourth century BC; the result is unintentionally hilarious, as it is clear that the artist's imagination was taxed to bursting point by the need to paint so many different faces without having an inkling as to what the subjects actually looked like. Legend has it that he trawled the streets of the Old Town for sitters to provide faces for the early obscure figures, and a frequently recurring feature in many of the portraits is a prominent nose, not dissimilar from that of his patron, Charles II. In the adjacent **King's Closet**, the artist's *The Finding of Moses* provides a biblical link to the portraits, the Scottish royal family claiming descent from Scota, the Egyptian pharaoh's daughter who discovered Moses in the bulrushes.

The oldest parts of the palace, the **Historical Apartments**, dating back to the sixteenth century, are mainly of note for their associations with Mary, Queen of Scots and in particular for the brutal murder, organized by her husband, Lord Darnley, of her private secretary, David Rizzio, who was stabbed 56 times and dragged from the small closet, through the **Queen's Bedchamber**, and into the **Outer Chamber**. Until a few years ago, visitors were shown apparently indelible bloodstains on the floor of the last, but these are now admitted to be fakes and have been covered up. A display cabinet in the same room shows some pieces of **needlework** woven by the deposed queen while in English captivity; another case has an outstanding **miniature portrait** of her by the French court painter, François Clouet.

HOLYROOD ABBEY

Map 5, B2.

In the grounds of the palace lie the wonderfully evocative ruins of **Holyrood Abbey**. Of King David's original Norman church, the only surviving fragment is a doorway in the far southeastern corner. Most of the remainder dates from a late twelfth- and early thirteenth-century rebuilding in the Early Gothic style.

The surviving parts of the **west front**, including one of the twin towers and the elaborately carved entrance portal, show how resplendent the abbey must once have been. Unfortunately, the building was all but destroyed during the Reformation. Charles I attempted to restore some semblance of unity by ordering the erection of the great east window and a new stone roof, but the latter collapsed in 1768, causing grievous damage to the rest of the structure. By this time, the Canongate congregation had another place of worship, and schemes to rebuild the abbey were abandoned.

THE SCOTTISH PARLIAMENT SITE

Map 5, B2.

Opposite the Palace, between Canongate and Holyrood Park, sprawls the massive construction site of the new **Scottish Parliament**. For decades, campaigners for home rule for Scotland advocated the Old Royal High School building on Calton Hill (see p.86) as the ideal place for the parliament. In the run-up to devolution, however, the Scottish Office unexpectedly announced that the school was too small to accommodate the proposed parliament and its offices, and various alternative sites were suggested, including the empty docklands at Leith. Eventually the present location – on the site of a disused brewery – was identified as the ideal site, and a competition to design the brand-new Parliament building was won by Catalan architect Enric Miralles, in association with Edinburgh-based architects RMJM. Their concept, a model of which can be viewed in the Scottish Parliament Visitor Centre on George IV Bridge (see box on p.25), centres on a series of petal-shaped buildings which have been compared (both favourably and unfavourably) to upturned boats. The structure will cost something in the region of £100 million, and is due to be completed by 2002, until which time the parliament is sitting in the Church of Scotland Assembly Hall (see p.23).

OUR DYNAMIC EARTH

Map 5, B3.

Although the largest, the new Parliament building is by no means the only newcomer to this historic area. On the Holyrood Road side of the construction site, a pin-cushion of white metal struts shelters **Our Dynamic Earth** (April–Oct daily 10am–6pm, Nov–March Wed–Sat 10am–5pm; £5.95, children £3.50, families £16.50), a high-tech attraction, aimed mainly at families, which delves into the natural world, looking at how the earth was created, and examining the different forms of life sustained on it. Visitors are taken in a "time machine" elevator to a room where the creation of the universe, fifteen billion years ago, is described using wide-screen video graphics, accompanied by eerie music and a deep-throated commentary. Subsequent galleries show how the earth and continents were formed, with the aid of crashing sound effects and a shaking floor, while the calmer grandeur of glaciers and oceans is explored through magnificent large-screen landscape footage. The "Casualties and Survivors" gallery traces the history of life on earth, from primordial swamps to life-size models of some of the odd creatures which once inhabited the earth. Further on, the polar regions and tropical jungles are imaginatively re-created, with interactive computer screens and special effects at every turn.

HOLYROOD PARK

Map 5.

Holyrood Park – or Queen's Park – a natural wilderness in the very heart of the modern city, is unquestionably one of Edinburgh's main assets. Packed into an area no more than five miles in diameter is an amazing variety of landscapes – mountains, crags, moorland, marshes, glens, lochs and fields – representing something of a microcosm of Scotland's scenery. The highest point is the summit of Arthur's Seat, situated in the southern part of the Park, though its lofty dominance means that the park as a whole is often referred to simply as "Arthur's Seat". The park is circled by a single tarred road, the **Queen's Drive**.

From the Palace gates, following Queen's Drive, in a clockwise direction, you arrive after around ten minutes' walk at **St Margaret's Loch**, a nineteenth-century man-made pond, above which stand the scanty ruins of **St Anthony's Chapel**, another fine vantage point. From here, the road's loop is one-way only, ascending to **Dunsapie Loch**, again an artificial stretch of water, which makes an excellent foil to the eponymous crag behind.

Arthur's Seat

Map 5, D6.

Arthur's Seat, a majestic extinct volcano, rising 823ft above sea level, is Edinburgh's single most prominent land-mark, resembling a huge crouched lion when seen from the west. There's no satisfactory story to explain the name: there's certainly little reason to associate it with the British king of the Holy Grail legends. One possibility is that it derives from the Gaelic phrase *Ard-na-Said*, meaning "Height of Arrows", from the days in the early twelfth century when the area was used as a hunting ground.

There are several ways up to the summit, the quickest of which is from Dunsapie Loch (see box opposite). The views from the top are all you'd expect, covering the entire city and much of the Firth of Forth; on a clear day, you can even see the southernmost mountains of the Highlands. The composer Felix Mendelssohn climbed Arthur's Seat in

Walks in Holyrood Park

One of the most popular walks in Holyrood Park is to the **summit of Arthur's Seat**, the highest point in the city. The easiest route is from the car park beside **Dunsapie Loch**. Less arduous than it looks, the climb takes about twenty minutes, starting off gently at first and then becoming steeper towards the summit. You can also start at **Duddingston**, from where a long flight of stairs and a steep path link up to the Dunsapie starting point.

A longer but more satisfying climb begins at the entrance to the park beside the Palace of Holyroodhouse: cross over to the south side of Queen's Drive, then take the path which passes St Margaret's Well, heading towards St Margaret's Loch and St Anthony's Chapel. Before reaching the chapel follow the path as it curves southwards into the flat glen called **Dry Dam**. From here it's a steady climb up the north face of Arthur's Seat to the top. The walk takes about one and a half hours altogether.

An equally satisfying walk is along the pathway called the **Radical Road** which runs along the base of the Salisbury Crags, a series of basalt rock formations, 400ft high. You can join the path at either the Holyrood or Newington end, and there's an easy return along the grassy verge beside the Queen's Drive. A wilder and lonelier alternative to the Radical Road is to traverse the top of the crags, though of course it's inadvisable to get too close to the edge, as the ground can be slippery and the rock unstable in places.

If you're keen to learn more about the formation and geology of Arthur's Seat, you could join one of Geowalk's **guided walks** led by a qualified geologist. The tours last one and a half hours and leave from the car park beside the Holyrood entrance to the park at 2pm on Wednesdays, Fridays and Sundays (℅0131/555 5488; £5).

July 1829, noting: "It is beautiful here! In the evening a cool breeze is wafted from the sea, and then all objects appear clearly and sharply defined against the gray sky; the lights from the windows glitter brilliantly."

DUDDINGSTON

Map 5, F6.

Continuing along Queen's Drive around Arthur's Seat you come to a roundabout. The turn-off here leads to another roundabout; taking the first exit, you pass beneath **Samson's Ribs**, a group of basalt pillars strikingly reminiscent of the Hebridean island of Staffa, and come to **Duddingston Loch**, the only natural stretch of water in the park, now a bird sanctuary. Above it, just outside the park boundary, perches **Duddingston Kirk**. Dating back in part to the twelfth century, the church is the focus of one of the most unspoilt old villages in Edinburgh. In the gateway of the church are a *loupin-on-stane*, a platform for mounting a horse, and *jougs*, an iron collar and chain set into the wall and formerly used for humiliating offenders. According to tradition, Bonnie Prince Charlie stayed in **no. 8 Duddingston Causeway**, a plain-looking house built in 1721, on the night before his victory at the battle of Prestonpans in 1745. Duddingston can be reached on foot through Holyrood Park; after a drink in the excellent *Sheep Heid Inn* (see p.210) take bus #42/46 from Duddingston Road West in either direction to get back to the city centre.

South of the Royal Mile

Before the elevated viaducts of George IV Bridge and Southbridge were built, the main thoroughfare immediately to the south of the Royal Mile was **Cowgate**, originally used for bringing cattle to market. Linked to the Holyrood area by its eastern extension, Holyrood Road, Cowgate is today a gloomy street even in daylight, hemmed in by tall buildings, and, with the exceptions of **St Cecilia's Hall** and the **Magdalen Chapel**, offers little in the way of sights. At night, however, though a little seedy, it's one of the city's prime spots for nightclubs. The western end of the street leads to the wide open space of **Grassmarket**, at the very foot of the Castle's intimidating southern crags, for centuries the place where livestock sales took place, and also the scene of executions and other grisly goings-on, such as the activities of the body-snatchers Burke and Hare. Further west lies the city's **theatre district**, centred on Lothian Road and Grindlay Street.

To the south of Grassmarket stand **Greyfriars Kirk** and the distinctive sandstone edifice of the **National Museum**

of **Scotland**, the new sanctum of the nation's most trea-
sured artefacts. Next door, the **Royal Museum of
Scotland** houses an amazing miscellany of displays and
objects from around the world. Just beyond it lies the
University of Edinburgh, which dominates this part of
town as far as the **Southside** area and the stretch of parkland known as the **Meadows**.

COWGATE

Map 3, H3.
Among Edinburgh's oldest surviving streets, **Cowgate** was
formerly one of the city's most prestigious addresses.
However, with the construction of Southbridge and
George IV Bridge to provide a link between the Old and
New towns, Cowgate was all but entombed below street
level. The water supply for the Old Town was diverted to
serve the new residences, resulting in severe shortage in the
lower parts of the old city, which led to sporadic outbreaks
of cholera in the 1840s. Hans Christian Andersen, who visited the city around this time, wrote, "poverty and misery
seem to peep out of the open hatches which normally serve
as windows".

St Cecilia's Hall

Map 3, H3. Wed & Sat 2–5pm; £3.
Standing at the corner of Cowgate and Niddry Street,
St Cecilia's Hall is Scotland's oldest purpose-built
concert hall. Established for the Musical Society of
Edinburgh in 1763, the hall thrived until the emergence
of the New Town attracted concert-goers away from the
area. After a spell as a Masonic Lodge, it was purchased
by Edinburgh University in 1966 and restored to its
original function.

For details of St Cecilia's Hall box office, see p.215.

Externally, the building looks unexciting: the original entrance on Niddry Street is blackened with grime, and the new one created in the 1960s resembles a public toilet. The interior, however, is a beautiful shallow-domed structure, which has been restored and extended to house the **Russell Collection** of antique keyboard instruments, comprising a variety of virginals, spinets, clavichords and harpsichords, most of which are in working order – as staff will happily demonstrate. At present, the collection is very low-key, but there are plans to upgrade it with the help of funding from the Lottery over the next few years.

Magdalen Chapel

Map 3, E4. Mon–Fri 9.30am–4.30pm; free.

Towards the western end of Cowgate stands the **Magdalen Chapel**, which was built between 1541 and 1544 with money bequeathed by Michael MacQueen, a prominent citizen; the tomb of his widow, Janet Rynd, is discreetly positioned in the southeast corner. Patronage of the almshouse chapel passed to the Incorporation of Hammermen, a guild to which most Edinburgh metal workers, other than goldsmiths, belonged. One of the focal points of the Reformation, the chapel was probably the setting for the first ever General Assembly of the Church of Scotland.

In the 1620s, the Hammermen added a handsome tower and steeple, and later transformed the chapel into their guildhall, which was suitably adorned with fine ironwork. The most important feature of the chapel is a set of four brilliantly coloured heraldic roundels on the south wall, the only pre-Reformation stained glass in Scotland to have survived in situ. Look out for the lower left-hand roundel, depicting the arms of the MacQueen family, which contains the heads of several savages.

The chapel has seen a variety of uses over the centuries: from serving as a mortuary for the bodies of Covenanters (see box on p.58) hanged in the Grassmarket, to being used to display mechanical curiosities in the eighteenth century and, latterly, as the base of the Edinburgh Medical Missionary Society. Recent restoration of the chapel, now used occasionally for concerts, has reversed a long-term decline.

GRASSMARKET

Map 3, C4.

At its western end, Cowgate opens out into **Grassmarket**, which has witnessed some of the murkier aspects of Edinburgh's turbulent history: the public gallows were located here, and it has been the scene of numerous riots and other disturbances down the centuries. It was here, for example, in 1736, that Captain Porteous was lynched after he had ordered shots to be fired at the crowd watching a public execution. In a now-vanished close just off the western end of Grassmarket the notorious body-snatchers William Burke and William Hare had their lair: they would lure victims here, murder them and then sell their bodies to the eminent physician Robert Knox. Eventually, Hare betrayed his partner, who was duly executed in 1829. Today, Grassmarket still has its seamy side, though the cluster of busy bars and restaurants along its northern side are evidence of a serious attempt to clean up its image.

At the northeastern corner of Grassmarket stand five old tenements of the old **West Bow**, which once zigzagged up to the Royal Mile – the rest of the thoroughfare was replaced in the 1840s by the curving **Victoria Street**, an unusual two-tier street, with arcaded shops below, and a pedestrian terrace above. Victoria Street sweeps up to

Grassmarket and Victoria Street shops

Grassmarket and **Victoria Street** are where you'll find the most eclectic and colourful range of shops in Edinburgh. Near the eastern end of Grassmarket (called, confusingly, the "West Bow"), look out for Armstrongs, which stocks secondhand **clothes**, from full tartan regalia to 70s fashions, and The Cooks Bookshop, owned by Clarissa Dickson Wright of TV programme *Two Fat Ladies*' fame, selling new and secondhand **books** on all matters culinary. Heading up cobbled Victoria Street, take a look into Robert Cresser at no. 40, a gloomy, timeless emporium dedicated to selling **brushes** of all kinds, shapes and sizes. Opposite this is the *Bow Bar*, one of Edinburgh's finest traditional **pubs**, with wooden panelling and charming old mirrors, while a little further up, back on the Castle side, stands Iain Mellis's superbly pungent **cheesemongery**, whose wooden shelves are piled high with an incredible selection of mainly British cheeses. The tall building across the street from this, Byzantium, harbours various shops and booths selling **jewellery** and **antiques**, and has a great **café** on the very top floor.

George IV Bridge and the **National Library of Scotland** (Mon–Sat 10am–5pm, Sun 2–5pm; free), which holds a rich collection of illuminated manuscripts, early printed books, historical documents, and the letters and papers of prominent Scottish literary figures.

LOTHIAN ROAD AND THE SOUTHWEST

Map 2, C7.

The area west of Grassmarket was formerly known as Portsburgh, nominally a separate burgh outside the city walls, though in practice it was a virtual fiefdom of Edinburgh. Since the 1880s and the construction of the Royal Lyceum Theatre on Grindlay Street, the area has gradually developed into something of a theatre district. More recently, the area around **Lothian Road**, which leads south from the west end of Princes Street, has seen a good deal of construction, most notably two large financial headquarters and the Edinburgh Conference Centre. The **Museum of Fire** (by appointment only; ©0131/228 2401; free), situated on Lauriston Place next to the Art School, records the history of the oldest municipal fire brigade in Britain, formed in 1824. It contains a small collection of well-preserved manual, horse-drawn and motorized fire appliances. South of this, on the far side of the huge Edinburgh Royal Infirmary and the main university campus, the open parkland areas of the **Meadows** and **Bruntsfield Links** mark the transition to Edinburgh's genteel Victorian villa suburbs. South of the Meadows, a plaque on the wall of Sciennes Hill House in Sciennes House Place records the only known meeting, in 1787, of Robert Burns and Sir Walter Scott. On the opposite side of the street is a tiny Jewish graveyard. Prominent among the suburbs is **Morningside**, whose prim and proper outlook was immortalized in Muriel Spark's *The Prime of Miss Jean Brodie*, and remains a favourite target for ridicule.

THE GREYFRIARS AREA

Map 3, E5.

At the southwestern corner of George IV Bridge stands the **statue of Greyfriars Bobby**, which ranks among Edinburgh's most sentimental tourist attractions. Bobby was a Skye terrier acquired as a working dog by a police constable named John Gray. When the latter died in 1858, Bobby began a vigil at his grave which he maintained until he died fourteen years later. In the process, he became an

Edinburgh celebrity, fed and cared for by locals who gave him a special collar (now in the Huntly House Museum; see p.39) to prevent him from being impounded as a stray. His statue was modelled from life, and erected soon after his death; his story has gained international renown, thanks to a number of cloying books and tear-jerking movies.

The grave Bobby mourned over is in the **Greyfriars Kirkyard**, entered through the gateway behind the statue. Many famous figures are buried here, including the poet and bestseller **Allan Ramsay Senior** and **James Craig**, designer of the New Town. Among the clutter of grandiose seventeenth- and eighteenth-century funerary monuments is the striking mausoleum of the Adam family of architects. Greyfriars Kirkyard is most closely associated, however, with the long struggle to establish **Presbyterianism** in Scotland: in 1638, it was the setting for the signing of the National Covenant, while in 1679, some 1200 Covenanters were imprisoned in the enclosure at the southwestern end of the yard. Set against the northern wall is the **Martyrs' Monument**, erected in 1706, with an inscription added in 1771, part of which reads:

"Here lies interr'd the dust of those who stood,
'Gainst perjury, resisting unto blood".

An example of a mort safe, a lockable iron structure designed to deter grave-robbers, can be seen beside the path running along the south side of the church. After the founding of Edinburgh University, a shortage of bodies to use for dissection led to grave-robbing, and as early as 1711, more than one hundred years before the heyday of Burke and Hare, the Royal College of Surgeons reported: "Of late there has been a violation of sepulchres in the Greyfriars Churchyard by some who most unchristianly have been stealing, or at least attempting to carry away, the bodies of the dead out of their graves."

THE GREYFRIARS AREA

The Covenanters

When Charles I, inspired by his belief in the divine right of kings, sought to impose a new *Book of Common Prayer* and episcopacy on the Scottish people in 1637, reaction was strong. Fuelled by anger at such high-handed interference, a number of leading figures in Scotland drew up a **National Covenant**, calling for "a glorious marriage of the kingdom and God" through the maintenance of Presbyterian church structures. It was signed in Greyfriars Kirkyard the following year by around 5000 people, and subsequently by some 300,000 across Scotland. In November 1638, the General Assembly of the Church of Scotland denounced Charles's Episcopalian reforms, and the **Covenanters** readied themselves for civil war against royalist forces. With the outbreak of the Civil War in England they forged links with the English opposition to Charles through the **Solemn League and Covenant** of 1643.

Following the execution of Charles I in 1649, Charles II's acquiescence to the Covenant persuaded the Scots to back their monarch. This set them against Oliver Cromwell, who sent an army north, defeated the Scottish army, and subdued large parts of Scotland, capturing Edinburgh Castle along the way.

After the restoration of the monarchy in 1660, Charles II reneged on his signing of the Covenant and sought to reintroduce episcopacy. The Covenanters were forced to hold prayer meetings outdoors in conventicles and were subject to repression for many years. After the battle of **Bothwell Bridge** in 1679, around 1200 Covenanters were detained in Greyfriars Kirkyard for four months. Many died; some who promised not to rebel again were released and the remainder were put on a ship for Barbados, which sank off the Orkney Islands leaving only forty survivors. Covenanter resistance weakened after this point with only a hard core, known as the Cameronians, surviving into the eighteenth century.

The graveyard rather overshadows **Greyfriars Kirk** itself, completed in 1620 – the first church to be built in Edinburgh after the Reformation. It's a real oddball in both layout and design, having a nave and aisles but no chancel, and adopting the anachronistic architectural language of the friary that preceded it, complete with medieval-looking windows, arches and buttresses.

At the western end of Greyfriars Kirkyard is one of the most significant surviving portions of the **Flodden Wall**, the city fortifications erected in the wake of Scotland's disastrous military defeat of 1513. When open, the gateway beyond offers a shortcut to **George Heriot's School**, otherwise approached from Lauriston Place to the south. Founded as a home for poor boys by "Jinglin Geordie" Heriot, James VI's goldsmith, it is now one of Edinburgh's most prestigious fee-paying schools. During the school summer holiday, senior pupils offer guided **tours** of the building (July to mid-Aug Mon–Fri 10am–noon & 1–4pm, Sat 10am–noon). At other times of the year the building is closed to visitors, although you can wander round the quadrangle, whose array of towers, turrets, chimneys, carved doorways and traceried windows is one of the finest achievements of the Scottish Renaissance.

THE NATIONAL MUSEUM OF SCOTLAND

Map 3, F5. Mon–Sat 10am–5pm, Tues 10am–8pm, Sun noon–5pm; £3, includes entry to Royal Museum of Scotland; free Tues 4.30–8pm; one-year season ticket £5.

Immediately opposite the statue of Greyfriars Bobby, on the south side of Chambers Street, stands the striking honey-coloured sandstone building of the **National Museum of Scotland**. Opened in 1998 to deserved acclaim, both for its elegant design and for its respectful but imaginative treatment of the nation's treasures, this is undoubtedly Scotland's premier museum. The fresh, open atmosphere of the building is

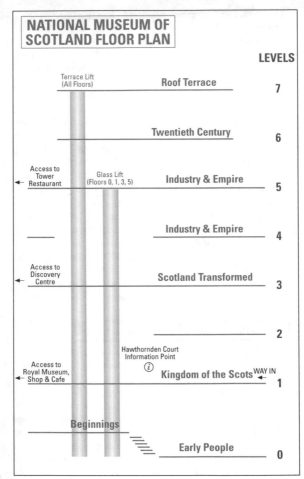

NATIONAL MUSEUM OF SCOTLAND FLOOR PLAN

LEVELS

Terrace Lift (All Floors)

Roof Terrace — 7

Twentieth Century — 6

Access to Tower Restaurant ←

Glass Lift (Floors 0, 1, 3, 5)

Industry & Empire — 5

Industry & Empire — 4

Access to Discovery Centre ←

Scotland Transformed — 3

— 2

Hawthornden Court Information Point

(i)

Access to Royal Museum, Shop & Cafe ←

Kingdom of the Scots ← WAY IN — 1

Beginnings

Early People — 0

combined with terrific features – specially commissioned art works; the **Discovery Centre**, specifically aimed at 5–14-year-olds; the **exhibIT** computer bank with databases of the museum's collections; and the **Tower Restaurant**, a sleek, stylish venue, with fabulous views, also open in the evenings (see p.178).

The lack of a figurehead national museum had been keenly felt by Scotland for decades, but it wasn't until the late 1980s that funding was made available, with construction beginning in 1996. Designed by architects Benson & Forsyth, it was built principally from sandstone quarried near Elgin in northeast Scotland. The most striking feature of the exterior is the cylindrical entrance tower, which breaks up the angular, modern lines of the building and echoes the shape of the Half Moon Battery of Edinburgh Castle. Tall windows reveal glimpses of the interior, an effect continued inside, where unexpected views of the floors above and below, as well as out onto the street, emphasize the interconnectedness of the layers of Scotland's history.

The main entrance to the museum is at the base of the tower, although it is also possible to enter through the neighbouring Royal Museum of Scotland (see p.65). The information desk in **Hawthornden Court**, the central atrium of the museum, is a useful orientation point. On this level you'll also find the museum shop, the sound guide desk and access to the Royal Museum's café. The glossy **brochure** on sale (£4.99) is more a photographic souvenir than a guidebook, but free guided tours on different themes take place throughout the day, and free audio headsets give detailed information on artefacts and displays.

Beginnings and early people

To get to the first section, "**Beginnings**", take the lift or stairs from Hawthornden Court down to Level 0. Here,

Scotland's story before the arrival of man is recounted with audiovisual displays, artistic re-creations and a selection of rocks and fossils, including some Lewisian gneiss, the oldest rock in Europe, and "Lizzie" (*Westlothiana lizziae*), the oldest known fossil reptile in the world.

The second section, "**Early People**", also on Level 0, covers the period from the arrival of the first people to the end of the first millennium AD. This, in many ways, is the most engrossing section of the entire museum, an eloquent testament to the remarkable craftsmanship, artistry and practicality of Scotland's early people. The best way to approach this section is from the doors of the main lift, where you are confronted by eight giant bronze figures in the distinctive post-industrial style of Edinburgh-born sculptor **Sir Eduardo Paolozzi**. Small display compartments containing artefacts such as necklaces and bracelets are incorporated into the bronze figures. The innovative use of contemporary art is continued with installations by the environmental artist **Andy Goldsworthy**, who shapes natural materials into sinuously beautiful geometrical patterns. Look out for *Hearth*, created from pieces of wood found on the construction site of the new museum, and *Enclosure*, four curved walls of slate roof tiles, and four separate panels of cracked clay set into the walls of the museum. Among the artefacts on display highlights include the **Trappain treasure** hoard, around 44lb of silver plates, cutlery and goblets found buried in East Lothian; the **Cramond Lioness**, a sculpture from a Roman tombstone found recently in the Firth of Forth; and the beautifully detailed gold, silver and amber **Hunterston brooch**, dating from around 700 AD and found on the Ayrshire coast.

The Kingdom of the Scots

"**The Kingdom of the Scots**" on Level 1 covers the period between Scotland's development as a single independent nation and the union with England in 1707. At the entrance to the section in Hawthornden Court stands the **Dupplin Cross**, a symbol of the different peoples who united under King Kenneth MacAlpin to form a single kingdom in 843. Many famous Scots are represented here, including Robert the Bruce – though not his near-contemporary William Wallace, because so few objects associated with him exist – and Mary, Queen of Scots and her son James VI, under whom the crowns of Scotland and England became united in 1603. Star exhibits include the **Monymusk reliquary**, an intricately decorated box said to have carried the remains of St Columba; the **Lewis chessmen**, exquisitely idiosyncratic twelfth-century pieces carved from walrus ivory; and the "**Maiden**", an early form of the guillotine, dating from the sixteenth century. The section looking at the role of the **church** in this period is notable not only for the craftsmanship of some of the objects, in particular the silver gilt **St Fillan's crozier**, but also for the way in which the displays on the National Covenant (see box on p.58) are cleverly juxtaposed with glimpses through the window of Greyfriars Kirkyard, the place where the Covenant was signed in 1638.

Also on this floor, the often overlooked heritage and society of the **Gaels**, the people who populated most of northern and western Scotland, is covered in "Na Gaidheil", with displays of beautifully patterned Highland brooches; claymores and dirks, the Highlander's fighting weapons; and an exquisite clarsach, or harp, dating from around 1500.

Scotland Transformed

Level 3 shows exhibits on the theme "**Scotland Transformed**", covering the century or so following the Union of Parliaments in 1707. This was the period which

SCOTLAND TRANSFORMED

saw the last of the Highland uprisings under Bonnie Prince Charlie, and also witnessed the expansion of trade links with the Americas and developments in industries such as weaving and iron and steel production. Dominating the floor is a reconstructed steam-driven **Newcomen engine** invented in the early eighteenth century and in popular use during the late eighteenth and early nineteenth century, and still being used to pump water from a coal mine in Ayrshire in 1901. Alongside it is part of a thatched, cruck-frame house of the 1720s, of a type in which many Scots still lived during the eighteenth century.

Industry and Empire

Following the early innovations of steam and mechanical engineering, Scotland went on to pioneer many aspects of heavy engineering, with ship and locomotive production to the fore. Largest of the exhibits in "**Industry and Empire**" is the steam locomotive *Ellesmere*, which has the honour of being the first object installed in the museum – it had to be lowered into place before the upper storeys could be built. As well as industrial progress, other fields are covered too, including domestic life, leisure activities and the influence of Scots outside Scotland, both as a result of emigration, and through such luminaries as James Watt, Charles Rennie Mackintosh (see p.126) and Robert Louis Stevenson (see p.33).

The Twentieth Century Gallery

For the **Twentieth Century Gallery** on Level 6, a range of Scots, from schoolchildren to celebrities, were asked to pick a single object to represent the twentieth century. Choices are intriguing, controversial and unexpected, from computers to football strips, cans of Irn Bru to a black

Saab convertible. Tony Blair, who went to Fettes school in Edinburgh, chose a Fender Stratocaster guitar, and former Edinburgh "milkie" Sean Connery a milk bottle. The obvious challenge is implicitly made: what would you choose, and why? Other features worth taking in here include a small **cinema** showing black-and-white documentary films about life in Scotland in the 1930s, and the often-overlooked but delightful **roof garden**, accessed by a lift. Up here, sweeping views open out to the Firth of Forth, the Pentland Hills, and across to the Castle and Royal Mile skyline.

THE ROYAL MUSEUM OF SCOTLAND

Map 3, F5. Mon–Sat 10am–5pm, Tues 10am–8pm, Sun noon–5pm; £3, includes entry to the National Museum of Scotland; free Tues 4.30–8pm; one-year season ticket £5.

Interlinked with the National Museum, though also with its own entrance, is the **Royal Museum of Scotland**, a dignified Venetian-style palace with a cast-iron interior, built in 1866 and extended in 1914. Intended as Scotland's answer to the museum complex in London's South Kensington, the Royal Museum contains an extraordinarily eclectic range of exhibits, from exotic stuffed animals to colonial loot. The neat slogan used to describe the different roles of the sister museums is that the National Museum shows Scotland to the world, and the Royal Museum shows the world to Scotland.

....

There is a café serving cakes, coffee and light snacks in the main hall of the Royal Museum, near the passage that links it to the National Museum.

....

The **sculpture** in the lofty entrance hall begins with a superb Assyrian relief from the royal palace at Nimrud, and ranges via classical Greece, Rome and Nubia to buddhas from Japan and Burma and a totem pole from British Columbia. Also on the ground floor are the **Power Collections**, which include a double-action beam engine designed by James Watt in 1786, a section of the Inchkeith lighthouse and the control desk from Hunterston A nuclear reactor.

Upstairs there's a fine array of Egyptian mummies, ceramics from ancient Greece to the present day, costumes, jewellery, natural-history displays and a splendid selection of European decorative art ranging from early medieval liturgical objects via Limoges enamels and sixteenth-century German woodcarving to stunning **French silverware** made during the reign of Louis XIV. Finally, on the top floor, you'll come to a distinguished collection of historic scientific instruments, a small selection of arms and armour, plus sections on geology, ethnology and Oriental arts. The Asian selection was boosted by the opening, in 1996, of the **Ivy Wu Gallery**, displaying the arts of China, Korea and Japan in a highly informative way. Look out for a splendid sixteenth-century Chinese throne and Buddhist art from each of the three nations.

THE UNIVERSITY

Map 3, G4.

Alongside the Royal Museum is the earliest surviving part of the **University of Edinburgh**, variously referred to as Old College or Old Quad, although nowadays it houses only a few university departments; the main campus colonizes the streets and squares to the south.

The Old College was designed by Robert Adam, but built after his death in a considerably modified form, owing to lack of cash, by William Playfair, one of Edinburgh's greatest architects. Playfair built just one of Adam's two

Darnley's murder

In January 1567, **Lord Darnley**, who had contracted smallpox, was brought to a church known as Kirk o'Field, close to what is now the quadrangle of Old College, in order to ensure that he did not infect his infant son in Holyrood. On the night of February 9, the building was destroyed by a huge explosion and the body of Darnley was found in the grounds outside. There were no signs of his body having been in an explosion: examination showed that he had been strangled. Mary, Queen of Scots, who had visited her husband on the evening in question and was later seen walking up Blackfriars Wynd, is generally considered to have been implicated in the murder. These allegations cannot be proved, but what is known is that Mary was by then involved with the Earl of Bothwell, who was almost certainly responsible for the deed. After his arrest and suspiciously speedy acquittal, Bothwell abducted Mary on her way from Stirling to Linlithgow, divorced his own wife and married the queen on May 15, 1567. Within a month Mary had surrendered to the enraged nobles of Scotland: Bothwell fled to Orkney and then Norway, where he died in captivity eleven years later.

quadrangles (the dome was not added until 1879). Playfair's magnificent **Upper Library** is now used mostly for ceremonial occasions.

The **Talbot Rice Art Gallery** (Tues–Sat noon–5pm; free) in the Old College displays some of the University's large art collection, including many splendid seventeenth-century paintings from the Low Countries, with Teniers, Steen and van de Velde well represented. The gallery also hosts touring and temporary exhibitions on a regular basis, and the show during the Festival is normally of a high standard.

THE SOUTHSIDE

Map 3, G5.

Located south of the University of Edinburgh, the **Southside** is a tenement suburb that grew up in the eighteenth century. Since the 1950s, the area has developed into a lively academic quarter, having been progressively colonized by the overspill of University buildings. One block up from the Old College is the glass-fronted **Festival Theatre**, a refurbished music hall which opened in 1994, giving the city a long-awaited venue for large-scale opera and dance. Opposite this is **Surgeons' Hall**, a handsome Ionic temple built by Playfair as the headquarters of the Royal College of Surgeons. Most of it is only accessible to the public one day a year, an exception being the museum, entered from 9 Hill Square (Mon–Fri 2–4pm; free), which has intriguing, if somewhat specialist, exhibits on the history of medicine.

The New Town

he **New Town**, itself well over two hundred years old, stands in total contrast to the Old Town: the layout is symmetrical, the streets broad and straight, and most of the buildings are Neoclassical. The entire area, right down to the names of its streets, is something of a celebration of the Union, which was then generally regarded as a proud development in Scotland's history. Though originally intended as a residential quarter, today the New Town is the bustling hub of the city's professional, commercial and business life, dominated by shops, banks and offices.

The New Town chiefly owes its existence to the vision of **George Drummond**, who made schemes for the expansion of the city soon after becoming Lord Provost in 1725. Work began on the draining of the Nor' Loch below the castle in 1759, a job that was to take some sixty years. The North Bridge, linking the Old Town with the port of Leith, was built between 1763 and 1772, and, in 1766, following a public competition, a plan for the New Town by a 20-year-old architect, **James Craig**, was chosen. Its gridiron pattern was perfectly matched to the site: the central **George Street**, flanked by showpiece squares, was laid out along the main ridge, with the parallel **Princes Street** and **Queen Street** on either side below, and two smaller streets, Thistle Street and Rose Street in between the three major thoroughfares. These smaller streets were for coach houses, artisans' dwellings and shops. Princes and Queen streets were built up on one side only, so as not to block the spectacular views of the Old Town and Fife. Architects were accordingly afforded a wonderful opportunity to play with vistas and spatial relationships, particularly well exploited by Robert Adam, who contributed extensively to the later phases of the project. The First New Town, as the area covered by Craig's plan came to be known, received a whole series of extensions in the first few decades of the nineteenth century, all in harmony with the Neoclassical style.

In many ways, the layout of the New Town is its own most remarkable sight, an extraordinary grouping of squares, circuses, terraces, crescents and parks, with a few set pieces such as **Register House**, the north frontage of **Charlotte Square** and the assemblage of curiosities on and around **Calton Hill**. It also contains an assortment of Victorian additions, notably the **Scott Monument**, as well as three of the city's most important public collections – the **National Gallery of Scotland**, the **Scottish National Portrait Gallery** and the **Scottish National Gallery of Modern Art**. On the northern edge of the New Town lies one of Edinburgh's greatest features – the **Royal Botanic Garden**, an oasis of calm in an otherwise busy city.

PRINCES STREET

Map 4, I6.

Although only allocated a subsidiary role in the original plan of the New Town, **Princes Street** had developed into Edinburgh's principal thoroughfare by the middle of the nineteenth century, a role it has retained ever since. Its unobstructed views across to the castle and the Old Town are undeniably magnificent. Indeed, without the views Princes Street would lose much of its appeal: its northern side, dominated for the most part by ugly department stores, is almost always crowded with shoppers, and few of the original eighteenth-century buildings remain.

It was the coming of the railway, which follows a parallel course to the south, that ensured Princes Street's rise to prominence. The tracks which run into Waverley Station at the eastern end of the street are well concealed at the far end of the sunken gardens that replaced the Nor' Loch. Known as the **Princes Street Gardens**, they provide ample space to relax or picnic during the summer. Thomas De Quincey, author of the classic account of drug addiction, *Confessions of an English Opium Eater* (1821), spent the last thirty years of his life in Edinburgh and is buried in the graveyard of **St Cuthbert's Church**, beneath the castle at the western end of the gardens.

The East End

Register House (map 4, K5; Mon–Fri 10am–4pm; free), Princes Street's most distinguished building, stands at the thoroughfare's extreme northeastern corner. Register House was designed in the 1770s by Robert Adam to hold Scotland's historic records, a function it has maintained ever since. Its exterior is a model of restrained Neoclassicism; the interior, centred on a glorious Roman rotunda, has a dome lavishly decorated with plasterwork and antique-style medallions. Unfortunately, the majesty of the building is marred by the **St James Centre** to the rear, a covered shopping arcade, a grey angular behemoth, woefully out of keeping with the elegant Georgian buildings around it and now regarded as the city's worst ever planning blunder.

....

For a review of *The Balmoral* and other good places to stay in the New Town see p.156.

....

Opposite Register House is one of the few buildings on the south side of Princes Street, *The Balmoral*, one of the most luxurious hotels in the city. Formerly the **North British Hotel**, and still popularly known as the "NB", its name was changed in a gesture of political correctness by its owners: North Britain was an alternative name for Scotland throughout the eighteenth and nineteenth centuries, and is regarded by Scots as an affront. Originally built by the owners of the North British Railway for travellers arriving at neighbouring Waverley station, *The Balmoral* maintains its association with the railway, and the timepiece on its bulky clock tower is always kept two minutes fast in order to encourage passengers to hurry to catch their trains. Alongside the hotel, **Princes Mall** (map 4, K6) is a sensitive modern redevelopment that carefully avoided repeating the mistakes of the St James Centre. The open-air piazza on its street-level roof is home to Edinburgh's Tourist Information Office and is a favourite haunt of street-theatre groups and other performing artists during the Festival.

The Scott Monument and the Royal Scottish Academy

Facing Jenners, the Victorian shopping emporium, and set within East Princes Street Gardens, the two hundred-foot-high **Scott Monument** (map 4, I6; March–May & Oct daily 10am–6pm; June–Sept Mon–Sat 9am–8pm, Sun 10am–6pm; Nov–Feb daily 10am–4pm; £2.50), the largest monument in the world to be erected to a writer, was built with donations from the public in memory of Scott within a few years of his death. Its magisterial, spire-like design is due to George Meikle Kemp, a carpenter and joiner whose only building this is; while it was still under construction, he stumbled into a canal one foggy evening and drowned. The architecture is closely modelled on Scott's beloved Melrose Abbey, while the rich sculptural decoration shows 16 Scottish writers and 64 characters from the *Waverley* novels. Underneath the archway stands a **statue** of Scott with his deerhound Maida, carved from a thirty-ton block of Carrara marble.

Following recent restoration work, the monument is fully on view again after being hidden by shrouds for a couple of years. Visitors are also able to climb the internal spiral staircase for some inspiring – if heady – vistas of the city below and hills and firths beyond.

The Princes Street Gardens are bisected by the **Mound**, which provides a road link between the Old and New towns. The Mound was formed, as its name suggests, from heaps of earth and other waste that were dumped here when the New Town was being built in the second half of the eighteenth century. It created a ramp between the Old and New Towns across the drained Nor' Loch, which became Princes Street Gardens.

At the junction of the Mound and Princes Street, Playfair's **Royal Scottish Academy**, or RSA (map 4, H7; Mon–Sat 10am–5pm, Sun 2–5pm; price varies), built in the style of a Doric temple, hosts the RSA annual exhibition from April to July and other temporary exhibitions during the rest of the year. The Academy is one of the Neoclassical buildings which helped give the city its tag "Athens of the North", though recently the building has fallen into a bad state of repair. The building's dignity isn't raised by the habitual use of its exterior as a public toilet, a gathering point for some of the city's homeless population and occasional flea market. From time to time there is talk of a possible merger with the National Gallery and even of closure, but no firm plans for its future have been made as yet.

Sir Walter Scott

Alongside Robert Burns and Robert Louis Stevenson, **Sir Walter Scott** (1771–1832) is part of Edinburgh's triumvirate of great literary figures, and of the three it is Scott who can claim to have had the most profound influence on English literature in general.

Born in a house on College Wynd (now Guthrie Street) to a solidly bourgeois family, Scott contracted polio as a child and was sent to recuperate at his grandfather's farm in the Borders, where his imagination was fired by tales of that area's history and legends. He returned to Edinburgh in 1779 to be educated at the High School and then Edinburgh University, where he studied law, qualifying as an advocate in 1792. His real interests remained elsewhere, however, and throughout the 1790s he transcribed hundreds of old Border ballads, publishing a three-volume collection entitled *Minstrelsy of the Scottish Borders* in 1802. An instant success, *Minstrelsy* was followed by Scott's own narrative poems *Lay of the Last Minstrel*, *Marmion* and *The Lady of the Lake*.

In 1797, Scott moved to 39 North Castle St in Edinburgh's New Town with his wife Charlotte, and divided his time between Edinburgh and his border seat at Abbotsford. Despite the popularity of his early work, and the fact that he had two prestigious paid jobs – one as the Sheriff-Depute of Selkirkshire, the other as clerk to the Court of Session in Edinburgh – Scott's finances remained shaky. From 1813, he was writing to pay the bills and thumped out a veritable flood of historical novels using his extensive knowledge of Scottish history and folklore. His best works came in the space of the next ten years, beginning with *Waverley* (1814), a runaway success despite the fact that it was published anonymously. This was followed by more novels "by the author of Waverley", including *Guy Mannering* (1815), *Rob Roy* and *The Heart of Midlothian* (both 1818), *Ivanhoe* (1819) and *Kenilworth* (1821). By this time Scott was the preeminent public figure in Edinburgh and Scottish life, organizing the successful search for the Honours of Scotland, discovered in Edinburgh Castle in 1818, the same year he was created a baronet, and co-ordinating the tartan-draped visit of George IV to Edinburgh in 1822. This event, seen as a watershed between the turbulent years of the Jacobite rebellions and Scotland's embrace of the more worldly vision of the United Kingdom, crowned Scott's romantic refashioning of his country's landscape and history, a vision which has endured as the prominent popular image of Scotland to this day. Only a few years later, however, a publishing venture Scott was involved in crashed, leaving him with huge debts which he vowed to pay off by writing. He buried himself in his craft, producing a succession of weighty tomes among which only *Tales of a Grandfather*, another reworking of Scottish legends, stands out, but in six years he earned over £50,000 for his creditors. Inevitably, however, his health suffered and his last years were plagued by illness. He died at Abbotsford in 1832 and was buried within the ruins of Dryburgh Abbey.

Although even his best-known works seem ponderous and heavy by today's standards, his undoubted lyricism and colourful, romantic plots can prove delightful to those with the patience to tackle them. Beyond that, however, his lasting importance is in his essential invention of the historical novel, a formula whose instant appeal and sustained hold over the bestselling lists of the day has been matched by very few authors since.

SIR WALTER SCOTT

THE NATIONAL GALLERY OF SCOTLAND

Map 4, H8. Mon–Sat 10am–5pm, Sun 2–5pm; free.

To the rear of the Royal Scottish Academy stands another of Playfair's constructions, the **National Gallery of Scotland**, built in the 1840s and now home to a choice display of paintings, many of which are on loan from the Duke of Sutherland. The knowledgeable staff wear tartan trousers, one of a series of innovations introduced by the flamboyant English director, Timothy Clifford. One of his more controversial decisions was to restore the original Playfair rooms on the ground floor to their 1840s appearance: the pictures are hung closely together, often on two levels, and interspersed with sculptures and *objets d'art* to produce a deliberately cluttered effect. As a result, lesser works, which would otherwise languish in the vaults, are also on display, though often a good fifteen feet up. Two small, late nineteenth-century works in room 12 – one anonymous, the other by A.E. Moffat – show the gallery as it was, with paintings stacked up even higher than at present.

Though individual works are frequently rearranged and well-known works are often out on loan, the layout is broadly chronological, starting in the upper rooms above the entrance, and continuing clockwise around the ground floor. The upper part of the rear extension is devoted to smaller panels of the eighteenth and nineteenth centuries, while the basement contains most of the Scottish collection.

Early Netherlandish and German works

Among the gallery's most valuable treasures are the Trinity Panels, the remaining parts of the only surviving pre-Reformation altarpiece made for a Scottish church. Painted by **Hugo van der Goes** in the mid-fifteenth century, they were commissioned for the Holy Trinity Collegiate Church by its provost Edward Bonkil. The finest and best preserved of the four panels shows Bonkil in the company of organ-playing angels. On the reverse sides are portraits of James III, his son (the future James IV) and Queen Margaret of Denmark. Their feebly characterized heads were modelled from life by an unknown local painter after the altar had been shipped to Edinburgh.

Of the later Netherlandish works, **Gerard David** is represented by the touchingly anecdotal *Three Legends of St Nicholas*, while the *Portrait of a Notary* by **Quentin Massys** is an excellent early example of northern European assimilation of the forms and techniques of the Italian Renaissance. Many of his German contemporaries developed their own variations on this style, among them **Cranach**, by whom there is a splendidly erotic *Venus and Cupid*, and **Holbein**, whose *Allegory of the Old and New Testaments* is a Protestant tract painted for an English patron.

The Italian Renaissance

The Italian section includes a wonderful array of **Renaissance** masterpieces, including *The Virgin Adoring the Child,* a beautiful composition set against a background of ruins, shown in strict perspective: although known to have been painted in the workshop of the great Florentine sculptor **Andrea del Verrocchio**, its authorship remains a mystery. Equally graceful are the three works by **Raphael**, particularly *The Bridgewater Madonna* and the tondo of *The Holy Family with a Palm Tree*, whose striking luminosity has been revealed after recent restoration.

Of the four mythological scenes by **Titian**, the allegorical *Three Ages of Man* is one of the most accomplished compositions of his early period, while the later *Venus Anadyomene* ranks among the great nudes of Western art, notwithstanding its rough state of preservation. The companion pair of

Diana and Acteon and *Diana and Calisto*, painted for Philip II of Spain, show the almost impressionistic freedom of his late style. **Bassano**'s truly regal *Adoration of the Kings*, a dramatic altarpiece depicting *The Descent from the Cross* by **Tintoretto**, and several other works by **Veronese**, complete a fine Venetian collection.

The seventeenth century

Among the seventeenth-century works is the gallery's most important sculpture, **Bernini**'s *Bust of Monsignor Carlo Antonio dal Pozzo*. **El Greco**'s *A Fable*, painted during his early years in Italy, is a mysterious subject whose exact meaning is unclear, while *The Saviour of the World* is a typically intense, visionary image from the artist's mature years in Spain. Indigenous Spanish art is represented by **Velázquez**'s *An Old Woman Cooking Eggs*, an astonishingly assured work for a lad of 19, and by **Zurbarán**'s *The Immaculate Conception*, part of his ambitious decorative scheme for the Carthusian monastery in Jerez. There are two small copper panels by the short-lived but enormously influential Rome-based German painter **Adam Elsheimer**; of these, *Il Contento*, showing Jupiter's descent to Earth to punish the ungodly, is a *tour de force* of technical precision.

Given its own room, *The Seven Sacraments* is a series of paintings by **Poussin** based on the artist's own extensive research into biblical times. The set, the second that Poussin painted, marks the first attempt to portray scenes from the life of Jesus and the early Christians in a historically authentic manner. The result is profoundly touching, with a myriad of imaginative and subtle details. Poussin's fellow Frenchman **Claude** is represented by his largest canvas, *Landscape with Apollo, the Muses and a River God*, which radiates his characteristically idealized vision of classical antiquity.

As for Poussin's and Claude's contemporaries in the Low Countries, **Rubens'** *The Feast of Herod* is an archetypal example of his grand manner, in which the gory subject matter is overshadowed by the depiction of the delights of the table. Like all his large works, it was executed with extensive studio assistance. Small-scale works include three sketches, among them the highly finished *Adoration of the Shepherds*. The trio of large upright canvases by **Van Dyck** date from his early Genoese period; of these, *The Lomellini Family* shows his mastery at creating a definitive dynastic image.

Among the four canvases by **Rembrandt** is a poignant *Self-Portrait Aged 51*, and the rather suggestive *Woman in Bed*, which probably represents the biblical figure of Sarah on her wedding night, waiting for her husband Tobias to put the devil to flight. *Christ in the House of Martha and Mary* is the largest and probably the earliest of the thirty or so surviving paintings of **Vermeer**; as the only one with a religious subject, it inspired a notorious series of forgeries by Han van Meegeren. There are two portraits by **Hals**, plus a brilliant caricature, *Verdonck*. There's also an excellent cross-section of the specialist Dutch painters of the age, highlights being the mischievous *School for Boys and Girls* by **Jan Steen**, and the strangely haunting *Interior of the Church of St Bavo in Haarlem* by **Pieter Saenredam**, one of the gallery's most expensive purchases.

The eighteenth and nineteenth centuries

Of the large-scale eighteenth-century works, **Tiepolo's** *The Finding of Moses*, a glorious bravura fantasy, stands out. Other decorative compositions of the same period are **Goya's** *The Doctor*, a cartoon for a tapestry design, and three large pastoral scenes by **Boucher**. However, the gems of the French section are the smaller panels, in particular

THE NATIONAL GALLERY OF SCOTLAND

Watteau's *Fêtes Vénitiennes*, an effervescent Rococo idyll, and **Chardin**'s *Vase of Flowers*, a copybook example of still-life painting. One of the gallery's most recent major purchases is **Canova**'s statue *The Three Graces*. However, as part of the purchase agreement it is on loan to the Victoria & Albert museum in London until 2006.

There's also a superb group of Impressionist and Post-Impressionist masterpieces, including a particularly good cross-section of the works of **Degas**, three outstanding examples of **Gauguin**, set respectively in Brittany, Martinique and Tahiti, and **Cézanne**'s *The Tall Trees* – a clear forerunner of modern abstraction.

English and American paintings

Surprisingly, the gallery has relatively few **English** paintings, but those that are on display here are impressive. **Hogarth**'s *Sarah Malcolm*, painted in Newgate Prison the day the murderess was executed, once belonged to Horace Walpole, who also commissioned **Reynolds**' *The Ladies Waldegrave*, a group portrait of his three great-nieces. **Gainsborough**'s *The Honourable Mrs Graham* is one of his most memorable society portraits ever, while **Constable** himself described *Dedham Vale* as being "perhaps my best". The gallery owns a wonderful array of **Turner** water-colours, but these are displayed each January only, as it is feared that strong light may damage them. Two of the artist's finest Roman views are displayed all year round.

Even more unexpected than the scarcity of English works is the presence of some exceptional **American** canvases: **Benjamin West**'s Romantic fantasy, *King Alexander III Rescued from a Stag*, **John Singer Sargent**'s brilliant *Lady Agnew of Lochnaw*, and **Frederic Edwin Church**'s *View of Niagara Falls from the American Side*. The last, having been kept in store for decades, was put back on display when the "rediscovery" of the artist in the late 1970s prompted astronomical bids from American museums keen to acquire the only work by the artist owned by a European gallery.

Scottish art

On the face of it, the gallery's **Scottish** collection, which represents the entire gamut of Scottish painting from seventeenth-century portraiture to the Arts and Crafts movement, is something of an anticlimax. There are, however, some important works – **Gavin Hamilton**'s *Achilles Mourning the Death of Patroclus*, for example, painted in Rome, is a particularly arresting image. **Allan Ramsay**, who became court painter to George III, is represented by his intimate *The Artist's Second Wife* and *Jean-Jacques Rousseau*, in which the philosopher is shown in Armenian costume.

Of **Sir Henry Raeburn**'s large portraits, note *Sir John Sinclair* and *Colonel Alistair MacDonell of Glengarry*, both of whom are shown in full Highland dress. Raeburn's technical mastery was equally sure when he was working on a small scale, as shown in one of the gallery's most popular pictures, *The Rev Robert Walker Skating on Duddingston Loch*.

Other Scottish painters represented include the versatile **Sir David Wilkie**, whose huge history painting, *Sir David Baird Discovering the Body of Sultan Tippo Saib*, stands in marked contrast to the early documentary and genre scenes displayed in the basement. **Alexander Nasmyth**'s tendency to gild the lily can be seen in his *View of Tantallon Castle and the Bass Rock*, where the dramatic scenery is further spiced up by the inclusion of a shipwreck. More recent Scottish work is best represented in works such as Sir William McTaggart's *The Storm*, and James Guthrie's *A Hind's Daughter*, along with Phoebe Anna Traquair's exquisite Arts and Crafts panels.

THE NATIONAL GALLERY OF SCOTLAND

GEORGE STREET AND CHARLOTTE SQUARE

George Street (map 4, C6), which runs parallel to Princes Street, was originally designed to be the centrepiece of the First New Town, joining two grand squares. Once the site of the city's most august financial institutions it has become in the last decade a marginally higher-brow version of Princes Street, and the big-money deals are now done in designer-label shops and refitted banks sell most of their liquid assets in pint glasses. At its eastern end lies **St Andrew Square** (map 4, I4), in the middle of which is a statue of Lord Melville, Pitt the Younger's Navy Treasurer. On the eastern side of the square stands a handsome eighteenth-century town mansion, designed by Sir William Chambers and headquarters of the Royal Bank of Scotland since 1825. On the south side of the street, the oval-shaped church of **St Andrew and St George** (map 4, H5) is chiefly famous as the scene of the 1843 General Assembly of the Church of Scotland, during which over four hundred ministers under the leadership of **Thomas Chalmers** walked out over the issue of patronage – they believed congregations rather than landowners had the right to choose their own ministers. With cheering crowds thronging the streets, the group walked down to a hall in Canonmills, where the "Free" Church of Scotland was established. A **statue** of Thomas Chalmers stands in the middle of the intersection between George and Castle streets. Famous visitors to George Street have included Percy Bysshe Shelley, who stayed at no. 60 with the 16-year-old Harriet Westbrook during the summer of 1811, and Charles Dickens, who gave a number of readings of his works in the Assembly Rooms in the 1840s and 1850s.

At the western end of George Street, **Charlotte Square** (map 4, B7) was designed by Robert Adam in 1791, a year before his death. For the most part, the architect's plans were faithfully implemented, an exception being the domed and porticoed church of St George, which was simplified on grounds of expense. The church's interior was gutted in the 1960s and refurbished as **West Register House** (map 4, A7), a kind of annexe to Register House at the opposite end of Princes Street; it also features changing documentary exhibitions (Mon–Fri 10am–4pm; free).

The Georgian House

Map 4, B6.

The north side of Charlotte Square has become the most exclusive address in the city. No. 6 is the official residence of the First Minister of the Scottish Parliament, and also where Scottish cabinet meetings take place. The upper storeys of no. 7 are the home of the Moderator of the General Assembly, the annually elected leader of the Church of Scotland. Restored by the NTS, the lower floors are open to the public under the name of the **Georgian House** (April–Oct Mon–Sat 10am–5pm, Sun 2–5pm; £4.40). The house's contents give a good idea of what the house must have looked like during the period of the first owner, John Lamont, chief of the Clan Lamont, who paid £1800 for it in 1796. The rooms are decked out in period furniture, including a working barrel organ which plays a selection of Scottish airs. There are a number of fine paintings, including portraits by Ramsay and Raeburn, seventeenth-century Dutch cabinet pictures, and a beautiful *Marriage of the Virgin* by El Greco's teacher, the Italian miniaturist Giulio Clovio. In the basement you can see the original wine cellar, lined with roughly made bins, and a kitchen, complete with an open fire for roasting and a separate oven for baking; video reconstructions of life below and above stairs are shown in a nearby room.

THE GEORGIAN HOUSE

THE SCOTTISH NATIONAL PORTRAIT GALLERY

Map 4, J3. Mon–Sat 10am–5pm, Sun 2–5pm; free.

At the far eastern end of Queen Street, parallel to George Street, stands the **Scottish National Portrait Gallery**. The building is itself a fascinating period piece, its red-sandstone exterior, modelled on the Doge's Palace in Venice, encrusted with statues of famous Scots – a theme taken up in the entrance hall, which has a mosaic-like frieze procession of great figures from Scotland's past, executed by William Hole. By the same artist, murals of stirring episodes from the nation's history adorn the balcony above. Temporary exhibitions are displayed in the galleries on the ground floor, which is where you'll also find the gallery shop and **café**, a favourite spot with locals.

The Upper Galleries

The permanent exhibitions are located on the two upper floors, and are devoted to **portraits**, accompanied by potted biographies, of famous Scots – a definition stretched to include anyone with the slightest Scottish connection. Taken as a whole, the gallery offers an engaging procession through Scottish history, with familiar images of famous Scots such as Mary, Queen of Scots; Robert Burns; and Bonnie Prince Charlie. The gallery owns two portraits of the last, one by Antonio David showing him as an aristocratic, rosy-cheeked twelve-year-old, the other, by Maurice-Quentin de la Tour, depicting him as an older, dashing warrior in armour.

From the seventeenth century, there's an excellent **Van Dyck** portrait of Charles Seton, second Earl of Dunfermline, and the tartan-clad Lord Mungo Murray, who died in the disastrous attempt to establish a Scottish colony in Panama. Eighteenth-century highlights include portraits of the philosopher-historian, David Hume by **Allan Ramsay**, and the bard Robert Burns by his friend **Alexander Nasmyth**. There are portraits by **Raeburn** of Sir Walter Scott, the fiddler Niel Gow and the artist himself. The star portrait from the nineteenth century is that of physician Sir Alexander Morison by his mad patient, the painter **Richard Dadd**. Twentieth-century portraits on the first floor include a very angular Alec Douglas-Home, briefly prime minister in the 1960s, Sean Connery depicted by the Scottish artist **John Bellany**, and photomontages of sporting stars Stephen Hendry and Alex Ferguson.

CALTON

Map 2, H4.

Of the various extensions to the New Town the most intriguing is **Calton**, which branches out from the eastern end of Princes Street and encircles a volcanic hill. It is an area of extraordinary showpiece architecture, dating from the time of the Napoleonic Wars or just after. Today, it is also the centre of a thriving gay scene (see p.228).

Waterloo Place (map 6, A7) forms a ceremonial way from Princes Street to Calton Hill, crossing the impressive Regent Bridge, whose parapets commemorate the victory over Napoleon in 1815. On the southern side of Waterloo Place lies the sombre and overgrown **Old Calton Burial Ground** (map 6, B7), in which you can see Robert Adam's plain, cylindrical memorial to David Hume and a monument, complete with a statue of Abraham Lincoln, to the Scots who died in the American Civil War. Hard up against the cemetery's eastern wall, perched above a sheer rockface, stands a picturesque castellated building which many visitors arriving at Waverley Station below mistake for Edinburgh Castle itself. In fact, it's the only surviving part of **Calton Jail**, formerly Edinburgh's main prison, built in 1791 and

CALTON

85

extended in 1817 when the Tolbooth jail on the High Street was taken down. Public executions used to take place on the prison roof until the 1860s, watched by crowds which gathered on Calton Hill. Next door is the massive **St Andrew's House**, built in the 1930s to house civil servants.

Further on, set majestically in a confined site below Calton Hill, is one of Edinburgh's greatest buildings, the Grecian **Old Royal High School** (map 6, F6), designed by Thomas Hamilton and modelled on the Temple of Theseus in Athens, with Doric columns dominating the central portico and matching colonnaded wings. The High School – alma mater to, among others, Robert Adam, Walter Scott and Alexander Graham Bell – started life as an adjunct to Holyrood Abbey; in 1578 it was given its own building just down the hill from where the present Old College of the University stands. In 1829, it moved into the splendid building on Calton Hill, and moved yet again in 1968 to new premises west of the city. For many years, it was assumed that the Old Royal High School building would be the site of Scotland's new parliament, but less than a year before the first elections it was announced that the venue was too small for the parliament envisaged, and that a brand-new building would be commissioned (see p.46). Now unwanted as a debating chamber, its future use is uncertain. Thomas Hamilton also built the **Robert Burns Monument**, a circular Corinthian temple, just across the road, modelled on the Monument to Lysicrates in Athens.

The upper part of **Calton Hill** is reached via a long flight of stairs from Waterloo Place, opposite the western end of St Andrew's House. Robert Louis Stevenson reckoned that Calton Hill was the best place to view Edinburgh, "since you can see the castle, which you lose from the castle, and Arthur's Seat, which you cannot see

CALTON

from Arthur's Seat". If the panoramas from ground level are spectacular enough, those from the top of the **Nelson Monument** (April–Sept Mon 1–6pm, Tues–Sat 10am–6pm; Oct–March Mon–Sat 10am–3pm; £1.50), on the right as you come to the top of the stairs, are even better. Begun just two years after Nelson's death, this is one of Edinburgh's oddest buildings, resembling a gigantic spyglass.

Alongside stands the **National Monument**, begun in 1822 by Playfair to plans by the English architect Charles Cockerell. It was intended to be a replica of the Parthenon, but funds ran out with only twelve columns completed. Susbsequent schemes to finish the monument similarly foundered, earning it the nickname "Edinburgh's Disgrace". On the opposite side of the hill, the grandeur of Playfair's classical **Monument to Dugald Stewart** seems totally disproportionate to the stature of the man it commemorates: a now-forgotten professor of philosophy at the University.

Playfair also built the **City Observatory**, the large complex beside the Monument to Dugald Stewart. Playfair built it for his uncle, the mathematician and astronomer John Playfair, whom he honoured in the cenotaph outside. Because of pollution and the advent of street lighting, which impaired views of the stars, the observatory proper had to be relocated to Blackford Hill, in the south of the city, before the end of the century, though the equipment here continues to be used by students. At the opposite end of the complex is the **Old Observatory**, one of the few surviving buildings by James Craig, designer of the New Town.

NORTHERN NEW TOWN

The Northern New Town, begun in 1801, was the earliest extension to the First New Town, and today roughly covers the area north of Queen Street, between India Street to the west and Broughton Street to the east, and stretches as far as Fettes Row to the north. The Northern New Town has survived in far better shape than its predecessor: with the exception of one street, almost all of it is intact, and it has managed to preserve its predominantly residential character.

One of the area's most intriguing buildings is the Neo-Norman **Mansfield Place Church** (map 2, G2), on the corner of Broughton and East London streets, designed in the late nineteenth century for the strange, now defunct Catholic Apostolic sect. Having lain redundant and neglected for more than three decades, the church became the obsession of local conservation groups, principally for its cycle of murals by the Dublin-born Phoebe Traquair, a leading light in the Scottish Arts and Crafts movement. Traquair laboured for eight years on this decorative scheme, which has all the freshness and luminosity of a medieval manuscript. The murals were almost lost owing to leaks and rot in the fabric of the building. It was only when the building was acquired by a trust in 1998 that its future was secured and the precious murals saved. The basement is currently used as a nightclub, but sometime in 2000 is due to be turned into a centre for Scottish voluntary groups. The upper level will also be completely refurbished and used as a large performance and exhibition space.

Dean Village and Stockbridge

Work began on the western end of the New Town, north of Charlotte Square and west of George Street, in 1822. Instead of the straight lines of the earlier sections, there were now the gracious curves of **Randolph Crescent**, **Ainslie Place** and the magnificent twelve-sided **Moray Place**, designed by the vainglorious James Gillespie

Graham, who described himself, with no authority to do so, as "architect in Scotland to the Prince Regent". Round the corner from Randolph Crescent, the four-arched **Dean Bridge**, a feat of 1830s engineering by Thomas Telford, carries the main road high above Edinburgh's placid little river, the **Water of Leith**. Down to the left lies **Dean Village** (map 2, A5), an old milling community that is one of central Edinburgh's most picturesque yet oddest corners. Its tight cobbled lanes and closes are surrounded by an assorted jumble of mews terraces and brick-built mill buildings rising up from the often gloomy valley floor, its atmosphere of terminal decay arrested by the conversion of some of the mills into chic flats. From Dean Village a riverside path leads to Stockbridge, passing en route **St Bernard's Well**, a pump room covered by a mock-Roman temple. Commissioned in 1788 by Lord Gardenstone to draw mineral waters from the Water of Leith, it has been recently restored, and is occasionally open (contact Water of Leith Conservation Trust ✆0131/445 7367 for details).

Stockbridge (map 2, B2), which straddles both sides of the Water of Leith on the other side of Dean Bridge, is another old village which has retained its distinctive identity, in spite of its absorption into the Georgian face of the New Town, and is particularly renowned for its antique shops and "alternative" outlets. The residential upper streets on the far side of the river were developed by Sir Henry Raeburn, who named the finest of them **Ann Street**. After Charlotte Square, Ann Street is the most prestigious address in Edinburgh – former residents including writers Thomas De Quincey and J.M. Ballantyne. Alone among New Town residences, the street's houses each have front gardens. Lower down, fringing the river between Stockbridge and Canonmills, are neat rows of two-storey terraces known as the "Stockbridge Colonies". Built in 1861 to house artisans – look out for the trade symbols engraved onto some of the gable ends along Glenogle Road – the Colonies are today something of a bohemian enclave, inhabited by a number of artists.

THE WEST END

The area to the west and northwest of the junction of Princes Street with Lothian Road, was the last part of the New Town to be built – between 1822 and 1850 – and deviated from the area's overriding Neoclassicism with a number of Victorian additions. One of these is the huge **St Mary's Episcopal Cathedral** (map 2, A6), built in the 1870s, its three spires a well-known landmark. The last major work of Sir George Gilbert Scott, the cathedral is built in imitation of the Early English Gothic style, and was, at the time of its construction, the most ambitious church built in Britain since the Reformation.

The northern part of the West End overlooks the deep, tree-lined gorge containing the Water of Leith, which is crossed by two major road bridges, Dean Bridge and, a little further west, Belford Bridge. On the northern side of the latter lie the **Scottish National Gallery of Modern Art** and its newly arrived satellite, the **Dean Gallery**.

The Scottish National Gallery of Modern Art

Map 2, A5. Mon–Sat 10am–5pm, Sun 2–5pm; free.

Set in spacious wooded grounds at the far northwestern fringe of the New Town, about ten minutes' walk from the cathedral and Dean Village, the **Scottish National Gallery of Modern Art** was established in 1959 as the first collection in Britain devoted solely to twentieth-century painting and sculpture. The grounds serve as a sculpture park, featuring works by Jacob Epstein, Henry Moore and Barbara Hepworth. Inside, the display space is divided between temporary loan exhibitions and selections from the gallery's own holdings; the latter are arranged thematically, but are almost constantly moved around. What you get to see at any particular time is therefore a matter of chance, though the most important works are nearly always on view.

French painting is particularly well represented, starting with **Bonnard**'s *Lane at Vernonnet* and **Vuillard**'s jewel-like *Two Seamstresses*. The collection includes a few examples of Fauvism, most notably **Matisse**'s *The Painting Lesson* and **Derain**'s dazzlingly brilliant *Collioure*, as well as a fine group of late canvases by **Léger**. Among some striking examples of German Expressionism are **Kirchner**'s *Japanese Theatre*, **Feininger**'s *Gelmeroda III*, and a wonderfully soulful wooden sculpture of a woman by **Barlach** entitled *The Terrible Year, 1937*. Highlights of the Surrealist section are **Magritte**'s haunting *Black Flag*, **Miró**'s seminal *Composition* and **Giacometti**'s repulsive *Woman with her Throat Cut*, while Cubism is represented by **Picasso**'s *Soles* and **Braque**'s *Candlestick*.

Of works by American artists, **Roy Lichtenstein**'s *In the Car* is a fine example of his Pop Art style, while **Duane Hanson**'s fibreglass *Tourists* is typically cruel. English artists on show include Sickert, Nicholson, Spencer, Freud and Hockney, but, as you'd expect, considerably more space is allocated to Scottish artists. Of particular note are the so-called Colourists – **S.J. Peploe**, **J.D. Fergusson**, **Francis Cadell** and **George Leslie Hunter** – whose works are attracting fancy prices on the art market, as well as ever-growing posthumous critical acclaim; although they did not form a recognizable school, these artists all worked in France and display considerable French influence in their warm, bright palettes. Also worth exploring is the vivid realism of the more recent Edinburgh School, whose members include **Anne Redpath**, **Sir Robin Philipson** and **William Gillies**. The gallery also

THE SCOTTISH NATIONAL GALLERY OF MODERN ART

shows works by many contemporary Scots, among them **John Bellany**, a portraitist of striking originality, and the poet-artist-gardener **Ian Hamilton Finlay**.

The Dean Gallery

Mon–Sat 10am–5pm, Sun 2–5pm; free.

Opposite the Modern Art gallery on the other side of Belford Road is the latest addition to the National Galleries of Scotland, the **Dean Gallery**, housed in an equally impressive Neoclassical building completed in 1833. Originally an orphanage and later an education centre, the building has been dramatically refurbished specifically to make room for the work of Edinburgh-born sculptor **Sir Eduardo Paolozzi**. The collection has been partly assembled from a bequest by Gabrielle Keiller (of the marmalade family), and partly from a gift of the artist himself, which included some three thousand sculptures, two thousand prints and drawings, and two thousand books.

Visitors are given an awesome introduction to Paolozzi's work by the huge *Vulcan*, a half-man, half-machine which stands in the Great Hall, immediately opposite the main entrance. No less persuasive of Paolozzi's dynamic creative talents are the rooms to the right of the main entrance, where his London studios have been expertly re-created, right down to the clutter of incomplete models and empty pots of glue. Hidden among this chaos is a large part of his bequest, with half-finished casts piled four or five deep on the floor and designs stacked randomly on shelves. In the adjoining room a much smaller selection of his sculptures and drawings are exhibited more formally.

Also on the ground floor is the **Roland Penrose Gallery**, which houses an impressive collection of Dada and Surrealist art; Penrose was a close friend and patron of many of the movements' leading figures. **Marcel Duchamp**, **Max Ernst** and **Man Ray** are all represented in the gallery. Look out also for **Dali**'s *The Signal of Anguish* and **Magritte**'s *Magic Mirror*, along with work by **Picasso** and **Miró**, including the former's montage *Head* – all these paintings are hung alongside an assortment of artefacts and ethnic souvenirs gathered by Penrose and his artist companions. In the adjoining **Gabrielle Keiller Library**, which contains a unique collection of Surrealist literature, manuscripts and correspondence, there is a wonderful pen-and-ink caricature of Picasso by **De Chirico**, as well as a series of Picasso's own cartoons satirizing General Franco. The rooms upstairs are given over to special exhibitions, which usually carry an entrance charge.

Getting to the Modern Art and Dean galleries

One of the pleasantest ways of getting to the Modern Art and Dean galleries is along the **Water of Leith walkway**. The walkway starts at the village of Balerno, west of the city at the foot of the Pentland Hills, and follows the River Leith to its mouth at the port of Leith. Two useful places to pick up the central section of the walkway are at **Canonmills** (map 2, D1), near the eastern gate of the Royal Botanic Garden, or **Stockbridge**, at the end of Saunders Street (map 2, B3); from either starting point follow the river upstream, leaving the walkway either at the *Hilton Hotel*, on the right-hand side shortly after you go under Belford Bridge, or at the marked path a few hundred metres further on which leads directly to the rear of the Modern Art gallery.

Alternatively, a **free bus** runs on the hour (Mon–Sat 10am–5pm, Sun 2–5pm) from outside the National Gallery on the Mound, stopping at the National Portrait Gallery on the way. The only regular **public transport** running along Belford Road is bus #13, which leaves from the western end of George Street.

THE ROYAL BOTANIC GARDEN

Map 2, C1. Daily: March & Sept 9.30am–6pm; April–Aug
9.30am–7pm; Oct & Feb 9.30am–5pm; Nov–Jan 9.30am–4pm; free.

Just beyond the northern boundaries of the New Town,
with entrances on Inverleith Row and Arboretum Place, is
the seventy-acre site of the **Royal Botanic Garden**, particularly renowned for its **rhododendrons**, which blaze
out in a glorious patchwork of colours in April and May. In
the heart of the grounds a group of hothouses, collectively
designated the **Glasshouse Experience** (daily: March–Oct
10am–5pm; Nov–Feb 10am–3.30pm; donation of £2.50
requested), display orchids and giant Amazonian water lilies.
One of the hothouses, the elegant 1850s glass-topped Palm
House, houses a 200-year-old West Indian palm tree. Many
of the most exotic plants were brought to Edinburgh by the
aptly named George Forrest, who made seven expeditions
to southwestern China between 1904 and 1932. There is
also a Chinese-style garden, featuring a pavilion, waterfall
and the world's biggest collection of Chinese wild plants
outside China.

....

**The *Terrace Café* at the Royal Botanic Garden offers
stunning views of the Royal Mile (see p.181).**

....

At the highest point of the gardens sits **Inverleith
House**, built in 1774, formerly an annexe to the Gallery of
Modern Art, and now used for exhibitions. From the lawn
to the south of the house, just next to a handy café, there
are marvellous views across to the Old Town, one of the
best places in the city to see the whole of the Royal Mile.
There is now a well-stocked gift and plant shop by the
western entrance.

The Suburbs

As the panoramas from some of the city's elevated spots indicate, there's a lot more to Edinburgh than its historic core. Best known and most intriguing of the suburbs is **Leith**, the port of Edinburgh situated a mile and a half from the east end of Princes Street down the wide boulevard called Leith Walk. Leith's transformation in the last twenty years from run-down docklands to the city's trendiest quarter has been dramatic. While in parts of the historic district low-quality housing, prostitutes and undeveloped wastelands give Leith a seedy edge straight out of the pages of *Trainspotting*, at the same time it also incorporates some of the most fashionable apartments and restaurants in the city, along with large dockland developments such as the new Scottish Office and the former Royal Yacht *Britannia*, now moored here permanently and open to the public. Nearby, on this part of the Forth coastline are the suburbs of **Newhaven**, which originated in the fifteenth century as a fishing village, and **Portobello**, a faded Victorian seaside resort, whose main appeal is its beach – the closest to the city centre.

South of the city lies a wide band of well-heeled residential suburbs, interspersed with large out-of-town shopping centres and the occasional sprawling, depressed housing estate, one of which, Craigmillar, lies near medieval

Craigmillar Castle one of Mary, Queen of Scots' favoured residences. Beyond the ring road which encloses Edinburgh to the south lies the Midlothian region, marked by small industrial sites, farmland and a series of commuter towns, including **Dalkeith**, with its attractive country park and nearby mining museum, and **Penicuik**, near which is the mysterious Rosslyn Chapel. Popular with residents of Edinburgh, the nearby Pentland Hills consist of ten square miles of Highlandesque scenery and offer some excellent walks and mountain-bike routes.

To the northwest of the city a series of attractive historic villages are strung out along the south side of the Firth of Forth, including **Cramond**, **Dalmeny** and **South Queensferry**, at the end of the majestic **Forth Rail Bridge**. The bridge is one of the man-made wonders of Scotland and is best seen from the parallel Road Bridge.

Getting there

The majority of Edinburgh's suburbs are well served by a comprehensive **bus** network, mostly radiating from St Andrew's Square or Princes Street in the city centre. The northwestern suburbs can also be reached by **train**. There is an extensive network of off-road **cycle paths** which link the city centre with most of the suburbs mentioned here, including Leith, the Pentlands and Cramond. The handy *Edinburgh Cycle Map* is available at most local bicycle and book shops and costs £3.

LEITH AND AROUND

Map 1, E4.

Until the early twentieth century, **Leith** was separate from Edinburgh. As Scotland's major east coast port, it played a key role in the nation's history: monarchs, armies and the lifeblood of continental trade arrived via its harbour. It even served as the seat of government for a time, and in 1833 finally became a burgh in its own right. In 1920, however, its physical proximity and the perceived advantages of municipal government saw it incorporated into the capital. In the decades that followed, it went into seemingly terminal decline: the population dropped dramatically, and much of its centre was ripped out, to be replaced by grim housing estates.

The 1980s, however, saw an astonishing turnaround. Against all the odds, a couple of waterfront bistros proved enormously successful; competitors followed apace, and by the end of the decade the port had acquired arguably the best concentration of restaurants and pubs in Edinburgh. The surviving historic monuments were spruced up and a host of housing developments built or restored. The renaissance of the area was crowned by the completion of a vast new building housing civil servants from the Scottish Office. The most recent developments have focused on the old harbour itself: a huge shopping and entertainment complex is currently being built near the berth of the former **Royal Yacht Britannia**.

Leith is a brisk twenty-minute walk from the city centre down Leith Walk (map 2, H3). At the top end of the road is a statue of Sherlock Holmes, erected in memory of his creator, Sir Arthur Conan Doyle, born nearby. The route is also well served by **buses**: #10 and #16 run from Princes Street and #22 leaves from St Andrew Square.

Around the port

Although most people come to Leith for its bars and restaurants, there's more that's worth exploring besides. The shipbuilding yards may have gone, and there are vast acres of wasteland and warehouses, but Leith remains a working port, and despite its rough-edged character there are a number of interesting historical buildings and expensive modern developments dotted around. The area boasts a number of showpiece Neoclassical buildings, which lie on or near **The Shore**, the tenement-lined road along the final stretch of the Water of Leith, just before it disgorges into the Firth of Forth. Note the former **Town Hall**, on the parallel Constitution Street, now the headquarters of the local constabulary, immortalized in the tongue twister, "The Leith police dismisseth us"; the classical Trinity House on Kirkgate, where Constitution Street meets Leith Walk, built in 1816; and the massive Customs House on Commercial Street, where Commercial Street meets The Shore. To the west of Customs House, set back from The Shore, is **Lamb's House**, a seventeenth-century mansion, built for the prosperous merchant Andro Lamb, and now an old people's day centre.

Just east of the police station lies **Leith Links**, an area of predominantly flat parkland. Documentary evidence suggests that The Links was a golf course in the fifteenth century, giving rise to Leith's claim to be the birthplace of the sport. Certainly the sport's first written rules were drawn up here in 1744, ten years before they were formalized in St Andrews.

The Royal Yacht Britannia

A little to the west of The Shore, moored alongside Ocean Drive near the huge Chancelot flour mills, is one of the world's most famous ships, the **Royal Yacht Britannia** (daily 10.30am–4.30pm; bookings advised ✆0131/555 5566; £7.50). Launched in 1953 at John Brown's Shipyard on Clydeside, the Royal Yacht *Britannia* was used by the royal family for 44 years for state visits, diplomatic functions and royal holidays. Leith acquired the yacht following her

THE ROYAL YACHT BRITANNIA

decommission in 1997. Many members of the royal family, however, felt that scuttling would have been a more dignified end. As it is, by day coachloads of visitors draw up and swarm over the once hallowed decks, while by night the function suites where kings and presidents were formerly entertained are now rented out as prestigious hospitality venues.

Visits to *Britannia* begin in a purpose-built **visitor centre**, on the quay alongside the ship, where you can see a reconstructed sergeant's mess and the royal barge, the small motor launch that used to ferry the Queen to and from the ship. There are also displays of royal holiday snaps and video clips of *Britannia*'s most famous moments, which included the evacuation of Aden in 1986 and the British handover of Hong Kong in 1997. On leaving the visitor centre you are given an audio handset and allowed to roam around the yacht. You can visit the **bridge**, the **admiral's quarters**, the **officers' mess** and most of the **state apartments**, including the state dining and drawing rooms, as well as the cabins used by the Queen and the Duke of Edinburgh, viewed through a glass partition. The yacht has been largely kept as she was when she was in service, with a well-preserved 1950s dowdiness, which the audio guide loyally attributes to the Queen's good taste and frugality in the lean postwar years. Certainly the atmosphere is a far cry from the opulent splendour which many expect, but it's by no means warm and homely. Interestingly, however, *Britannia* was the one place where the Queen said she could truly relax.

Among the quirkier aspects of *Britannia*'s history you learn that a full Marine Band was always part of the three-hundred-strong crew; hand signals were used by the sailors to communicate orders, as shouting was forbidden; and a special solid mahogany rail was built onto the royal bridge to allow the Queen to stand on deck as *Britannia* came

THE ROYAL YACHT BRITANNIA

into port, without fear of a gust of wind lifting the royal skirt.

Regular shuttle **buses** operated by both Guide Friday and LRT run between Waverley Bridge and *Britannia*. Other buses (see p.97) from the centre stop at the junction of Commercial Street and North Junction Street, from where it's a five-minute walk down to the visitor centre.

Newhaven

Map 1, D4.

The suburb immediately to the west of Leith, **Newhaven**, was originally a village built by James IV at the start of the sixteenth century as an alternative shipbuilding centre to Leith: his massive warship, the *Michael*, capable of carrying 120 gunners, 300 mariners and 1000 troops, and said to have used up all the trees in Fife, was built here. The village also used to be a ferry station and an important fishing centre, landing some six million oysters a year at the height of its success in the 1860s. Today, although a few boats still operate from the harbour, the fish market is no more, and the last of the colourfully dressed fishwives has long since retired. A variety of costumes and other memorabilia of the village's only industry can be found in the small **Newhaven Heritage Museum** (daily noon–5pm; free), a fascinating collection staffed by enthusiastic members of local fishing families.

Portobello

Map 1, F4.

Among Edinburgh's least expected assets is its beach, most of which falls within **Portobello**, about three miles east of the centre of town. Founded in 1739 on wasteland between

Leith and Musselburgh, the area was named after the naval victory of Puerto Bello in Panama. In Victorian times and even in the early part of this century, Portobello was a busy resort, known as "Brighton of the North". Today, in spite of a few tacky amusement arcades and a half-hearted funfair, it retains a certain faded charm, and a walk along the promenade is a pleasure at any time of the year.

The streets running down to the beach are an interesting mishmash of Georgian and Victorian houses. The odd-looking **Tower** near the western end of the promenade was built in 1785 as a summer house, using stones from assorted demolished medieval houses, including, so tradition has it, the Mercat Cross, the old buildings of Edinburgh University and even parts of St Andrews Cathedral. Nearby, in Bridge Street, a plaque marks the birthplace of music-hall giant **Sir Harry Lauder** (1870–1950), responsible for famously sentimental songs such as *Roamin' in the Gloamin* and *I Love a Lassie*. Portobello is easily reached from the city centre by **buses** #15, #26, #42 or #86.

CRAIGMILLAR CASTLE

Map 1, E5. April–Sept daily 9.30am–6pm; Oct–March Mon–Wed & Sat 9.30am–4pm, Thurs 9.30am–noon, Sun 2–4pm; £1.80.

Craigmillar Castle, where the murder of Lord Darnley, second husband of Mary, Queen of Scots was plotted, lies in a green belt five miles southeast of the centre. It's one of the best-preserved medieval fortresses in Scotland, and before Queen Victoria set her heart on Balmoral, she considered usinwg it as her royal castle north of the border – a possibility which seems odd now given the castle's proximity to the ugly council-house estate of Craigmillar, one of Edinburgh's most deprived districts.

The oldest part of the castle is the L-shaped **tower house**, which dates back to the early 1400s: it remains substantially intact, and the great hall, with its resplendent late Gothic chimneypiece, is in good enough shape to be rented out for functions. A few decades after Craigmillar's completion, the tower house was surrounded by a quadrangular wall with cylindrical corner towers pierced by some of the earliest surviving gunholes in Britain. The west range was remodelled as an aristocratic mansion in the mid-seventeenth century, but its owners abandoned the place a hundred years later, leaving it to picturesque decay.

To get to the castle, take **bus** #30, #33 or #82, or any bus heading for Hawick or Jedburgh, from the city centre to the district called Little France. From here the castle is a ten-minute walk along Craigmillar Castle Road.

THE SOUTHERN HILLS

The **hills** in Edinburgh's southern suburbs offer good and not overly demanding walking opportunities, with plenty of sweeping panoramic views. Two miles due south of the city centre, just a short walk south of Morningside, is Blackford Hill, on the upper slopes of which stands the **Royal Observatory** (Mon–Sat 10am–5pm, Sun noon–5pm; £3). The visitor centre here seeks to explain the mysteries of the solar system by means of various hands-on exhibits and CD-ROMs, and you also get to see the observatory's two main telescopes. Buses #24 and #41 run from the city centre to Blackford Avenue, at the foot of Blackford Hill.

At the foot of the hill, the bird sanctuary of Blackford Pond is the starting point for one of the many trails running through the **Hermitage of Braid** local nature reserve, a lovely shady area around a mile long, along the course of the Braid Burn. The reserve is named after a castellated eighteenth-century mansion located on the burn, about halfway along, and which now serves as a **visitor centre** (April–Oct Mon–Fri 10am–4pm, Sun noon–5pm; Nov–March daily 11am–4pm; café Sun only noon–4pm).

Further south are the **Pentland Hills**, or the Pentlands, a chain some eighteen miles long and five wide, offering the most extensive **hill-walking** within easy reach of Edinburgh. The well-managed paths and tracks crisscross a series of hills which rise to 1898ft (579m), often powdered with snow in winter. It's also a great place for **mountain bikers** to get off-road and uphill. The best map of the region is the Ordnance Survey Landranger **map** no. 66.

A good starting point for walks is **Flotterstone**, ten miles south of the city centre on the A702, and served by bus #315. Flotterstone is an old staging post on the route south: there's been an inn here since the seventeenth century, and the present *Flotterstone Inn* is a good spot for a drink or a pub meal after your exertions. Numerous walks, from gentle strolls along well-marked paths to a ten-mile traverse of the hills and moors, are outlined in a pamphlet available from Flotterstone Regional Park Information Centre (daily: May–Sept 9am–7pm; Oct–April 9am–5pm), just past the *Flotterstone Inn*. One suggested walk is described in the box overleaf.

An alternative entry point to the Pentland Hills – and with slightly better bus connections to the city centre (buses #4, #15, #16 and #27) – is **Swanston**, an unspoiled, highly exclusive hamlet of whitewashed thatched roof dwellings separated from the rest of the city by almost a mile of farmland. **Robert Louis Stevenson** (see box on p.33) spent his boyhood summers in Swanston Cottage, immortalized in his novel *St Ives*.

You can also get a taste of the Pentlands scenery from the dry-ski slopes at **Hillend** country park, at the northeastern end of the Pentlands range. From the car park by the ski centre take the path up the right-hand side of the dry-ski

Hiking and biking in the Pentlands

The following suggested round-trip **hike** in the Pentlands lasts
around four hours and takes in hills, reservoirs and moorland.
From **Flotterstone** (see overleaf) car park a pleasant side road
leads up to Glencorse Reservoir. The road swings round it,
then goes through a tight pass and on to Loganlee Reservoir.
A path leads on from the west end of the reservoir through a
short pass called Green Cleugh to come out on the far side of
the Pentland range, where the large expanse of Threipmuir
Reservoir stretches out in front of you. Cross a bridge over a
"neck" in the reservoir; the path heads inland for a while, but
take the first right to return to the reservoir and then follow it to
Harlaw Reservoir beyond. At the far end of Harlaw Reservoir is
another small ranger centre; from here, take the path to your
right over flat moorland and through the pass between Bell's
Hill and Harbour Hill. The path runs down a burn to rejoin
Glencorse Reservoir.

It is possible to **bike** along the same route, though for a
more testing circuit start from the car park at **Nine Mile Burn**,
six miles south of Flotterstone. There's a long, steep uphill
start along a rough, often muddy path to the top of Cap Law
on the main Pentland ridge. Carry on across the plateau and
then down the back of Hare Hill to Threipmuir Reservoir, crossing the bridge over the "neck". Head along the tarred road for
half a mile, turning left at the T-junction onto the Old Road,
which after some distance becomes a jeep track. Continue
along this track till you get to a signpost at Listonshields. Turn
left here in the direction of North Esk Reservoir, and immediately after passing the reservoir, take the left-hand path which
crosses the river and climbs briefly over the shoulder of Spittal
Hill. You then have an exhilarating downhill run past Spittal
farm back to your starting point.

slopes, turning left shortly after crossing a stile to reach a viewpoint with outstanding views over Edinburgh and Fife. An easier way way into the range is to take the **chair-lift** from the ski centre (Mon–Fri 1–9pm, Sun 10am–7pm; £1.20). For downhill thrills and spills there's a hairy 600-metre **downhill mountain-bike course** beside the slopes. The chair-lift is fitted with special hooks which can carry your bike to the top: tickets cost £4 for the first hour and £1.50 for each hour thereafter. There is no bike-rental facility at Hillend so you'll have to bring your own or rent one in town. **Buses** #4 and #15 run from the city to the ski centre, and the hourly Lowland Omnibus #315 also stops here before carrying on to Flotterstone.

MIDLOTHIAN

Immediately south of Edinburgh lies the old county of **Midlothian**, once called Edinburghshire. It's one of the hilliest parts of the Central Lowlands, with the Pentland chain running down its western side, and the Moorfoot Hills defining its boundary with the Borders to the south. Though predominantly rural, it contains a belt of former mining communities, still struggling to come to terms with the recent decline of the coal industry. The history of mining in the area is recorded in the excellent mining museum near **Dalkeith**, one of the major towns in the region. Such charms as the area has are mostly low-key, with the exception of the riotously ornate chapel at **Roslin**.

Dalkeith and around

Dalkeith, eight miles southeast of central Edinburgh – to which it is linked by regular buses (#3, #30, #82) – grew up in the Middle Ages as a baronial burgh under the successive control of the Douglases and Buccleuchs. Today it's a bustling shopping centre, with an unusually broad High Street at its heart.

At the far end of the street is the entrance to **Dalkeith Country Park** (April–Oct daily 10am–6pm; £2), the estate of the Dukes of Buccleuch, whose seat, the early eighteenth-century **Dalkeith Palace**, can only be seen from the outside. You can, however, visit its one-time chapel, now the Episcopalian parish church of **St Mary**, adorned inside with extremely rich furnishings. Further north, Robert Adam's **Montagu Bridge** straddles the River North Esk in a graceful arch; beyond are some derelict but once wonderfully grandiose garden follies. There is also a large woodland playground, suitable for all but the youngest children.

A mile or so south of Dalkeith lies **Newtongrange**, whose Lady Victoria Colliery is now open to the public as the **Scottish Mining Museum** (Feb–Nov daily 10am–5pm; £4), with a 1625-foot shaft, and a winding tower powered by Scotland's largest steam engine. A brand-new visitor centre brings the life of the mine and the local community to life, helped by some entertaining innovation, including "magic helmets", with which you can go on shift and experience a virtual reality tour of life below ground.

Roslin

The tranquil village of **Roslin** lies seven miles south of the centre of Edinburgh, from where it can be reached by bus #87A. Regular Eastern Scottish services from St Andrew Square also run to the neighbouring town of Penicuik. An otherwise nondescript place, the village has two unusual claims to fame: it was near here, at the Roslin Institute, that the world's first cloned sheep, Dolly, was created in 1997; and it also boasts the mysterious, richly decorated late-Gothic **Rosslyn Chapel** (Mon–Sat 10am–5pm, Sun noon–4.45pm; £3). Only the choir, Lady Chapel and part

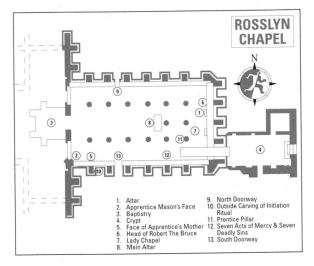

1. Altar
2. Apprentice Mason's Face
3. Baptistry
4. Crypt
5. Face of Apprentice's Mother
6. Head of Robert The Bruce
7. Lady Chapel
8. Main Altar
9. North Doorway
10. Outside Carving of Initiation Ritual
11. Prentice Pillar
12. Seven Acts of Mercy & Seven Deadly Sins
13. South Doorway

of the transepts were built of what was intended to be a huge collegiate church dedicated to St Matthew: construction halted soon after the founder's death in 1484, and the vestry built onto the facade nearly four hundred years later is the sole subsequent addition. After a long period of neglect, a massive restoration project has recently been undertaken: a canopy has been placed over the chapel which will remain in place for several years in order to dry out the saturated ceiling and walls, and other essential repairs are due to be carried out within the chapel.

The outside of the chapel bristles with pinnacles, gargoyles, flying buttresses and canopies, while inside, the foliage carving is particularly outstanding, with botanically accurate depictions of over a dozen different leaves and plants. Among them are cacti and Indian corn, providing fairly convincing

ROSLIN

evidence that the founder's grandfather, the daring sea adventurer Prince Henry of Orkney, did indeed, as legend has it, set foot in the New World a century before Columbus. The rich and subtle figurative sculptures have given Rosslyn the nickname of "a Bible in stone", though they're more allegorical than literal, with portrayals of the Dance of Death, the Seven Acts of Mercy and the Seven Deadly Sins.

The greatest and most original carving of all is the extraordinary knotted **Prentice Pillar** at the southeastern corner of the Lady Chapel. According to local legend, the pillar was made by an apprentice during the absence of the master mason, who killed him in a fit of jealousy on seeing the finished work. A tiny head of a man with a slashed forehead, set at the apex of the ceiling at the far northwestern corner of the building, is popularly supposed to represent the apprentice, his murderer the corresponding head at the opposite side. The entwined dragons at the foot are symbols of Satan, and were probably inspired by Norse mythology.

The chapel's unconventional and sometimes disturbing carvings and designs have led to all kinds of theories about the chapel's function, symbolism and hidden secrets. The number of Masonic images has given rise to speculation that the chapel is connected to the Knights Templar and may be the home of the Ark of the Covenant, while others claim it may be where the true Stone of Destiny is kept – the implication being that the stone stolen by Edward I which now sits in Edinburgh Castle is but a fake. Other theories involve the Turin Shroud and reported sightings of UFOs over Midlothian.

CRAMOND AND LAURISTON CASTLE

Map 1, C4.

Cramond is one of the city's most atmospheric – and poshest – old villages. The enduring image of this village is of step-gabled whitewashed houses rising uphill from the waterfront. It also boasts the foundations of a Roman fort, a medieval bridge and tower house, as well as a seventeenth-century church, inn and mansion. In December 1996, a wonderful Roman sculpture of a lioness devouring a man was discovered in the River Almond here: it is thought that it was simply thrown into the river after the departure of the Romans. The sculpture is now on display in the National Museum of Scotland on Chambers Street (see p.59).

There are a number of interesting short walks in the area: across the causeway at low tide to uninhabited (except for seabirds) **Cramond Island**; eastwards along the seafront towards the gasometers of Granton with sweeping views out to sea; and upstream along the River Almond past former mills and their adjoining cottages towards the sixteenth-century bridge Old Cramond Brig. Each of these walks should take you around an hour.

Lauriston Castle

Map 1, C4. visit by guided tour only (40min) April–Oct daily except Fri 11am–1pm & 2–5pm; Nov–March Sat & Sun 2–4pm; £4.50. Bus #40 from the city centre.

Roughly five miles west of the city centre and a mile east of Cramond stands **Lauriston Castle**, a country mansion set in its own parkland overlooking the Firth of Forth. The original sixteenth-century tower house forms the centrepiece of what is otherwise a neo-Jacobean structure, which in 1902 became the retirement home of a prosperous local cabinet-maker. He decked out the interior with his private collection of furniture and antiques, including Flemish tapestries and ornaments made of Blue John from Derbyshire. He also added a number of domestic features ranging from central heating and secondary glazing to an

LAURISTON CASTLE

en-suite Edwardian bathroom incorporating a flushing toilet and a splendidly sturdy bath-cum-shower. On the death in 1926 of the last private owners, Lauriston Castle was gifted to the nation and the interior has been left untouched.

The castle is set in large well-kept **grounds** (daily 9am–dusk; free), including croquet lawns, offering wonderful views down to the Firth of Forth and across to Fife.

DALMENY

Map 1, B4.

In 1975, Edinburgh's boundaries were extended to include a number of towns and villages which were formerly part of West Lothian. Among them was **Dalmeny**, two miles west of Cramond, which can be reached directly from the city centre by bus (#43 SMT) or train. Another option is to take the coastal path from Cramond, which passes through the estate of **Dalmeny House** (July & Aug only Mon & Tues noon–5.30pm, Sun 1–5.30pm; £3.60), the seat of the earls of Rosebery. Built in 1815 by the English architect William Wilkins, it was the first stately home in Scotland to be built in Tudor Gothic Revival style, and features a picturesque turreted roofline, fan vaulting and hammerbeam ceilings. The family portraits include one by Raeburn of the fourth earl, who commissioned the house, and one by Millais of the fifth earl, the Earl of Rosebery, a former British prime minister. There are also likenesses of other famous society figures by Reynolds, Gainsborough and Lawrence. Among the furnishings are a set of tapestries made from cartoons by Goya, and the Rothschild Collection of eighteenth-century French furniture and *objets d'art*. There's also a fascinating collection of objects associated with Napoleon Bonaparte – including some of the items he used during his exile in St Helena. These were amassed by the fifth earl, who wrote a biography of the emperor.

Dalmeny **village** is a quiet community built around a spacious green. Its focal point is the mid-twelfth-century **St Cuthbert's Kirk**, a wonderful Norman church that has remained more or less intact. Although very weather-beaten, the south doorway is particularly notable for its illustrations of strange beasts. More vivedly grotesque carvings can be seen inside on the chancel corbels and arch.

SOUTH QUEENSFERRY AND AROUND

Map 1, B3.

The compact little town of **South Queensferry** was named after St Margaret, the eleventh-century queen, who used the town as a crossing point for her frequent trips between her palaces in Edinburgh and Dunfermline. Squeezed into the narrow gap between the seashore and the hillside above, the town's **High Street** is lined by a picturesque array of old buildings, among them an unusual two-tiered row of shops, the roofs of the lower level serving as the walkway for the upper storey. The small **museum** at 53 High St (Mon & Thurs–Sat 10am–1pm & 2.15–5pm, Sun 2–5pm; free) contains relics of the town's history and traces the history of the building of its two bridges.

Everything in South Queensferry is overshadowed, quite literally, by the two great bridges, each about a mile and a half in length, which traverse the Firth of Forth at its narrowest point. The cantilevered **Forth Rail Bridge**, built between 1883 and 1890 by Sir John Fowler and Benjamin Baker, ranks among the supreme achievements of Victorian engineering. Some £33.5 million was spent in the construction of a bridge that manages to exude grace as well as might. Derived from American models, the suspension format chosen for the **Forth Road**

Bridge makes a perfect complement to the older structure. Erected between 1958 and 1964, it finally killed off the 900-year-old ferry service, and now attracts a heavy volume of traffic. It's well worth walking across the Road Bridge's footpath to Fife for tremendous views of the Rail Bridge and the Forth estuary.

The Forth Rail Bridge

The late-Victorian railway boom saw the development of train lines to many parts of Scotland, as well as continual investment to upgrade and improve important existing routes. One of the most important of these was the East Coast line from Edinburgh to Aberdeen, which took a long diversion around the Firth of Forth via Stirling. The first plans for a **suspension bridge** to carry a railway line across the Firth of Forth were ripped up in 1879 when the collapse of the Tay Rail Bridge over the Tay Estuary at Dundee shocked the authorities into commissioning John Fowler and Benjamin Baker's dramatic cantilevered steel bridge, which used over 50,000 tons of steel and 6.5 million rivets – making it twice as strong as experts deemed it needed to be. Its construction was eagerly followed by the inhabitants of Edinburgh and Fife, and after it was opened in 1890, people would take a train to North Queensferry simply to say they'd crossed the bridge. It was widely acknowledged as a triumphant symbol of Scottish engineering prowess, with the great French engineer Alexandre-Gustave Eiffel describing it as "the greatest wonder of the century", although not everyone took to it: the artist William Morris called it "the supremest specimen of all ugliness". Today, 190 trains cross the bridge every day, and maintenance is a time-consuming business: as soon as it's received a new lick of paint it's time to start again at the other end.

Inchcolm

Map 1, C3.
From South Queensferry's Hawes Pier, just west of the Forth Rail Bridge, pleasure boats leave for a variety of **cruises on the Forth** (Easter, May & June Sat & Sun; July to mid-Sept daily; ℂ0131/331 4857; £7.50–10). Be sure to check in advance, as sailings are always subject to cancellation in bad weather.

The most enticing destination is the island of **Inchcolm**, whose beautiful ruined **abbey** was founded in 1123 by King Alexander I in gratitude for the hospitality he received from a hermit when his ship was forced ashore in a storm. The hermit's cell survives at the northwestern corner of the island. The best-preserved medieval monastic complex in Scotland, the abbey's surviving buildings date from the thirteenth to the fifteenth centuries, and include a splendid octagonal chapterhouse. Although the church is almost totally dilapidated, its tower can be ascended for a great aerial view of the island, which is populated by a variety of nesting birds and a colony of grey seals.

Hopetoun House

Map 1, A3. April–Sept daily 10am–5.30pm; Oct Sat & Sun 10am–5.30pm; house and grounds £5; grounds only £2.80.
One of Scotland's grandest stately homes, **Hopetoun House**, lies immediately beyond the western edge of South Queensferry. The original house was built at the turn of the eighteenth century for the first Earl of Hopetoun by Sir William Bruce, the architect of Holyroodhouse (see p.43). A couple of decades later, William Adam carried out an enormous extension, engulfing the house in a curvaceous main facade and two projecting wings – superb facsimiles of Roman Baroque pomp and swagger.

The grounds of Hopetoun House are used for concerts during the summer; phone ©0131/331 2451 for details.

The interiors were designed by Adam, and decorated by his sons after their father's death. The scale and lavishness of the decoration make for a stark contrast with the intimacy of those designed by Bruce. Particularly impressive are the Red and Yellow **Drawing Rooms**, with their splendid ceilings by the young Robert Adam. Among the house's furnishings are seventeenth-century tapestries, Meissen porcelain and a distinguished collection of paintings, including portraits by Gainsborough, Ramsay and Raeburn. The grounds of Hopetoun House are also open to the public, and provide magnificent walks along the banks of the Forth and great opportunities for picnics. From the northwestern corner of the grounds, look upriver to the ship-like shape of the fifteenth-century **Blackness Castle**. Walking back towards the house you can see the only surviving feature of Bruce's design, the west face of the central section of the building.

Day-trips from Edinburgh

Relatively short distances and good transport links make many parts of south and central Scotland feasible day-trips from Edinburgh. Within easy reach of the capital lie sights as diverse as Glasgow's post-industrial cultural scene, the world-famous golf courses of St Andrews and the beguiling countryside of the Highlands to the north and the Borders region to the south.

Less than an hour's travel west of Edinburgh is **Glasgow**, the largest city in Scotland and long a rival to the capital in terms of prestige, influence and importance. The many contrasts between the two cities are in their own way a compelling reason to pay a visit to Glasgow, where decades of industrial decline have given way in recent years to a reawakened appreciation of the city's stunning Victorian and early twentieth-century design and architecture. One of the most important legacies of this period are the unique and flamboyant buildings designed by Art Nouveau visionary Charles Rennie Mackintosh. Other attractions include a wealth of museums and art galleries, including the diverse Burrell Collection, the city's medieval cathedral, and, for those making an evening as well as a day of their visit, there's an opportunity to tap into Glasgow's hip and vibrant nightlife.

The essential day-trip for those interested in the main events in Scottish history is to **Stirling**, with its fine castle and battle sites, also less than an hour from Edinburgh, in the northwest. North of here it's possible to get a taste of the spectacular landscapes of the **Highlands**, and a trip to any of the areas south of **Crianlarich** and **Pitlochry** is eminently feasible in a day. The rolling hills of the **Borders** region south of the capital and the North Sea coastline of **East Lothian** offer some equally attractive countryside dotted with historic castles and ruined abbeys. Between Edinburgh and Stirling, **Linlithgow's palace** has long-standing connections with the Stewart dynasty, while traces of medieval Scotland can also be found at **St Andrews**, perched on the east coast thirty miles northeast of Edinburgh. The site of Scotland's oldest university and some atmospheric ruins, the town is also world-famous as the home of golf.

Transport links from Edinburgh to Glasgow, Stirling, Linlithgow and parts of East Lothian by both train and bus are regular and efficient; services further afield, including those to St Andrews and the Borders, tend to be less so.

GLASGOW

Glasgow is separated from Edinburgh by a mere forty miles and can be reached by train in under an hour. However, for two cities so geographically close the contrasts could hardly be more marked. Edinburgh is well-heeled establishment, Glasgow is industrial grit; Edinburgh has professions, Glasgow workers; Edinburgh is tweedy, Glasgow trendy; Edinburgh is rugby, Glasgow football.

Although Glasgow doesn't have the same dramatic visual impact as Edinburgh, a bit of time spent getting to know its idiosyncratic, creative vibe found in its grand municipal buildings as well as its hyper-cool "style-bars" is invariably repaid. In a day you should easily be able to take in the area known as **Merchant City**, home of Glasgow's prosperous traders in the eighteenth-century; the medieval **Cathedral**; and **Glasgow Green**, a city-centre patch of common land flanked by the River Clyde. Visitors interested in finding out more about Glasgow's outstanding Victorian and early twentieth-century architecture will find plenty of outstanding examples, many of them the work of the world-famous designer Charles Rennie Mackintosh, who took Glasgow architecture to the forefront of early twentieth-century design with buildings such as the School of Art and the recently redeveloped Lighthouse building.

A more laid-back side of Glasgow can be found in its **West End**, the student quarter, which is studded with a series of excellent art galleries and museums. The city's most impressive museum, the **Burrell Collection**, is, however, further out of town, but it's well worth the time spent getting there not just for the eclectic treasures gathered under its roof but also its unexpected parkland setting.

With regular trains running back to Edinburgh as late as 11.30pm, you could consider sampling some of Glasgow's **nightlife**, consistently sparkier and more cutting-edge than Edinburgh's, or taking in some of the city's innovative and high-quality theatre and live music.

Arrival and information

Trains to Glasgow run every fifteen minutes from Edinburgh's Waverley and Haymarket stations until around 11pm, and pull into **Glasgow Queen Street Station**, on the corner of George Square, right at the heart of the city. A ten-minute walk away is **Glasgow Central Station**, the main terminus for trains to the south. **Buses** also run regularly, departing from Edinburgh's St Andrews Square and arriving at Glasgow's **Buchanan Street** bus station, just to the north of Queen Street station.

The city's efficient **tourist information office** is at 11 George Square (May, June & Sept Mon–Sat 9am–6pm, Sun 10am–6pm; July & Aug Mon–Sat 9am–8pm, Sun 10am–6pm; Oct–April Mon–Sat 9am–6pm; ©0141/204 4400). Ask here for the free *Guide to Getting Around Glasgow*, which contains brief details about public transport and an excellent fold-out map of the city centre and West End.

Orientation and city transport

The **centre** of Glasgow is a sprawling place, built upon some punishingly steep hills, and with no really obvious focus, although centrally located **George Square** is a useful orientation point. East of this lies the **Merchant City**, where Glasgow's rise as a mercantile centre can be traced, and the **Cathedral**, the main sight in the oldest part of the city. Just over a mile west of Queen Street station the city's **West End** begins; home of the university and very much the student quarter of Glasgow, it exudes a decorous air, with graceful avenues, parks and interesting shops and cafés. South of the River Clyde lie the once-notorious suburbs of **Govan** and the **Gorbals**. These in turn give way to middle-class areas and the rolling green acres of **Pollok Park**, home of the famous **Burrell Collection**.

Although it can be tough negotiating the steep hills, **walking** is the best way of exploring any one part of the city. However, as the main sights are scattered throughout the city – the West End, for example, is a good thirty-minute walk from the centre – you'll probably need to make use of the **Underground**, whose stations are marked with a large orange U. There's a flat fare of 80p, or you can buy a **day ticket** for £2.50. The most useful stations are **Buchanan Street**, which is near George Square and connected to Queen Street railway station by a moving walkway; **St Enoch**, at the junction of Buchanan Street pedestrian precinct and Argyle Street; and **Hillhead**, bang in the heart of the West End.

For getting to areas further out, such as the Burrell Collection or Mackintosh's House for an Art Lover, you'll find the suburban **train** network swift and convenient. The Roundabout Glasgow Ticket (£3.50) gives unlimited travel for a day on the Underground and local rail services. The city's **bus** network is comprehensive but confusing – information on relevant services is given at some bus stops, though the tourist office will help you find the right service to take you to a specific destination.

Open-topped **tour buses**, run by rivals Discovering Glasgow and Guide Friday (both April–Oct Mon–Sat 9.30am–4pm; £6.50), leave on the hour and half-hour from George Square. They run a continuous route around all the major attractions in the city centre and West End, allowing you to get on and off as you please.

City Centre

Glasgow's large city centre is the densest in Scotland, with offices, shops and traffic bound in a rigorous grid-pattern of streets – possibly inspired by Edinburgh's New Town. Glasgow has one of the best collections of Victorian buildings in the world; the city's booming trade and industry at the end of the nineteenth century and beginning of the twentieth allowed merchants to commission the finest architects of the day. Nowhere is the confidence of the era more apparent than in **George Square** (map 7, K6): dominating this continental-style plaza is the florid splendour of the **City Chambers**, opened in 1888, at the square's eastern

CITY CENTRE

end. Its intricately detailed facade contains friezes depicting the four nations (England, Ireland, Scotland, Wales) of the then United Kingdom at the feet of the throned queen, the British colonies and allegorical figures representing Religion, Virtue and Knowledge. It's worth taking a free guided tour (Mon–Fri 10.30am & 2.30pm; ✆0141/227 4017) of the labyrinthine interior to get a look at the acres of intricate gold leaf and Italian marble.

The grid of streets that lies immediately southeast of the City Chambers is known as the **Merchant City** (map 7, K6), where wealthy eighteenth-century tobacco merchants built warehouses and homes. In the last decade or so it has been sandblasted and swabbed clean, and yuppie apartments, expensive designer shops and bijou cafés give the area a pervasive air of sophistication and chic. A *Merchant City Trail* leaflet, guiding you around a dozen of the most interesting buildings in the area, can be picked up from **Hutcheson Hall**, at 158 Ingram St (Mon–Sat 10am–5pm).

The oldest part of the city lies to the east of the Merchant City, centred on the stumpy-spired **Glasgow Cathedral** (map 7, N5; April–Sept Mon–Sat 9.30am–6pm, Sun 2–5pm; Oct–March Mon–Sat 9.30am–4pm, Sun 2–4pm). The first cathedral on this spot was built in 1136, although the existing building, dedicated to the city's patron saint and reputed founder, St Mungo, dates back to the late fifteenth century. Inside, the impressively lofty nave of the **upper church** contrasts with the **lower church**, with its dark and musty **chapel**, one of the most glorious examples of medieval architecture in Scotland, housing the tomb of St Mungo. Next to the Cathedral the atmospheric **Necropolis**, a hillside graveyard filled with gloomy catacombs and Neoclassical temples, reflects the vanity of the nineteenth-century industrialists buried here. The climb to the summit is worth it for the superb views over the cathedral and city.

Heading down the High Street from the Cathedral, you'll come to **Glasgow Cross**, the city's principal intersection until the middle of the nineteenth century. The turreted seventeenth-century **Tolbooth Steeple** still stands here, although the rest of the building has long since disappeared. Further east, down Gallowgate, sprawls the **East End**, once a densely packed industrial area which essentially created the city's wealth. Today, isolated pubs, tatty shops and cafés sit amidst industrial dereliction, though the nearby open spaces of **Glasgow Green**, reputedly the oldest public park in Britain, offer a welcome contrast. Various memorials, some in a bad state of repair, are dotted around the lawns, while the **People's Palace Museum** (map 7, M8; Mon–Sat 10am–5pm, Sun 11am–5pm; free), at the northern end of the Green, is a wonderfully haphazard evocation of the city's history. It was purpose-built as a museum back in 1898 – almost a century before the rest of the country caught on to the fashion for social history collections.

The best way to return to George Square is to head along the banks of the **Clyde**, a river whose intimate connections with the city range from the fish which appears on Glasgow's coat of arms to the ships which once packed the quaysides from the centre all the way downriver to the Firth of Clyde. As you make your way back through town, Glasgow's lively and off-beat **Gallery of Modern Art** (map 7, J6; Mon–Sat 10am–5pm, Sun 11am–5pm; free), on Royal Exchange Square off Queen Street, just south of George Square, is a good place to catch up on works such as the large-scale socially committed art of the "Glasgow Pups" – Peter Howson, Adrian Wiszniewski, Ken Currie and Stephen Campbell – as well as the evocative black-and-white urban photographs of Sebastião Salgado and the inspired art-from-nature intallations of Andy Goldsworthy. Alternatively, you might prefer to explore the designer stores of the Merchant City and the large shopping arcades

CITY CENTRE

on Argyle and Buchanan streets, notably **Princes Square** (map 7, J6), one of Britain's most stylish and imaginative shopping centres.

West End

The urbane veneer and leafy parks of the **West End** of Glasgow seem a world away from the tightly packed centre. In the 1800s, the city's focus moved west as wealthy merchants established huge estates away from the soot and grime of city life, and in 1870 the ancient university was moved from its cramped home near the cathedral to a spacious new site overlooking the River Kelvin. The hub of life in this part of Glasgow is **Byres Road**, running down from Great Western Road past Hillhead Underground station, where shops, restaurants, cafés, some enticing pubs and hordes of roving young people, including thousands of students, give the area a real sense of style.

The principal attraction in the district is the huge, red-brick fantasy castle of **Kelvingrove Museum and Art Gallery** (map 7, D4; Mon–Sat 10am–5pm, Sun 11am–5pm – though likely to be closed for much of 2000 for renovations; for up-to-date information, phone the tourist information office on ©0141/332 7133; free), a brash statement of Glasgow's nineteenth-century self-confidence, built to house the 1888 International Exhibition. Located in Kelvingrove Park, not far from the university, it's most easily reached from the centre by Underground to Kelvin Hall station. The central hall on the ground floor is an impressive, airy introduction to the place. Most of the art collection is upstairs: highlights include some superb Italian paintings, notably Botticelli's delicate *Annunciation*, Rembrandt's tender portrait, *The Man in Armour*, various works by Courbet, Corot, Degas and Monet, and a good representation of Scottish work, ranging from Sir Henry

Raeburn's magnificent *Mr and Mrs Robert N. Campbell of Kailzie*, through the distinctive work of the Glasgow Boys such as Guthrie, Lavery and Crawhall, to the grittier *Two Children* by Joan Eardley, which makes use of collage and thick paint to convey the energy of Gorbals children in the 1960s.

Opposite Kelvingrove Museum and Art Gallery, the **Transport Museum** (map 7, C4; Mon–Sat 10am–5pm, Sun 11am–5pm; free) contains an entertaining collection of trains, cars, trams and other old Glaswegian ephemera, including intricate models of vessels forged in Glasgow's famous shipyards – everything from tiny schooners to the *QE2*. A cinema shows fascinating films of old Glasgow life, with crackly footage of Sauchiehall Street packed solid with trams and shoppers and hordes of pasty-faced Glaswegians setting off for their annual jaunts down the coast.

Within the precincts of the university – Sir George Gilbert Scott's dramatic black Gothic quadrangle and spire perched on the hill behind Kelvingrove – is the **Hunterian Art Gallery** (map 7, D2; Mon–Sat 9.30am–5pm; free). To get here from Kelvingrove, follow the tree-lined Kelvin Way then climb up University Avenue. The gallery is best known for its wonderful works by James Abbott McNeill Whistler. Especially compelling are Whistler's portraits of women: in addition to their fey and occasionally winsome qualities the subjects are often imbued with a resolute strength. Also displayed are the quasi-Impressionist Scottish landscapes of William McTaggart, a forerunner of two important Scottish groups, the Glasgow Boys and the Scottish Colourists, both represented here. Attached to the gallery is **Mackintosh House**, a re-creation of the interior of the now-demolished Glasgow home of Margaret and Charles Rennie Mackintosh, containing over sixty pieces of Mackintosh furniture on three floors.

WEST END

123

Burrell Collection

Glasgow's most outstanding collection of art is to be found at
the **Burrell Collection** (map 7, B9; Mon–Sat 10am–5pm,
Sun 11am–5pm; free), the accumulated treasures of shipping
magnate Sir William Burrell (1861–1958). The gallery is
located in Pollok Country Park, three miles south of the city.
You'll be hard pushed to see this in addition to a full tour of
either the city centre or the West End, although you could
combine it with two other architectural triumphs south of
the river, Mackintosh's House for an Art Lover (see p.126)
and Alexander Thomson's Holmwood House (see opposite).

A superbly designed gallery, built in 1983, houses the collection, with large picture windows giving sweeping views
over the park and serving as a tranquil backdrop to the
objects inside. Sir William's tastes were eclectic and broad.
The **Ancient Civilizations** collection – a catch-all title for
Greek, Roman and earlier artefacts – includes an exquisite
mosaic Roman cockerel from the first century BC and a
4000-year-old Mesopotamian lion's head. The large
Oriental Art section ranges from Neolithic jades and Tang
funerary horses to cloisonné. Near Eastern art is also represented in a dazzling array of turquoise- and cobalt-decorat-
ed jugs, and a swath of intricate carpets. A sculpture court
centred on the huge **Warwick Vase** from Hadrian's Villa in
Tivoli includes Rodin's *The Age of Bronze*, *A Call to Arms*
and the famous *Thinker*, while nearby a trio of dark and
sombre panelled rooms have been re-erected in faithful
detail from the Burrells' Hutton Castle home, their heavy
tapestries, antique furniture and fireplaces displaying the
same extraordinary taste as the rest of the museum. Among
the highlights of Sir William's weighty painting collection
are one of Rembrandt's evocative early self-portraits, Degas'
thoughtful and perceptive *Portrait of Émile Duranty*, along
with work by Pissarro, Manet and Boudin.

You can get to the Burrell by taking **bus** #34 or #34A from Govan Underground station – you'll need to get out at the park gate nearest to the Burrell on Haggs Road. Pollokshaws West station beside the Pollokshaws Road gate is served by regular **trains** from Glasgow Central. In addition, buses #45, #48 or #57 connect Union Street in the city centre with Pollokshaws West station. From both the park gates a free half-hourly minibus runs between 10am and 4.30pm to the Burrell Collection, or you can walk through the grounds to the gallery in about twenty minutes.

Holmwood House

Just over two miles southeast of the Burrell Collection in the suburb of Cathcart sits **Holmwood House** (April–Oct daily 1.30–5.30pm; £3.20), the finest domestic design by rediscovered Glasgow architect Alexander "Greek" Thomson. Long overshadowed by Charles Rennie Mackintosh, Thomson took the principles of Greek architecture, reprocessing them in a highly unique manner and applying his ideas to a wide range of buildings, from the lowly tenement to churches. Recently restored and opened to the public, Holmwood is a showcase for Thomson's bold classical concepts, with exterior pillars on two levels and a raised main door, as well as his detailed and highly imaginative interiors. The restoration is ongoing, as you'll see from the patches of exquisite stencilling revealed beneath the wallpaper, and the fact that the rooms are unfurnished. One room upstairs is given over to a series of displays about Thomson and the history of the house, while the most impressive rooms are on the downstairs level, where the **parlour** boasts a delightful round bay window and the **dining room** has a frieze of scenes from the *Iliad*.

To get to Holmwood from the Burrell Collection, exit Pollok Park at the Pollokshaws Road gate, then follow this

HOLMWOOD HOUSE

Charles Rennie Mackintosh

Glasgow is synonymous with the work of architect **Charles Rennie Mackintosh** (1868–1928), whose idiosyncratic fusing of Scots Baronial with Gothic and Art Nouveau makes him one of the most important designers of the twentieth century, and outstanding examples of his work are found all over the city.

The finest display of his visionary style is surely the **Glasgow School of Art**, designed in 1896. Student-led guided tours (Mon–Fri 11am & 2pm, Sat 10.30am & 11.30am; booking advised; ✆0141/353 4526; £5) offer a taste of his innate ability to blend function with superb artistry. Another early commission, **The Lighthouse**, on Mitchell Lane (Mon, Wed, Fri & Sat 10.30am–6pm, Tues 11am–6pm, Thurs 10.30am–8pm, Sun noon–5pm; free), now houses Scotland's Centre for Architecture, Design and the City, and incorporates a **Mackintosh Interpretation Centre** (£2.50), where you can learn more about the man and his work.

Other Mackintosh highlights around the city are the **House for an Art Lover** (April–Sept Sat–Thurs 10am–4pm; Oct–March daily 10am–4pm; ✆0141/353 4449; £3.50), in Bellahouston Park on the south side of the Clyde, which was designed by Mackintosh in 1901 for a German competition, but not actually built until 1996; and the **Scotland Street School Museum of Education** (Mon–Sat 10am–5pm, Sun 2–5pm; free), located opposite the Shields Road Underground station. At the Hunterian Art Gallery next to the university you can see the **Mackintosh House**, a re-creation of the interior of the artist's now-demolished Glasgow home, with over sixty pieces of Mackintosh furniture on three floors. A popular place for tea, the **Willow Tea Rooms** (daily 9.30am–5pm), 217 Sauchiehall St, are a faithful reconstruction on the site of Mackintosh's 1904 original.

road back towards the city for just under half a mile to reach Shawlands train station. Regular services run from here to Cathcart station, which can also be reached directly from Central Station. From Cathcart station to Holmwood it's a ten-minute walk south along Rhannan Road, turning left onto Millholm Road and then right into the driveway of the house.

Nightlife and entertainment

While Glasgow has nothing to match the Edinburgh Festival for an explosion of theatre and the arts, it still manages to pump out an impressive breadth of art, theatre, film and music round the calendar, a cultural integrity recognized, and to some extent sustained, by the city's reign as European City of Culture in 1990. It is the home of both Scottish Opera and the Royal Scottish National Orchestra and has two major **music** venues – the Royal Concert Hall and the Clyde Auditorium (or the "Armadillo" as it's popularly known). It also boasts two of Scotland's most consistently innovative and trendy **theatres**, the Citizens' and the Tramway. You can find **details** of the city's events in the *Herald* or *Evening Times* newspapers, or the comprehensive fortnightly listings magazine, *The List* (£1.95), which also covers Edinburgh. To book **tickets** for theatre productions or big concerts, call the Ticket Centre (Mon–Sat 9am–6pm, Sun noon–5pm; phone bookings Mon–Sat 9am–9pm, Sun noon–6pm; ✆0141/287 5511).

The city's **music and clubbing scene** is highly rated; Glasgow consistently attracts some of the top DJs from around the world, while various small live music venues have almost become used to nurturing local talent such as Deacon Blue, Texas, Belle and Sebastian and Mogwai. Most of Glasgow's nightclubs are in the heart of the main shopping areas off Argyle and Buchanan streets, with a further concentration on Sauchiehall Street near Charing Cross on the western side of the city centre. Establishments are pretty mixed, and although there's still a stack of outdated mega-discos with rigorous dress codes the last couple of years have seen the arrival of far more stylish haunts. Hours hover from around 11pm to 3am, though some places are open until 5am, and cover charges are variable – expect to pay around £3 during the week, and up to £10 at the weekend.

Eating and drinking also benefit from Glaswegians' renowned sense of style and enjoyment of a good night out. The most fashionable restaurants and bars (often referred to as "style bars") are found in the Merchant City, while the West End is also a great place to head, with its mix of students and yuppies guaranteeing a lively atmosphere.

STIRLING

Stirling looks a bit like a smaller version of Edinburgh, with its crag-top castle, steep, cobbled streets and mixed community of locals and students. While it lacks the cosmopolitan edge of the capital, the town is rich in history and was the scene of two of the most significant battles in Scottish history. A day-trip to Stirling should take in the **castle** – a more explorable and interesting citadel than even Edinburgh's – and either the **Wallace Monument**, the hilltop monolith built in memory of the Scottish leader William Wallace, or **Bannockburn**, the field where the famous Scottish victory under Robert the Bruce in 1314 was won.

Arrival, information and getting around

From Edinburgh there are regular trains (45min) and buses (1hr) to Stirling: the **railway station** is near the centre of town on Station Road, while the **bus station** is nearby on Goosecroft Road.

Stirling's **tourist information office**, (June & Sept
Mon–Sat 9am–6pm, Sun 10am–4pm; July & Aug Mon–Sat
9am–7.30pm, Sun 9.30am–6.30pm; Oct–May Mon–Sat
10am–5pm; ✆01786/475019), at 41 Dumbarton Rd in the
heart of the town, serves Loch Lomond, Stirling and the
Trossachs. It has a wide range of books, maps and leaflets, as
well as a free accommodation-booking service.

Stirling is very compact and the sights are easily seen on
foot, though to avoid the steep hills you could take the
"hop on, hop off" **Heritage Bus** service (June–Sept
10am–5pm; £6), whose circular route takes in the castle,
Wallace Monument, Stirling University, and the bus and
railway stations.

The Castle

Map 8, B4. Daily: April–Sept 9.30am–6.30pm; Oct–March
9.30am–5pm; £4.50.

As one of the most important bridging points across the
River Forth, with the Highlands in view to the north
and Edinburgh visible to the southeast, Stirling is one of
the most strategically significant places in Scotland, and
was the site of vital Scottish victories at the **battles of
Stirling Bridge** in 1297 and **Bannockburn** in 1314.
The possession of **Stirling Castle** was vital for any army
wanting to control the gateway to the Highlands. The
daunting rock on which it sits was first fortified during
the Iron Age, though what you see now dates largely
from the fifteenth and sixteenth centuries. The castle is
presently undergoing a massive restoration (due to be
completed in 2001), and parts of it may be inaccessible
when you visit.

It's a ten-minute walk to the castle up the hill from the
railway station; the **visitor centre** on the esplanade shows
an introductory film giving a potted history of the castle,

THE CASTLE

but the best place to get an impression of the castle's gradual expansion is in the courtyard known as the **Upper Square**. Here you can see the magnificent **Great Hall** (1501–3), perhaps the finest medieval secular building in Scotland, and the **Palace** (1540–42), its exterior richly decorated with grotesque carved figures, including, in the left-hand corner, the glaring bearded figure of James V in the dress of a commoner. Inside, in the royal apartments are the **Stirling Heads**, 56 elegantly carved oak medallions, which once comprised the ceiling of the Presence Chamber, where visitors were presented to royalty. The **Chapel Royal** (1594), built by James VI for the baptism of his son, has a delightful interior, with a seventeenth-century fresco of elaborate scrolls and patterns.

The castle also houses the impressive **Argyll and Sutherland Highlanders Museum** and the restored castle **kitchens**, which re-create the preparations for the spectacular Renaissance banquet given by Mary, Queen of Scots for the baptism of the future James VI. In addition, the **views** from various points are fantastic, with sweeping panoramas of the Trossachs to the north and the industrialized lowlands to the south.

The rest of the town

Heading downhill from the castle along St John Street, you'll encounter the whinstone boulders of the **town walls**, built in the mid-sixteenth century and intended to ward off the advances of Henry VIII, who had set his sights on the young Mary as a wife for his son, Edward. A short walk further on takes you to the best of the various historic buildings and museums in the old centre of Stirling – the impressive **Old Town Jail** (map 8, D6; daily: April–Sept 9.30am–6pm; Oct–March 9.30am–4pm; guided tours every 30min; £2.75), the history of which is brought to life by enthusiastic actors. Take the glass lift up to the prison roof to admire spectacular views across Stirling and the Forth Valley.

Back on the ground, **Broad Street** was the site of the marketplace and centre of the medieval town. The further downhill you go the more recent the buildings become. The town's main **shopping** area is along Port Street and Murray Place, while the **Smith Art Gallery and Museum** (map 8, C6; Tues–Sat 10.30am–5pm, Sun 2–5pm; free) is a short walk west up Dumbarton Road. Founded in 1874, the museum houses a permanent exhibition relating the history of Stirling, as well as changing displays of arts and crafts, contemporary art and photography.

The fifteenth-century **Old Bridge** (map 8, F2) over the Forth lies to the north on the edge of the town centre, a twenty-minute walk from Murray Place. Although once the most important river crossing in Scotland – the lowest bridging point on the Forth until the new bridge was built in 1831 – it now stands virtually forgotten, an almost incidental reminder of Stirling's former importance. An earlier, wooden **bridge** nearby was the focus of the Battle of Stirling Bridge in 1297, where William Wallace (the subject of Mel Gibson's Oscar-winning but wildly inaccurate film, *Braveheart*) defeated the English.

Wallace's victory at Stirling Bridge is marked by the prominent **Wallace Monument** (daily: March–May & Oct 10am–5pm; June & Sept 10am–6pm; July & Aug 9.30am–6.30pm; Nov & Dec 10am–4pm; £3), a mile and a half north of here on the top of Abbey Craig, the place from which the Scottish hero led his troops to victory. If you can manage the climb – 246 spiral steps up – there are superb views across to Fife and Ben Lomond from the top of the 220-foot tower. A shuttle bus (75p return) runs from the base of the hill to the tower every ten minutes, saving you the initial steep climb.

The Scots' other great battlefield triumph is remembered a couple of miles south of Stirling, just north of the village of **Bannockburn**. Here, the **Bannockburn Heritage Centre** (April–Oct daily 10am–5.30pm; March, Nov & Dec daily 11am–3pm; £2.30) recalls Robert the Bruce's victory on June 24, 1314. It was this battle, the climax of the Wars of Independence, which united the Scots under Bruce and led to independence under the Declaration of Arbroath (1320) and the Treaty of Northampton (1328). Pondering the scene is an equestrian statue of Bruce, on the spot from where he is said to have commanded the battle, fought on the boggy carse down towards the burn. Bannockburn can be reached by **buses** #51 and #52, which leave Stirling every half-hour.

The Highlands

The spectacular scenery of the **Highlands**, with its beguiling mix of bare hills, green glens and silvery lochs and rivers, is one of Scotland's major draws. The distances involved, however, as well as the relative infrequency of public transport, mean that only certain parts of the region are achievable in a day-trip from Edinburgh.

The most accessible area from the capital is the **Trossachs** region, situated in the centre of the country to the northwest of Stirling. The two focal points here are the towns of **Callander** and **Aberfoyle**, both of which have tourist information centres where you can pick up details about good local walks and viewpoints. One of the Trossachs' most enticing peaks is Ben Ledi (2857ft). A clear path leads up from the Stank car park, at the southern tip of Loch Lubnaig, a mile and a half beyond Callander. For a longer day, you could hike to the top of Stuc a' Croin (3199ft), which enjoys the status of being the closest Munro to Edinburgh – a Munro is a hill in Scotland over 3000ft in height, of which there are 284 in total. The best way into the Trossachs is by bus from Stirling.

Another option is the countryside around **Loch Lomond**, most easily reached from Glasgow, where the largest area of freshwater in the country is framed by some grand hills, including Ben Lomond. There are road and rail links up the west side of Loch Lomond to **Crianlarich**, a small village surrounded by impressive mountains, most notably the twin peaks Ben More (3852ft) and Stob Binnien (3822ft), two of the country's most distinctive summits.

In the Central Highlands, a reasonable target is the town of **Pitlochry**, 25 miles north of Perth on the main A9 towards Inverness, and served by both trains and buses. While its centre is rather overrun by tourist shops, Pitlochry lies close to some lovely elevated countryside. Overlooking the town is Ben Vrackie (2733ft), best reached from the Killiecrankie Visitor Centre, on the northern side of Loch Faskally, north of Pitlochry.

If you're prepared to spend a lot of time on the road, a good option for a packed day of Highland sightseeing is to join a **guided minibus day tour** from Edinburgh.

Safety in the Highlands

If you do decide to go walking in the hills, it is essential to go **properly equipped**: you should have stout footwear, warm and waterproof clothing (the weather can change dramatically in the course of a day), something to eat and drink, and a good map – such as the Ordance Survey Landranger series, which covers the country. You should also check the **weather forecast** before you go, and be prepared to turn back if the weather turns poor.

Various daily trips to places such as Glencoe, Loch Tay and Loch Lomond are offered by Rabbies Trail Burners (℡0131/226 3133) and Timberbush Tours (℡0131/555 4075) — both charge around £20–25 per person. There are also companies that offer **guided day walking trips** into the Highlands, with transport included: in Edinburgh contact Walkabout Scotland (℡0131/661 7168), while from Stirling contact C-N-Do (℡01786/445703).

ST ANDREWS

Only thirty miles from Edinburgh as the crow flies, though frustratingly tiresome to get to by road or rail, **St Andrews** is Scotland's oldest university town and a pilgrimage centre for golfers from all over the world. According to legend, the town was founded in the fourth century, when St Regulus, a custodian of the bones of the apostle Andrew, was instructed in a vision to carry the relics to the edge of the western world, but was shipwrecked on rocks close to the present harbour. He built a shrine to the saint on what subsequently became the site of the cathedral; St Andrew became Scotland's patron saint and the town its ecclesiastical capital.

Arrival and information

The nearest **railway station** is on the Edinburgh–Dundee–Aberdeen line at Leuchars, five miles northwest, from where regular (but not always connecting) buses make the fifteen-minute trip into town. Frequent **buses** from Edinburgh and Dundee terminate at the bus station on City Road at the west end of Market Street.

The **tourist information office**, 70 Market St (April & May Mon–Sat 9.30am–6pm, Sun 11am–4pm; June to mid-Oct Mon–Sat 9.30am–7pm, Sun 11am–6pm; mid-Oct to

March Mon–Sat 9.30am–5pm; ℂ01334/472021), holds comprehensive information about St Andrews and north-east Fife.

The Town

Perched on the edge of the North Sea and hemmed in on two sides by rugged seashore, the centre of St Andrews still follows its medieval layout, with three main thorough-fares, North Street, South Street and Market Street, run-ning west to east towards the ruined cathedral. Narrow alleys connect the cobbled streets, while attic windows and gable ends shape the rooftops, and here and there you'll see old wooden doors with heavy knockers and black iron hinges.

The most significant of the town's early medieval sights is the ruined Gothic **St Andrews Cathedral** (April–Sept Mon–Sat 9.30am–6pm, Sun noon–6pm; Oct–March Mon–Sat 9.30am–4pm, Sun 2–4pm; £1.80, joint ticket with St Andrew's Castle £3.50; cathedral grounds Sun only 9am–6.30pm; free), at the eastern end of town. What you see today gives only an idea of the former importance of what was once the largest cathedral in Scotland. Consecrated in 1318 in the presence of Robert the Bruce, it was plundered and left to ruin during the Reformation. In front of the great east window a slab is all that remains of the high altar, where the relics of St Andrew were once enshrined. Previously, it is believed that they were kept in **St Rule's Tower**, the austere Romanesque monolith next to the cathedral, which was built as part of an abbey in 1130. From the top of the tower (a climb of 157 steps), there's a good view of the town and surroundings. Around the entire complex is a sturdy wall dating from the six-teenth century, over half a mile long and with three gate-ways.

THE TOWN

The ruins of **St Andrew's Castle** (April–Sept Mon–Sat 9.30am–6pm, Sun 9.30am–4pm; Oct–March Mon–Sat 9.30am–4pm, Sun 2–4pm; £2.50) lie a little to the north, on the coast, with a drop to the sea on three sides and a moat on the fourth. It was founded in 1200 and extended over the centuries. There's not a great deal left, as it fell into ruin in the seventeenth century, and apart from the four-teenth-century Fore Tower most of what can be seen dates from the sixteenth century.

For all its golfing connections, the atmosphere of the town of St Andrews is dominated by its **university**, the oldest in Scotland, founded in 1410 by Bishop Henry Wardlaw. The first building was on the site of the Old University Library and by the end of the Middle Ages three colleges had been built: St Salvator's (1450) on North Street, St Leonard's (1512) on The Pens, and St Mary's (1538) on South Street. At the time of the Reformation, St Mary's became a seminary of Protestant theology, and today it houses the university's Faculty of Divinity. The quad here has beautiful gardens and some magnificent old trees, per-fect for flopping under on a warm day. A **guided tour** of the university buildings starts from the International Office, Butts Wynd, near St Salvator's Chapel (June–Aug Mon–Sat 11am & 2.30pm, also at 4.30pm on request; £3), or you can wander freely around the buildings at your own pace.

There are plenty of other excellent walks around the town, in particular the clifftop path between the castle and the har-bour, and along either of the town's superb sandy beaches: the East Sands stretch south from the harbour, while the West Sands run along the seaward edge of the Old Course.

Golf in St Andrews

St Andrew's **Royal and Ancient Golf Club** (or "R&A") is the governing body for golf the world over, dating back to a meeting in 1754 of 22 of the local gentry, who founded the Society of St Andrews Golfers, being "admirers of the ancient and healthful exercise of golf", although the game itself has been played here since the fifteenth century. The approach to the town from the west runs adjacent to the famous **Old Course**, one of six courses in the immediate vicinity of the town. The Old Course's strictly private **clubhouse**, a stolid, square building dating from 1854, is at the eastern end of the course overlooking both the eighteenth green and the long beach made famous by the film *Chariots of Fire*. The first British Open Championship was held here in 1873, having been inaugurated in 1860 at Prestwick in Ayrshire, and since then the British Open has been held here regularly. Pictures of golfing greats from Tom Morris to Tiger Woods, along with clubs and a variety of memorabilia which they donated, are displayed in the admirable **British Golf Museum** (April–Oct daily 9.30am–5.30pm; Nov–March Thurs–Mon 11am–3pm; £3.75), on Bruce Embankment, on the waterfront below the clubhouse. There are also plenty of hands-on exhibits, including computers, video screens and footage of British Open championships.

If being in St Andrews inspires you to take to the fairways, it is possible to play any of the town's courses, including the Old Course, though for this you must have a letter of introduction from your club and put your name into a ballot to play on any given day. Even then the green fees are £72. The other courses are generally more accessible; for more information call the St Andrews Golf Line on ©01334/472021. Other facilities include various driving ranges, as well as the National Golf Centre at Drumoig, eight miles away, which has an indoor short game practice facility, while the less ambitious can try out the wonderful eighteen-hole putting course called the Himalayas, situated right next to the Old Course.

GOLF IN ST ANDREWS

LINLITHGOW PALACE

April–Sept daily 9.30am–6.30pm; Oct–March Mon–Sat
9.30am–4.30pm, Sun 2–4.30pm; £2.50.

Romantically set on the edge of Linlithgow Loch, sixteen miles due west of Edinburgh, **Linlithgow Palace** is a splendid fifteenth-century ruin associated with some of Scotland's best-known historical figures – including the ubiquitous Mary, Queen of Scots, who was born here in 1542. A royal manor house is believed to have existed on this site since the time of David I. Fire razed the manor in 1424, after which James I began construction of the present palace, a process that continued through two centuries and the reign of no fewer than eight monarchs. From the top of the northwest tower, Queen Margaret looked out in vain for the return of James IV from the field of Flodden in 1513. The ornate octagonal **fountain** in the inner courtyard, with its wonderfully intricate figures and medallion heads, flowed with wine for the wedding of James V and Mary of Guise. The last reigning monarch to stay in the palace was Charles I in 1633. Bonnie Prince Charlie stayed for a night in 1745, and the following year, in their haste to head north in pursuit of remaining Jacobites, the Duke of Cumberland's troops left the palace on fire – it has been in ruins ever since.

The rooflessness of the castle creates unexpected vistas and the elegant rooms with their intriguing spiral staircases are labyrinthine. The galleried **Great Hall** is magnificent, as is the adjoining kitchen, which has a truly cavernous fireplace. Don't miss the dank downstairs **brewery**, which produced vast quantities of ale; 24 gallons was apparently a good nightly consumption in the sixteenth century.

Linlithgow is twenty minutes by rail from Waverley and there are **trains** throughout the day, approximately every half-hour.

EAST LOTHIAN

East Lothian consists of the coastal strip and hinterland immediately east of Edinburgh. It's largely made up of rolling, fertile farm land, though the best reason for heading out here is for the coastline, particularly between Aberlady and North Berwick, where you'll find long sandy **beaches** and bracing **clifftop walks**, dramatic volcanic outcrops such as the **Bass Rock**, and the romantic ruined medieval castles of **Dirleton** and **Tantallon**. Two worthwhile diversions inland off the A1 are **Lennoxlove House** with its well-known restaurant, and the Iron Age fort on **Trappain Law**. Buses from Edinburgh meander along the east coast, connecting most of the points of interest as far as **North Berwick**. You can also catch a train here or to **Dunbar**.

Aberlady to Dirleton Castle

The best of the coastline begins at **Aberlady**, an elongated conservation village of Gothic-style cottages and mansions, just sixteen miles from Edinburgh. The salt marshes and sand dunes of the adjacent **Aberlady Bay Nature Reserve**, a bird-watchers' haven, mark the site of a medieval harbour. From the nature reserve it's a couple of miles east to **Gullane**, the location of a number of golf courses, including the famous shoreline links of **Muirfield Golf Course**, a regular venue for the British Open established in the late 1800s. Another draw are the fine sandy **beaches** of Gullane Bay, great for blustery walks and views out across the Firth of Forth.

Two miles east of Gullane nestles the genteel hamlet of **Dirleton**, where you'll find **Dirleton Castle** (daily: April–Sept 9.30am–6.30pm; Oct–March daily 9.30am–4.30pm; £2.50), largely in ruins, but well worth the expedition for its wonderful walled gardens. As you pass

EAST LOTHIAN

through the gatehouse, look upwards to the "murder hole", a circular opening in the roof, once used for dropping objects onto the heads of unwelcome visitors. Inside, turn left to see the **Lord's Hall**, a large room with a beautiful domed ceiling. This is part of the original castle built in the early thirteenth century by the de Vaux family. Over the next two hundred years, the Halyburtons built the eastern front, notable for the massive **Great Hall**. The most recent part of the castle is the **Ruthven Lodging**, a Renaissance house north of the original tower, built for the Ruthven family, whose propensity for skulduggery, including the murder of **David Rizzio** and the kidnapping of **James IV**, eventually led to the confiscation of the castle in 1600. Fifty years later, Dirleton, like nearby Tantallon Castle, was bombarded by Cromwell's troops and destroyed.

The well-tended **gardens** contain a sixteenth-century bowling green, a belvedere, just inside the entrance, and a 400-year-old dovecote. If the weather's good you can take the mile-long path from the village church to the sandy, rock-framed beach at **Yellowcraigs**, which overlooks **Fidra Island**, a large lump of basalt, home to thousands of seabirds.

North Berwick and the Bass Rock

There are more sandy beaches at **North Berwick**, two miles east of Dirleton, a coastal town with a somewhat faded, old-fashioned air, its guest houses and hotels extending along the shore in all their Victorian and Edwardian sobriety, though the main draws are two volcanic heaps: the **Bass Rock**, a 350ft-high chunk of basalt three miles out to sea, and **North Berwick Law**, a 613ft-high hill behind the town, from which, on a clear day, you can enjoy views out across the Firth of Forth to Fife and along the coast to Arthur's Seat and the capital.

Resembling a giant molar, the **Bass Rock** has served as a prison, a fortress and a monastic retreat, with a natural tunnel running east to west under the chapel building. Now it is home to millions of nesting seabirds, with Scotland's second-largest gannet colony after St Kilda in tight competition with razorbills, terns, puffins, guillemots and fulmars. Weather permitting, there are regular ninety-minute **boat trips** around the island from North Berwick harbour (Easter to early Oct daily; £3.50). A new **Scottish Seabird Centre**, which will show live pictures from cameras stationed on the rock, as well as offering background information on the birds you can see on the rock and on the nearby coast, is being established at North Berwick and is due for completion in 2000.

Tantallon Castle

April–Sept daily 9.30am–6.30pm; Oct–March Mon–Wed & Sat 9.30am–4.30pm, Thurs 9.30am–noon, Sun 2–4.30pm; £2.50.

The melodramatic pinkish sandstone ruins of **Tantallon Castle** lie three miles east of North Berwick on the A198. With a sheer drop down to the sea on three sides and a sequence of moats and ditches on the fourth, the castle's desolate invincibility is daunting, especially when the wind howls over the remaining battlements and the surf crashes on the rocks far below.

Built at the end of the fourteenth century, the castle was a stronghold of the Douglases, the Earls of Angus, one of the most powerful noble families in Scotland. A Douglas had been regent early in the reign of James II and guardian to James IV, while another had married James IV's widow, Margaret Tudor – their grandson was Lord Darnley, second husband of Mary, Queen of Scots and father of James VI (James I of England). The castle was besieged several times before it was finally destroyed by Cromwell in 1651 after a

TANTALLON CASTLE

twelve-day bombardment. The ruins, including a seven-teenth-century dovecote, left untouched by Cromwell's men, enjoy a wonderfully photogenic setting, with the Bass Rock and the Firth of Forth in the background. You can reach Tantallon Castle from North Berwick by the Dunbar **bus** (Mon–Sat 6 daily, Sun 2 daily), which takes fifteen minutes, or you can walk there from town along the cliffs in around an hour.

Dunbar

Twelve miles further along the coast lies **Dunbar**. The town's claim to fame is its connections with **John Muir**, the explorer and naturalist who created the United States national park system. **John Muir House** at 128 High St (June–Sept Mon–Sat 11am–1pm & 2–5pm, Sun 2–5pm; free), his birthplace, has been refurbished in period detail and contains a tiny museum dedicated to the pioneer's life and work. A more appropriate tribute is the **country park** in Muir's honour, where an easy three-mile walk west of the harbour takes you past the town's ruined castle then along a rugged stretch of coast to the sands of **Belhaven Bay**. There are various cosy pubs in town, many of which sell the excellent locally-brewed Belhaven range of beers.

Lennoxlove House and Trapain Law

The inland route through East Lothian along the fast A1 isn't nearly as scenic as the coastal alternative, though if you're exploring the area there are a couple of worthwhile diversions. A mile south of the town of Haddington and around sixteen miles east of Edinburgh, is **Lennoxlove House** (Easter–Oct Wed, Sat & Sun 2–5pm; £3.50), a sprawling pile incorporating a medieval tower house which has a splendid fine and applied art collection belonging to the Duke of Hamilton. The main reason most folk come here, however, is to eat at *The Garden Café* (Tues–Sun 11am–5pm), run by Clarissa Dickson Wright, star of TV's *Two Fat Ladies* cookery show.

Five miles further east, a moderately easy six-mile walk from the village of East Linton takes you along the River Tyne and up the 221ft-high **Trapain Law**, a relatively low hill, which nevertheless commands wide views of the entire East Lothian area. On the summit you can still make out the remains of an Iron Age fort, which excavations have shown to be the headquarters of the Votadini, the dominant tribe in southeast Scotland at the time. In 1919, one of the richest hordes of Roman silver found in Britain was dug up here – the Trapain silver collection can be seen in the National Museum of Scotland in Edinburgh (see p.59).

THE BORDERS

South of Edinburgh, beyond the Pentland and Moorfoot hills, nestles the valley of the **Tweed River**, the heart of the **Borders** region of Scotland, famous for its fishing. For many, this area has some of the most tranquil and beguiling scenery in the country. Broadly known as the Southern Uplands, the Border hills are characteristically bare and rounded – in contrast to the craggier peaks of the Highlands – and form the backdrop to a rich, turbulent history of border skirmishes and religious and internecine feuding.

From the capital, the most worthwhile targets of a day-trip are one or more of the famous ruined **abbeys** of **Melrose**, **Dryburgh** and **Jedburgh**, along with the impressive stately homes of **Abbotsford**, Sir Walter Scott's beloved country seat, and **Traquair**, with its appealingly quirky history and tiny brewery. The whole region is also great for **walking**, either up into the hills or along sections

Tourist information in the Borders

Galashiels, 3 St John's St (April–June & Sept Mon–Sat
10am–5pm, Sun 2–4pm; July & Aug Mon–Sat 10am–6pm, Sun
1–5pm; Oct Mon–Sat 10am–12.30pm & 1.30–4.30pm;
℃01896/755551).

   Melrose, adjacent to the abbey ruins (March–May & Oct
Mon–Sat 10am–5pm, Sun 10am–1pm; June Mon–Sat
10am–6pm, Sun 10am–2pm; July & Aug Mon–Sat
9.30am–6.30pm, Sun 10am–6pm; Sept Mon–Sat 10am–6pm,
Sun 10am–2pm; ℃01896/822555).

   Jedburgh, Murray's Green (April, May & Oct Mon–Sat
10am–5pm, Sun noon–4pm; June & Sept Mon–Sat
9.30am–6pm, Sun noon–4pm; July & Aug Mon–Fri
9am–8.30pm, Sat 9am–7pm, Sun 10am–7pm; Nov–March
Mon–Fri 10am–4.30pm; ℃01835/863435).

of riverside, particularly the Tweed, which has a well-
marked walkway and cycle path. For more details on local
walks, contact one of the **local tourist information
offices** (see box above).

   The region isn't that well served by public **transport**.
There are no trains, and while buses run south from
Edinburgh to Galashiels on a fairly regular basis, picking up
connections to places beyond this normally requires some
careful planning. For full details contact Traveline
(℃0131/225 3858) or one of the local tourist information
offices.

Melrose Abbey

April–Sept daily 9.30am–6.30pm; Oct–March Mon–Sat
9.30am–4.30pm, Sun 2–4.30pm; £3.50.

Three miles east of Galashiels, the small town of **Melrose** is tucked in between the Tweed and the three-peaked Eildon Hills. Behind the town square, the pink- and ochre-tinted stone ruins of **Melrose Abbey** soar above their riverside surroundings. Founded in 1136 by David I, the abbey grew rich selling wool and hides to Flanders, but its prosperity was fragile: the English repeatedly razed Melrose, most viciously under Richard II in 1385 and the Earl of Hertford in 1545. Most of the present remains date from the inter-vening period, when extensive rebuilding abandoned the original austerity for an elaborate Gothic style, inspired by the abbeys of northern England. The site is dominated by the **Abbey Church**, marked out by its elegant window arches. Unfortunately, the grand piers of the **monk's choir** are disfigured by the masonry of a later parish church. Better preserved is the adjacent **presbytery**, its dignified lines illuminated by a magnificent perpendicular window, under which the heart of Robert the Bruce is buried. In the **south transept**, another fine fifteenth-century window sprouts yet more delicate, foliate tracery, while outside, all sorts of **gargoyles** frolic along the majestic lines of the church – one of the most peculiar is the pig playing the bagpipes on the roof on the south side of the nave.

Dryburgh Abbey

April–Sept daily 9.30am–6.30pm; Oct–March Mon–Sat 9.30am–4.30pm, Sun 2–4.30pm; £2.50.

If you're driving the three miles from Melrose to Dryburgh, you'll pass **Scott's View**, a viewing point overlooking the Tweed Valley, where Sir Walter Scott often picnicked and where his horse stopped out of habit during the great writer's funeral procession. The best way to get to Dryburgh by public transport is to take the Jedburgh **bus** (Mon–Sat hourly, Sun 8 daily; 10min) as far as St Boswells, then walk a mile or so to a footbridge across the Tweed and the tiny village of Dryburgh.

Here, the remains of **Dryburgh Abbey** occupy an idyllic position against a hilly backdrop, with ancient cedar trees and wide lawns flattering the reddish hues of the stonework. The Premonstratensians, or White Canons, founded the abbey in the twelfth century, but they were never as successful – or apparently as devout – as their Cistercian neighbours in Melrose. Their chronicles detail interminable disputes about land and money – in one incident, a fourteenth-century canon called Marcus flattened the abbot with his fist. Demolished and rebuilt on several occasions, the abbey incorporates several architectural styles, as illustrated in the shattered **church**, where the clumsy decoration of the main entrance contrasts with the spirited dog's-tooth motif around the east processional doorway. The battered north transept contains the grave of **Sir Walter Scott**, while close by lies Field Marshal Haig, the World War I commander. The east processional doorway leads through to the **monastic buildings**, a two-storey ensemble that provides an insight into the lives of the monks. The real highlight is the barrel-vaulted **chapterhouse**, complete with low stone benches, grouped windows and carved arcades.

Jedburgh Abbey

April–Sept Mon–Sat 9.30am–6.30pm, Sun 2–6.30pm; Oct–March Mon–Sat 9.30am–4.30pm, Sun 2–4.30pm; £3.

Eight miles south of Dryburgh and just ten miles north of the border with England, **Jedburgh** nestles in the valley of the Jed Water near its confluence with the Teviot. The remains of **Jedburgh Abbey**, right in the centre of town, date from the twelfth century. The abbey was burnt and badly damaged on a number of occasions, the worst damage being inflicted by the English in 1544–45 during English king Henry VIII's "rough wooing" of Mary, Queen of Scots (see p.283 for more details). The monastic way of life, however, had already fallen prey to corruption, and only a few canons remained living in the ruins of the abbey until the monastery closed in 1560 with the Reformation. However, the Abbey Church remained a parish kirk for another three centuries and is particularly well preserved.

Entry to the site is through the **visitor centre** at the bottom of the hill. The **Abbey Church** is entered through the east processional doorway, remarkably, still in its original condition. The splendidly proportioned three-storey nave is a fine example of the transition from Romanesque to Gothic design; even more impressive is the east end of the church, where the squat central tower is underpinned by the monumental circular pillars and truncated arches of the earlier, twelfth-century choir.

Abbotsford House

March–May & Oct Mon–Sat 10am–5pm, Sun 2–5pm; June–Sept daily 10am–5pm; £3.50.

Memorably set on the banks of the Tweed just outside Galashiels, **Abbotsford House** was designed to satisfy the Romantic inclinations of Sir Walter Scott, who lived here from 1812 until his death twenty years later. Abbotsford took twelve years to evolve, with the fanciful turrets and castellations of the Scots Baronial exterior incorporating copies of medieval originals: the entrance porch imitates that of Linlithgow Palace and the screen wall in the garden echoes Melrose Abbey's cloister. Scott was proud of his creation, writing to a friend, "It is a kind of conundrum castle to be sure [which] pleases a fantastic person in style and manner."

Inside, visitors start in the wood-panelled **study**, with its small writing desk made of salvage from the Spanish Armada. The library boasts Scott's collection of more than nine thousand rare books and an extraordinary assortment

ABBOTSFORD HOUSE

of Scottish memorabilia, including Rob Roy's purse and *skene dhu* (knife); a lock of Bonnie Prince Charlie's hair and his *quaich* (drinking cup); Flora Macdonald's pocket-book; the inlaid pearl crucifix that accompanied Mary, Queen of Scots to the scaffold; and even a piece of oatcake found in the pocket of a dead Highlander at Culloden. You can also see Henry Raeburn's famous portrait of Scott hanging in the **drawing room**, and all sorts of weapons – notably Rob Roy's sword, dagger and gun – in the **armoury**. In the barbaric-looking **entrance hall**, hung with elk and wild cattle skulls, is a cast of the head of Robert the Bruce.

Traquair House

April, May & Sept daily 12.30–5.30pm; June–Aug daily 10.30am–5.30pm; Oct Fri–Sun 2–5pm; £5; grounds only £2.

Peeping out from the trees a mile or so south of Innerleithen, a town twelve miles west of Galashiels and six miles east of Peebles, **Traquair House** is the oldest continuously inhabited house in Scotland, and has been in the hands of the same family – the Maxwell Stuarts – since 1491. The first of the line, **James**, first Laird of Traquair, inherited an elementary fortified tower, which his powerful descendants gradually converted into a mansion, visited, it is said, by 27 monarchs, including Mary, Queen of Scots, and one or two aspirant ones, including Bonnie Prince Charlie.

Traquair's main appeal lies in its ancient shape and structure. The whitewashed facade is strikingly handsome, with narrow windows and trim turrets surrounding the tiniest of front doors – an organic, homogeneous edifice that's a welcome change from other grandiose stately homes. Inside, the house has kept many of its oldest features. You can see original vaulted cellars, where locals once hid their cattle from raiders; the twisting main staircase as well as the earlier medieval version, later a secret escape route for persecuted Catholics; a carefully camouflaged priest's hole; and even a **priest's room** where a string of resident chaplains lived in hiding until the Catholic Emancipation Act freed things up in 1829. Of the furniture and fittings, the carved oak door at the foot of the stairs is outstanding, as are the Dutch trompe l'oeil carvings in the **still room** and the bright-yellow four-poster of the **king's room**, with a bedspread allegedly embroidered by Mary, Queen of Scots.

It's worth sparing time for the surrounding **gardens** where you'll find a maze, several craft workshops and a **working brewery**, dating back to 1566, and which had lain unused for 150 years. The present owner restored it and opened it to the public in 1965, claiming it to be the only British brewery that still ferments totally in oak. You can taste the ales in the Brewery House (April & May daily 12.30–5.30pm; June–Aug daily 10.30am–5.30pm; Oct Fri–Sun 12.30–5.30pm), and buy them from the tearoom and gift shop. There's also a redundant avenue which leads to the locked **Bear Gates**; Bonnie Prince Charlie, who stayed here for a night in 1745 while his army was in Edinburgh, left the house through the gates, and the then owner promised to keep them locked till a Stuart should ascend the throne.

LISTINGS

Accommodation

As you'd expect of one of Britain's most visited cities, Edinburgh offers an extensive choice of **accommodation**. In addition to the city's large central **hotels**, there's a wide choice of smaller hotels and **guest houses**, with a dozen rooms or fewer, as well as numerous private houses offering **bed and breakfast**. Budget travellers have a decent range of **backpacker hostels** to choose from, and there are four **campsites**, attached to caravan parks, within commuting distance of the city. The number of **self-catering** options has increased recently, and there's a wide variety of **campus accommodation** available during the summer months, though, surpisingly, this is neither as cheap nor as convenient as might be expected.

The highest concentration of places to stay can be found immediately north of Haymarket Station, the eastern and northern reaches of the New Town, and in the south, around the suburbs of Bruntsfield and Newington, about a mile from the centre. Other popular areas, slightly further out, are Ferry Road, to the north of town, and the seaside suburbs of Portobello and Joppa – around three miles from the centre.

You should be able to find accommodation reasonably easily for most of the year. However, **advance reservations** are recommended during summer months, especially during the

Festival. The tourist information office (see p.6) gives out accommodation lists for free, and can reserve any type of accommodation in advance for a £5 fee: call in personally when you arrive or write in advance to Edinburgh Marketing Central Reservations Department, 3 Princes St, Edinburgh EH2 2QP (℗0131/473 3800, *www.edinburgh.org*), stating requirements. An accommodation reservation service is also run by Capital Holidays, in Waverley Station (daily 9am–5pm; ℗0131/556 0030), which makes no charge for bookings, but requires the first night to be paid in full in advance by credit card. Agencies that can help with accommodation specifically during the Festival include Festival Beds (℗0131/225 1011), an Edinburgh University-run service specializing in private accommodation, and the Fringe Office (℗0131/226 5257, *www.edfringe.com*), whose Internet notice board also advertises rooms for the Festival. It's also worth checking the **classified sections** in publications such as *Private Eye* and *Time Out* and some of the broadsheet newspapers. If you're planning to be in Edinburgh for the duration of the Festival, it's worth considering **renting a flat**. Inevitably, prices are inflated, but if there's a group of you it can work out significantly cheaper and more flexible than a B&B.

Accommodation price codes

Accommodation **prices** have been graded with the codes below, according to the cost of the least expensive double room in high season.

① under £40	⑥ £90–110
② £40–50	⑦ £110–150
③ £50–60	⑧ £150–200
④ £60–70	⑨ £200 and over
⑤ £70–90	

HOTELS

Edinburgh's large central **hotels** tend to fall into two categories: grand, traditional establishments at the upper end of the market, and modern, continental-style hotels in the middle price range. A number of stylish upmarket hotels have recently arrived around the edges of the city centre in places such as Leith and the West End, while in the suburbs and beyond the country-house hotel style dominates.

OLD TOWN

Apex International
Map 3, C4. 31–35 Grassmarket ℡0131/300 3456, fax 220 5345, *mail@apexhotels.co.uk*
Formerly a student residence, this large, new business-oriented hotel is handy for the bars and restaurants of Grassmarket. Upper rooms and the rooftop bar/restaurant have views across to the Castle. ⑥.

Bank Hotel
Map 3, G3. 1 South Bridge ℡0131/556 9043.
Unique location in a 1920s bank at the crossroads of the Royal Mile and South Bridge, with *Logie Baird's* bar downstairs and nine unusual but comfortable rooms upstairs each tastefully decorated on the theme of a famous Scot. ⑤.

Ibis Hotel
Map 3, G3. 6 Hunter Square ℡0131/240 7000.
Part of the French economy hotel chain, offering functional, though well-presented, rooms right at the heart of the Old Town. Buffet-style continental breakfast costs extra. ③.

Point Hotel
Map 3, A5. 34–59 Bread St ℡0131/221 9919, fax 221 9929.

Chic, modern conversion of a former Co-op, this large hotel is handily located for theatreland. The lively ground-floor restaurant serves high-quality, good-value set-price dinners. ⑥.

Tailors Hall Hotel

Map 3, F4. 139 Cowgate ℗0131/622 6800.

Don't let the location in dingy Cowgate put you off – this hotel has stylish and modern rooms in the shell of a 1621 trades hall and brewery, next door to the lively mock-Gothic *Three Sisters Bar*. ⑥.

NEW TOWN

Albany Hotel

Map 4, J2. 39–43 Albany St ℗0131/556 0397, fax 557 6633.

Three Georgian houses make up this hotel situated in a central yet quiet location. The high-ceilinged rooms have recently undergone a complete revamp. ⑦.

The Balmoral

Map 4, K6. 1 Princes St ℗0131/556 2414, fax 557 3747, *www.rfhotels.com*

Originally known as the *North British*, this Edinburgh landmark is the finest grand hotel in the city. Everything, from the thistle-green décor in the rooms to the stained-glass windows in the main stairwell, exudes a refined Scottish elegance. *The Balmoral* boasts nearly two hundred rooms, full business facilities, a swimming pool and gym, and two highly rated restaurants. Its famous 192ft-high clock tower runs two minutes fast for the benefit of those hurrying to catch a train at Waverley Station. ⑧.

The Bonham

Map 2, A5. 35 Drumsheugh Gardens ℗0131/226 6050, *reserve@thebonham.com*

One of Edinburgh's most stylish upmarket hotels, cheekily hiding behind a grand West End Victorian facade. Original art and styling in the rooms, mixing period and modern furniture. Internet and email link-ups in each room. ⑧.

Caledonian Hotel

Map 4, B9. Princes St ℗0131/459 9988.
Built by the railway for the well-to-do travelling between London and their Highland estates, this red-sandstone building is a local landmark, lording it over the west end of Princes Street. The hotel is popular with visiting celebrities such as Sean Connery and has good facilities, including a business suite, pool, gym and top-class restaurant. ⑨.

Frederick House Hotel

Map 4, E5. 42 Frederick St ℗0131/226 1999,
frederickhouse@ednet.co.uk
A smart, well-priced hotel in a superb location just off George Street. The décor is overly-grand, but the rooms are large and well-equipped. No breakfast in the hotel, but continental breakfasts served across the road at *Café Rouge*. ④.

Howard Hotel

Map 4, G1. 34 Great King St ℗0131/557 3500,
reserve@thehoward.com
Elegant and exclusive town-house hotel with only fifteen rooms. Lavishly decorated and furnished, and serving classy modern Scottish food in restaurant *36* in the basement. ⑨.

Old Waverley Hotel

Map 4, J6. 43 Princes St ℗0131/556 4648.
Long-established city-centre hotel with over sixty neat, fully equipped but slightly bland rooms. Some funky décor has been added to the public areas in a recent upgrade, but its best selling point is its location: right across from Waverley Station and

the Scott Monument with sweeping city views from the front-facing rooms. ⑧.

Parliament House Hotel

Map 2, G4. 15 Calton Hill ℗0131/478 4000, *phadams@aol.com*

A little further from the new Scottish Parliament building than was envisaged when it opened, this is a well-presented upscale hotel, discreetly situated on a cobbled lane between Princes Street and Calton Hill. It has an easy-going atmosphere and attentive staff. ⑦.

LEITH

Malmaison Hotel

Map 1, E4. 1 Tower Place ℗0131/468 5000, *edinburgh@malmaison.com*

In spite of its unlikely setting near Leith docks, this hotel is the height of sophistication. Each room boasts bright, bold original designs, as well as CD players, cable TV and top-quality furniture and linen. You can also make use of the gym, room service, Parisian brasserie and café-bar. The staff are exceptionally helpful. ⑦.

SOUTH OF THE CENTRE

Allison House Hotel

Map 1, E5. 15–17 Mayfield Gardens, Mayfield ℗0131/667 8049, *dh007ljh@msn.com*

Well-run and recently expanded hotel on one of the main bus routes into town. It has an "honesty" bar – guests serve themselves and pay on departure, and it also offers free car parking. ④.

Bruntsfield Hotel

Map 1, D5. 69–74 Bruntsfield Place, Bruntsfield ℗0131/229 1393, *bruntsfield@queensferry-hotels.co.uk*

Located a mile south of Princes Street, this hotel overlooks

Bruntsfield Links, an extension of the Meadows, and is handy for Bruntsfield's attractive row of delis, bars and restaurants. The fifty rooms are comfortable and furnished in traditional style. ⑦.

Prestonfield House Hotel

Map 1, E5. Priestfield Rd ⓒ0131/668 3346.

Luxury hotel in a seventeenth-century mansion set in its own park below Arthur's Seat. Peacocks strut around on the lawns and Highland cattle low in the adjacent fields. A new wing, sympathetic to the old building, has been added, raising the number of rooms from 5 to 31. ⑦.

GUEST HOUSES

Although the price of staying at one of Edinburgh's many **guest houses** or small hotels is rising steadily, they are relatively good value for money and generally have much more atmosphere than the large modern city hotels. Many are large, elegant Georgian or Victorian houses, located in the **New Town** and slightly further out on the major routes into Edinburgh, notably in the south of the city round **Newington** and **Bruntsfield**, and in the north on **Ferry Road**. Also included below are a few notable **B&Bs**. The tourist office has fuller lists of member B&Bs, and can help you with bookings (see p.6).

NEW TOWN

Ardenlee Guest House

Map 2, E2. 9 Eyre Place ⓒ0131/556 2838.

A four-storey guest house near the Royal Botanic Garden. The décor of the rooms is restrained but attractive, and the dining room has a display of old and new maps of Edinburgh. Vegetarian options on offer for breakfast, and large family rooms are available. Private parking. Non-smoking. ③.

Brodies Guest House

Map 2, F2. 22 East Claremont St ℰ0131/556 4032,
rose.olbert@seqnet.co.uk
Friendly B&B in an attractive terraced Victorian town house on the eastern edge of the New Town. The rooms are plain but neat, and there's a small, quiet garden at the back. ③.

Claymore Hotel

Map 2, I3. 6 Royal Terrace ℰ0131/556 2693.
Family-run town-house hotel located on a prestigious terrace on the northern side of Calton Hill. Has twelve decent-sized and recently upgraded en-suite rooms and a pleasant conservatory for breakfast. ⑤.

Davenport House

Map 2, I3. 58 Great King St ℰ0131/558 8495,
davenporthouse@btinternet.com
A grand, regally decorated guest house in an attractive Georgian town house; a well priced and intimate alternative to some of the nearby hotels. ④.

Dene Guest House

Map 2, E2. 7 Eyre Place ℰ0131/556 2700.
Well priced B&B on the fringe of the New Town, ten minutes' walk from Princes Street. Some of the rooms are tastefully furnished; all are adequate. The owners are welcoming and helpful. ②.

Frasers B&B

Map 2, F2. 7 Bellevue Place ℰ0131/556 5123.
Three smallish but clean and tastefully decorated rooms in a good location near Broughton Street. ②.

Greenside Hotel

Map 2, I3. 9 Royal Terrace ℂ & fax 0131/557 0022.
Another of the small Royal Terrace hotels with great views from the top floors across to Leith and beyond to the Firth of Forth. There are fifteen rooms, all en suite, some large enough for families. Evening meals are available in the residents' bar, while snacks can be rustled up at any time. Value for money considering the location. ④.

Sibbet House

Map 4, F2. 26 Northumberland St ℂ0131/556 1078,
sibbet.house@zetnet.co.uk
Small, sumptuous family guest house, with beautifully decorated rooms and high standards. Breakfast is around one large communal table. Non-smoking. ⑥.

Six Mary's Place

Map 2, B3. 6 Mary's Place, Raeburn Place ℂ0131/332 8965,
sixmarysplace@btinternet.com
A collectively run, "alternative" guest house in Stockbridge renowned for excellent vegetarian breakfasts served in the bright conservatory; evening meals are also available. On summer evenings you can relax in the garden. Non-smoking. ③.

Stuart House

Map 2, F2. 12 East Claremont St ℂ0131/557 9030,
stuartho@globalnet.co.uk
Bright and welcoming, if slightly over-elaborate Georgian terrace house in eastern New Town, a few minutes' walk from lively Broughton Street. Non-smoking. ④.

LEITH AND INVERLEITH

A-Haven Town House

Map 1, D4. 180 Ferry Rd, Leith ℂ0131/554 6559,
reservations@a-haven.co.uk

A very friendly place, with eleven rooms, among the best of a number of guest houses on the main east–west artery of north Edinburgh. Does filling breakfasts. ⑤.

Ashlyn Guest House

Map 1, D4. 42 Inverleith Row, Inverleith ©0131/552 2954.
Right by the Royal Botanic Garden, and about twenty minutes' walk from the centre. Good-quality, intimate guest house with some genuinely elegant furnishings. Non-smoking. ③.

Bar Java

Map 1, E4. 48–50 Constitution St, Leith ©0131/467 7527, *www.scoot.co.uk/bar_java/*
Simple but bright rooms above one of Leith's funkiest bars. Great breakfasts are served, and food and drink are available till late in the bar itself. ②.

Camore Hotel

Map 1, E4. 7 Links Gardens, Leith ©0131/554 7897.
Georgian house with many attractive original features including marble fireplaces. Also has great views over Leith Links, Calton Hill and Arthur's Seat. ③.

Ravensdown Guest House

Map 1, E4. 248 Ferry Rd, Inverleith ©0131/552 5438.
Located far enough west to offer a fine panoramic view across Inverleith playing fields to the city centre. Provides good quality bed-and-breakfast accommodation. Non-smoking. ②.

SOUTH OF THE CENTRE

Ashdene House

Map 1, E5. 23 Fountainhall Rd, Grange ©0131/667 6026, *Ashdene_House_Edinburgh@compuserve.com*

Well-run, non-smoking and environmentally friendly guest house in the quiet southern suburbs. All five rooms are en suite and have a pleasant, unfussy décor. ③.

Finlay Guest House

Map 2, C9. 4 Hartington Place, Viewforth ©0131/229 1620, *finlays@btinternet.com*

Pleasant, well-priced B&B near Bruntsfield about twenty minutes' walk from town. All the rooms are decently furnished and have TVs; both smoking and non-smoking rooms are available, and some have en-suite bathrooms. ③.

The Greenhouse

Map 2, C9. 14 Hartington Gardens, Viewforth ©0131/622 7634, *greenhouse_edin@hotmail.com*

Edinburgh's most fully vegetarian/vegan guest house, right down to the soaps and duvets, though a relaxed rather than right-on atmosphere prevails. The rooms are neat and tastefully furnished, with fresh fruit and flowers in each. ③.

Hopetoun Guest House

Map 1, E5. 37 Mayfield Rd, Newington ©0131/667 7691, *hopetoun@aol.com*

Bright guest house with just three rooms sharing two bathrooms. It has great views of Arthur's Seat and Blackford Hill, and there are plenty of buses into the centre. Non-smoking. ②.

Ravensneuk Guest House

Map 1, E5. 11 Blacket Ave, Newington © & fax 0131/667 5347. Built in 1836 in an exclusive conservation area, family-run *Ravensneuk Guest House* is close to Holyrood Park and the city centre. It has seven rooms, three of which are en suite. Fresh fruit salad and yogurt are available for breakfast. Non-smoking. ②.

The Stuarts B&B

Map 2, D9. 17 Glengyle Terrace, Bruntsfield ℂ0131/229 9559, *reservations@the-stuarts.com*

A friendly, expertly run five-star bed and breakfast in central Edinburgh, with three comfortable and well-equipped, if pricey, rooms in a basement beside Bruntsfield Links. ⑥.

Teviotdale House Hotel

Map 1, E5. 53 Grange Loan, Grange ℂ0131/667 4376, *teviotdale.house@btinternet.com*

Peaceful non-smoking hotel, offering luxurious standards at reasonable prices. Serves particularly good, huge home-cooked Scottish breakfasts. ③.

EAST OF THE CENTRE

Devon House Guest House

Map 1, F4. 2 Pittville St, Portobello ℂ & fax 0131/669 6067.

On a quiet side street, with pleasant parks and great walks along the promenade nearby. Good breakfast menu. ②.

Joppa Turrets Guest House

Map 1, F4. 1 Lower Joppa, Joppa ℂ0131/669 5806, *stanley@joppaturrets.demon.co.uk*

A well-appointed, quiet guest house right by the beach in Joppa, five miles east of the city centre, with fantastic views across the Firth of Forth. ②.

Stra'ven Guest House

Map 1, F4. 3 North Brunstane Rd, Joppa ℂ0131/669 5580, fax 657 2517.

Very close to the beach, with seven rooms and a large, magnificent lounge. Very relaxed atmosphere. Unrestricted parking. Non-smoking. ②.

SELF-CATERING APARTMENTS

Self-catering apartments offer good value if you're in a group or after a level of independence and privacy you can't always get in guest houses or hotels. In Edinburgh two distinct styles of self-catering accommodation can be found: smart, modern apartments full of mod-cons, aimed mainly at visiting business travellers; and holiday lets which make a feature of their historical character, but generally have a minimum stay in summer of a week and need to be booked quite a long time in advance.

Canon Court Apartments

Map 2, E1. 20 Canonmills ℗0131/474 7000, *canon.court@dial.pipex.com*

Two modern blocks containing smart, comfortable self-contained two- or three-room apartments on the northern edge of the New Town, near the Water of Leith. All units have cable TV, a CD player, fully equipped kitchens and security door entry. There's also free parking alongside. Prices start at £89 a night for a two-room apartment or £148 a night for two bedrooms with a sleeper couch in the living room.

Gladstone's Land

Map 3, D3. Contact the National Trust for Scotland, 5 Charlotte Square ℗0131/243 9331.

A two-room self-catering apartment in Gladstone's Land, a magnificent seventeenth-century mansion (see p.24). Minimum stay one week in summer and three nights in winter. Sleeps two and costs from £350 per week.

Rosslyn Castle

Map 1, E6. Roslin, Midlothian ℗01628/825925.

This fifteenth-century castle is dramatically sited on a rock high above the River Esk and just five minutes' walk from Rosslyn

Chapel (see p.106), seven miles from the city centre. Sleeps up to seven people and costs £650–1269 a week; minimum stay three nights.

West End Apartments

Map 2, A4. c/o Brian Matheson, 2 Learmonth Terrace, Comely Bank ✆0131/332 0717 or 226 6512, *brian@sias.co.uk*

Five decent, well-equipped apartments in a West End town house; minimum let two nights. Sleeps up to five and costs £200–800 per week.

CAMPUS ACCOMMODATION

With a large number of students studying in Scotland's capital, **campus accommodation** is available at certain times of the year. The kind of accommodation on offer varies from tiny single rooms in long lonely corridors to relatively comfortable places in small, shared apartments. Much of what's available, however, is quite a trek from the centre of town, though there are one or two more central options, such as Pollock Halls by Arthur's Seat.

Heriot-Watt University

Map 1, C5. Riccarton Campus, Currie ✆0131/451 3669.

Sited some way out at the extreme western fringe of the city, but offering comfortable, en-suite rooms, available all year round. In addition, simpler student accommodation is available during university holidays. Transport links include trains from Curriehill and buses #22/22A, #45 and #65. ②–③.

Napier University

Map 1, D5. 219 Colinton Rd, Merchiston ✆0131/455 4921.

Halls of residence (①) in a reasonable location in the southern inner suburbs, available July to mid-Sept only. Minimum stay two nights. Buses #23 and #37 will take you to Princes Street.

Also available during the same period are three–five person self-catering flats (℡0131/455 4427) in more central locations near Haymarket. Minimum stay one week; from £300 per week.

University of Edinburgh Pollock Halls of Residence

Map 5, B7. 18 Holyrood Park Rd, Newington ℡0131/651 2011.
This is unquestionably the best setting of any of the campuses, right beside the Royal Commonwealth Pool and Holyrood Park. It's quite expensive for campus accommodation, though rates do include breakfast. Open Easter and late June to mid-Sept only. ⑤.

HOSTELS

Edinburgh now has a wealth of **hostels**, including two grand SYHA-run establishments and a cluster of independent outfits on or near the Royal Mile. All have dorms with bunkbeds and large communal kitchens and living areas. Most hostels these days provide bedding, and many have private four-bed or double rooms available, though these tend to be priced at the same level as cheaper guest houses. Expect to pay around £10 a night for a dorm bed, though prices rise during the Festival by a couple of pounds, and some places now charge more in a bid to make the hostel slightly more upmarket. The hostels listed here are open all year round unless otherwise indicated. We've also indicated those that have a curfew.

Argyle Backpackers Hotel

Map 1, D5. 14 Argyle Place, Marchmont ℡0131/667 9991, argyle@sol.co.uk
Pleasantly located in studenty Marchmont near the Meadows, this is a quieter, less intense version of the typical backpackers' hostel, with only three nine-bed dorms and a good selection of

double, twin and four-bed rooms, though prices are a pound or two more than elsewhere. Communal areas include a bright conservatory.

Belford Hostel

Map 2, A6. 6–8 Douglas Gardens, West End ☏0131/225 6209, booking hotline ☏0800/096 6868, *info@hoppo.com*
Housed in a converted Arts and Crafts church, just west of the centre close to St Mary's Cathedral and the Gallery of Modern Art. The dorms are in box rooms with the vaulted church ceiling above.

Bruntsfield Hostel

Map 2, D9. 7 Bruntsfield Crescent, Bruntsfield ☏0131/447 2994, central reservations ☏0541/553255.
Large SYHA hostel overlooking Bruntsfield Links, a mile south of Princes Street. It's served by buses #11, #15 or #16. There's a 2am curfew, and breakfast is included in the price.

Castle Rock Hostel

Map 3, D4. 15 Johnston Terrace, Old Town ☏0131/225 9666.
Busy two-hundred-bed hostel tucked below the Castle ramparts. Dorms are large and bright, and the communal areas include a games room with pool and ping-pong tables.

Cowgate Tourist Hostel

Map 3, F4. 112 Cowgate, Old Town ☏0131/226 2153.
Basic, low-cost accommodation in small apartments with kitchens, in the heart of the Old Town. Laundry facilities. Open July–Sept only.

Edinburgh Backpackers Hostel

Map 3, F2. 65 Cockburn St, Old Town ☏0131/220 1717, booking hotline ☏0800/096 6868, *info@hoppo.com*
Big hostel in a great central location down a side street off the

HOSTELS

Royal Mile. Accommodation is mostly in large, bright dorms, although a few doubles are available.

Eglinton Hostel

Map 2, A7. 18 Eglinton Crescent, Haymarket ☏0131/337 1120, central reservations ☏0541/553255.

Slightly more expensive and more central of the two main SYHA hostels, in a characterful town house west of the centre, near Haymarket Station. The curfew is 2am; breakfast is included in price.

High Street Hostel

Map 3, H3. 8 Blackfriars St, Old Town ☏0131/557 3984.

Large, lively and well-known hostel in a sixteenth-century building just off the Royal Mile.

Royal Mile Backpackers

Map 3, G2. 105 High St, Old Town ☏0131/557 6120.

Small, friendly hostel popular with longer-term residents, with limited communal areas, but shared facilities with the nearby *High Street Hostel*.

Student residences

Map 3, I4 and G3. New Arthur Place, Pleasance; 4 Robertson Close, Cowgate ☏0131/337 1120, central reservations ☏0541/553255.

As well as running the *Bruntsfield* and *Eglinton* hostels, SYHA takes over two central student residences during July and August – one on The Pleasance and one on Cowgate; both have over a hundred single bedrooms for £16 per night.

CAMPSITES

There are four well-equipped caravan parks with **campsites** on the fringes of Edinburgh: one in the west, one in the east and two in the north of the city. Although each is a fair distance from the centre of town, all are well served by buses. You can expect to pay under £10 a night for a tent.

Drummohr Caravan Park

Map 1, F4. Levenhall, Musselburgh ©0131/665 6867.
A large, pleasant site in this coastal satellite town to the east of Edinburgh, with excellent transport connections to the city; it's served by buses #15, #15A, #26, #44, #66 (SMT) and #85. Open March–Oct.

Mortonhall Caravan Park

Map 1, B6. 38 Mortonhall Gate, East Frogston Rd ©0131/664 1533.
Five miles from the centre in the south of the city near the Braid Hills; take bus #11 from Princes Street. There are around 250 places, a play area, laundry facilities and three toilet/shower blocks. Open March–Oct.

Silverknowes Caravan Site

Map 1, C4. Marine Drive, Silverknowes ©0131/312 6874.
Very busy campsite in the northwest of the city. Close to the sea and Lauriston Castle. It's not a great part of town, but you're close to the sea and Lauriston Castle, and it's just a half-hour bus (#14) journey into the centre. Room for a hundred tents. Open April–Sept.

Slatebairns Caravan Club Site

Map 1, E6. Roslin, Midlothian ©0131/440 2192.
This is an attractive countryside site with good facilities for caravans and tents, and is only seven miles from the city centre (bus #87A). Open Easter–Oct.

Eating

It wasn't that long ago that eating out in Edinburgh meant either a stuffy, expensive restaurant or a tearoom serving little but sad-looking sandwiches and mugs of tea. Nowadays, however, the capital offers a much wider variety of eating places. There's a thriving **café culture**: tables and chairs spill onto the pavements during the summer months, and customers can order tasty, contemporary food at most times of day and night. Small, casual **diners and bistros** have also begun to proliferate, many offering good-value set menus. **Traditional Scottish cooking**, using fresh local produce, can still be found at some of the more formal restaurants, and a number of places are giving their menus a more contemporary slant. There are plenty of **fish** specialists – seafood fans should head to **Leith**, whose waterside restaurants serve consistently good food. International cuisine, ranging from Spanish to Southeast Asian, can be found, and the city's ethnic communities, despite their small size, are well represented: in particular, there are some great **Italian** trattorias and a host of excellent **Indian** restaurants. **Vegetarians** and vegans are also well catered for. It's worth bearing in mind that most **pubs** (which are covered in the following chapter) serve food, and that many have restaurants attached. The large city-centre hotels also have restaurants, though most of these are extremely expensive.

In the listings below, we've used broad **price categorizations** to indicate how much you can expect to pay for a two-course meal, excluding the cost of **drink**: **inexpensive** means you can expect to pay under £10; **moderate** £10–20; **expensive** £20–30; and **very expensive** over £30. Some places will add on a ten percent service charge to the bill; if they haven't, it's usual to leave a **tip** of around the same amount.

The majority of places reviewed below accept all major types of **credit cards**; we've indicated those which don't. Most of Edinburgh's restaurants **open** from noon to 2.30pm and 6pm to 11pm and close on Sundays, except where otherwise stated in the reviews. During the Festival, however, the majority of restaurants stay open all day until the early hours.

OLD TOWN

Terrific cafés and some of the city's best upmarket Scottish and French restaurants are concentrated in the atmospheric streets of the **Old Town**. There's also a wide range of other cuisines on offer, including a couple of excellent vegetarian places. Tollcross, handy for the city's theatres, also has a sprinkling of good restaurants, including some notable Chinese options.

BRASSERIES AND CAFÉS

blue

Map 2, C7. 10 Cambridge St ©0131/221 1222.
Sun & Mon 10am–midnight, Tues–Sat 10am–1am. Moderate.
In the same building as the avant-garde Traverse Theatre, *blue* has a stunning glass and pale-wood décor and equally impressive food – original and tasty dishes such as wood pigeon with shiitake mushrooms or venison and redcurrant sausages and mash for under £10.

Clarinda's

Map 3, I8. 69 Canongate ℗0131/557 1888.

Mon–Sat 9am–4.45pm, Sun 10am–4.45pm. Inexpensive.

Located near the foot of the Royal Mile, this snug café serves breakfasts, excellent home baking and light lunches. Its traditional service is a bit old-fashioned, but it's friendly and popular with locals.

Common Grounds

Map 3, E3. 2–3 North Bank St ℗0131/226 1146.

Mon–Fri 9am–10pm, Sat & Sun 10am–8pm. Inexpensive.

An American-style coffee shop on two levels, non-smoking upstairs. The menu includes filled croissants, quiches and a good range of coffees – anyone struggling to stay awake through a session of the nearby Parliament should try the "Keith Richards", which contains four shots of espresso. Live music Friday evenings.

Deacon's House Café

Map 3, D8. 3 Brodie's Close, 304 Lawnmarket ℗0131/226 1894.

Daily 9am–early evening, later during the Festival. Inexpensive.

Quiet licensed café off the Royal Mile, claiming to have been the workshop of the infamous Deacon Brodie (see p.27). You can get light snacks, home baking and even a nip of whisky here.

Elephant House

Map 3, E4. 21 George IV Bridge ℗0131/220 5355.

Mon–Fri 8am–11pm, Sat & Sun 10am–11pm. Inexpensive.

Images of elephants plaster the walls, and students huddle round the wooden tables in this highly popular café, offering a large selection of coffees and teas, with croissants and pastries, as well as light meals and daily specials. The large room at the back can be a bit smoky, but there are great views of the Castle, piles of newspapers to read, art on the wall to muse over and

OLD TOWN: BRASSERIES AND CAFÉS

earnest philosophical discussions to be overheard at the next table.

Lower Aisle
Map 3, E8. Beneath High Kirk of St Giles, High St ©0131/225 5147
Mon–Fri 9.30am–4.30pm, Sun 9am–2pm (closed Sat). Inexpensive.
Popular with bewigged advocates from the High Court, this café in the crypt serves good-value light lunches and excellent home-baked food.

Ndebele
Map 2, D9. 57 Home St, Tollcross ©0131/221 1141.
Daily 10am–10pm. Inexpensive.
Funky South African café offering tasty sandwiches, snacks and salads, delicious fruit juices and a wide selection of teas and coffees. The name comes from a colourful Southern African tribe – the owners claim the pun on "In da belly" is unintentional.

Netherbow Café
Map 3, G8. Netherbow Arts Centre, 43 High St ©0131/556 9579.
Daily 10am–4pm. Inexpensive.
Located right beside John Knox's house on the Royal Mile, this café serves excellent wholefood, vegetarian soups and light meals. Outside seating in a courtyard during summer months.

Patisserie Florentin
Map 3, D8. 8–10 St Giles St ©0131/225 6267.
Daily 7am–11pm. Inexpensive.
French-style café on two floors, just off the High Street. Exquisite pastries and delicious coffee are served downstairs, hot food is available upstairs. Frequented by office workers during the day, it becomes a trendy hangout at night, especially during the Festival when it's open until 3am.

CHINESE

Jasmine

Map 2, C7. 32 Grindlay St ℗0131/229 5757.
Mon–Fri noon–2pm & 5–11.30pm, Sat & Sun 2–11.30pm.
Moderate.
Well-situated for the Lothian Road cinemas and theatreland,
this is a good-value restaurant, with a strong line in fresh fish.
The décor is modern and unclichéd, the service friendly.

Oriental Dining Centre

Map 2, C8. 8–14a Morrison St, Tollcross ℗0131/221 1288.
Noodle Shack: Mon–Sat 5.30pm–2am; restaurant: daily
noon–midnight; Henry's: daily noon–3am. All
inexpensive–moderate.
Three distinct restaurants in one building, the most popular
being the *Ho-Ho-Mei Noodle Shack*. Also contains the *Rainbow
Arch Gourmet Restaurant* – try the three-course banquet for two
for around £20 – and *Henry's Dim Sum Cellar*, which also has a
popular bar.

FRENCH

Bleu

Map 3, D3. 36–38 Victoria St ℗0131/226 1900.
Daily 9am–late. Moderate.
From the creator of the original *Pierre Victoire* comes a newer,
trendier way to eat French – *bouchées* (mouthfuls), which are
bigger than a starter and smaller than a main. The style is more
minimalist than Gallic, and it's at its best when busy and lively.

Grain Store

Map 3, E3. 30 Victoria St ℗0131/225 7635.
Daily noon–3pm & 6–11pm. Moderate.
A reasonably priced, solid Scottish/French restaurant in a large

alcoved first-floor room. Starters include salads and seafood; for
the main course try guinea fowl and venison or a vegetarian
special. The superb cheeseboard is put together from Iain
Mellis's wonderful shop below (see p.248).

Le Sept
Map 3, E8. 7 Old Fishmarket Close ©0131/225 5428.
Mon–Thurs noon–1.45pm & 6–10pm, Fri noon–11pm, Sat
noon–10.30pm, Sun 12.30–9.30pm. Moderate.
A long-established French brasserie tucked down a cobbled
close off the Royal Mile near the Fringe Office. Three-course
set lunch for £6, with three-course set evening meal for
around £15 Sun–Thurs; à la carte only Fri–Sun.

Pierre Victoire
Map 3, E3. 10 Victoria St ©0131/225 1721.
Daily noon–3pm & 5.30–11pm. Moderate.
The *PV* phenomenon started here, and lives on despite a recent
brush with the bankers, doing what it does best – great French
food in an easy-going atmosphere, at decent prices.

INDIAN

Shamiana
Map 2, D9. 14 Brougham Place, Tollcross ©0131/228 2265.
Mon–Sat 6–9pm, Sun 6–8pm. Moderate.
Established, first-class North Indian and Kashmiri restaurant
located midway between the King's and Lyceum theatres.
Although it's one of the more expensive places in this category,
and has an oddly stark interior, it's well worth it. Choice dishes
include Royal Chicken and Chashini Tikka.

For reviews of the best child-friendly cafés and
restaurants, see p.238.

OLD TOWN: INDIAN

Caffe Sardi
Map 3, E5. 18–20 Forrest Rd ✆0131/220 5553.
Mon–Sat 9.30am–11pm. Moderate.
Good fresh food is served throughout the day, with original
twists given to the usual Italian stand-bys. The three-course
evening set menu is around £10.

Mamma's
Map 3, C4. 30 Grassmarket ✆0131/225 6464.
Sun–Thurs noon–10.30pm, Fri & Sat noon–11pm.
Inexpensive–moderate.
Ever fancied haggis pizza? You can choose your own dream
combination from 49 toppings (at the last count) at this lively
American-style pizzeria, popular with students and larger
groups. There are tables outside in the summer. Basically a
good, fun place to eat.

The Atrium
Map 2, C7. 10 Cambridge St ✆0131/228 8882.
Mon–Fri noon–2.30pm 6–10.30pm, Sat 6–10.30pm. Very
expensive.
Serving innovative *nouvelle cuisine* and focusing on high-quality
Scottish produce, this award-winning restaurant is considered by
many to be the city's best. The chunky tables are made from railway sleepers, and the interior is lit by flaming torches. Typical
offerings are seabream with celeriac purée and candied celery.

Creelers
Map 3, F8. 3 Hunter Square ✆0131/220 4447.
Mon–Thurs noon–2.30pm & 5.30–10.30pm, Fri & Sat noon–2.30pm
& 5.30–11pm, Sun 5.30–10.30pm. Moderate–expensive.

OLD TOWN: ITALIAN, SCOTTISH

Excellent seafood restaurant priding itself on fresh produce brought in from a sister restaurant/fish shop on Arran. A bistro section is located at the front, with a more expensive restaurant at the back. Some tables outside in the summer.

Point Hotel
Map 2, D8. 34 Bread St ℂ0131/221 5555.
Mon–Wed noon–2pm & 6–9.30pm, Thurs–Sun noon–2pm & 6–10.30pm. Moderate.
A restaurant with a classy, modernist décor, white linen table-cloths and smartly dressed waiters, serving impressive food based on fresh local fish and meat. Its three-course set menu for just £12 is one of the best-value deals in town.

The Tower
Map 3, E5. Museum of Scotland, Chambers St ℂ0131/225 3003.
Daily noon–11pm. Expensive.
On Level 5 of the new Museum of Scotland, with views of the Castle, *The Tower* serves modern Scottish food in a self-consciously chic setting.

The Witchery by the Castle
Map 3, C3. 352 Castlehill, Royal Mile ℂ0131/225 5613.
Daily noon–4pm & 5.30–11.30pm. Expensive.
Gothic panelling, tapestries and heavy stonework only a broomstick-hop from the Castle. The superb fish and game dishes are pricey, but you can steal a sense of it all with a pre- or post-theatre set menu (£10).

SPANISH

Igg's
Map 3, H2. 15 Jeffrey St ℂ0131/557 8184.
Mon–Sat noon–2.30pm & 6–10.30pm. Expensive.
A Spanish-owned hybrid, offering tapas snacks and

Mediterranean dishes, plus traditional Scottish food. Good lunchtime tapas from around £5.

VEGETARIAN

Bann's Vegetarian Café
Map 3, F8. 5 Hunter Square ©0131/226 1122.
Daily 10am–11pm. Moderate.
Reliable, informal café, halfway up the Royal Mile, with a frequently changing but always original and appealing menu, including veggie burgers, curries, enchiladas and organic beer and wine. You can eat well for under £12. Tables outside in the summer months.

Black Bo's
Map 3, H3. 57–61 Blackfriars St ©0131/557 6136.
Mon–Sat noon–2pm & 6–10.30pm, Sun 6–10.30pm. Moderate.
Friendly service at this non-meat diner, serving up inventive cooking, such as roast vegetable roulade, in an earthy setting of stone floors, dark wood and rustic colours.

NEW TOWN

With everything from Japanese and North African to organic Scottish food, the **New Town** and its satellites **Stockbridge** and **Broughton** boast a wide variety of top-notch eateries, and prices are often cheaper than in the Old Town.

BRASSERIES AND CAFÉS

Bell's Diner
Map 2, C3. 7 St Stephen St ©0131/225 8116.
Mon–Fri 6–11pm, Sat & Sun noon–11pm. Moderate.
An unpretentious and perennially popular little diner tucked

away in Stockbridge. It doesn't have a wide-ranging menu, but sticks to what it does best: good, inexpensive burgers, plus a wide choice of steaks and pancakes.

Cyberia

Map 4, G6. 88 Hanover St ℡0131/220 4403,
manager@cybersurf.co.uk
Mon–Sat 10am–10pm, Sun noon–7pm. Inexpensive.
A light and airy Internet café, offering a decent range of teas, coffees, croissants and sandwiches. Half an hour surfing the Net costs from £2.50. The café is licensed, has art exhibitions and offers training courses for Internet novices.

The Gallery Café

Map 1, D4. Scottish National Gallery of Modern Art, Belford Rd ℡0131/332 8600.
Mon–Sat 10am–4.30pm, Sun 2–4.30pm. Moderate.
With its sleek interior, enticing cakes and light but imaginative lunches, this is far more than a standard refreshment stop for gallery visitors, and attracts reassuring numbers of locals.

Glass & Thompson

Map 4, F3. 2 Dundas St ℡0131/557 0909.
Mon–Fri 8.30am–6.30pm, Sat 8.30am–5.30pm, Sun 11am–4.30pm. Inexpensive.
An airy deli devoted to the most exquisite food – from huge bowls of olives to a groaning cheese counter. Scattered tables and chairs mean you can linger over a made-to-order sandwich, various irresistible cakes and coffee.

Laigh Bake House

Map 4, G5. 117a Hanover St ℡0131/225 1552.
Mon–Sat 8.30am–5pm. Inexpensive.
A long-established, homely New Town café, with flagstone floor and cast-iron stoves, best known for its wonderful home-

baked scones and cakes, and serving good organic salads and soups, too.

L'Alba d'Oro

Map 2, D2. 5 Henderson Row ⊘0131/557 2580.
Mon–Fri noon–2pm & 6pm–midnight, Sat & Sun noon–midnight.
Inexpensive.
Italian voices throng the air in this classic takeaway, with fish and chips served on one side, and pizzas, filled Italian rolls and ready-made pasta dishes on the other.

Lost Sock Diner

Map 2, G2. 11 East London St, Broughton ⊘0131/557 6097.
Mon 9am–4pm, Tues–Sat 9am–10pm, Sun 10am–5pm.
Inexpensive.
Fill up on burgers, wraps and parsnip chips, all at surprisingly low prices, while your dirty clothes take a spin in the adjacent laundry.

Starbucks Coffee

Map 4, D7. Waterstone's, 128 Princes St ⊘0131/226 3610.
Mon–Sat 8am–8pm, Sun 10.30am–6pm. Inexpensive.
The bookstore/coffee shop idea isn't that original these days, but this one is made memorable by excellent coffee and the views across Princes Street Gardens to the Castle.

Terrace Café

Map 2, C1. Royal Botanic Garden ⊘0131/552 0616.
Daily: March–Oct 10am–5pm; Nov–Feb 10am–2.30pm.
Inexpensive.
Superior spot, with outside tables offering stunning views of the city skyline, serving reasonable but not ground-breaking food. Sandwiches, baked potatoes, quiches and cakes are available, along with juices and snacks for younger visitors.

NEW TOWN: BRASSERIES AND CAFÉS

Valvona and Crolla

Map 2, H2. 19 Elm Row, on Leith Walk ℂ0131/556 6066.

Mon–Sat 8am–5pm. Moderate.

At the back of an exquisite Italian deli, a café serving authentic and delicious breakfasts, lunches and snacks. The best advert for the café is the walk through the shop – with display cabinets full of sublime olives, meats and cheeses.

CHINESE

Bamboo Garden

Map 4, E5. 57a Frederick St ℂ0131/225 2382.

Mon–Thurs noon–2pm & 5.30–11pm, Fri & Sat noon–11.30pm, Sun 5.30–11.30pm. Moderate.

Members of Edinburgh's Chinese community gather in this inexpensive basement restaurant for great dim sum at weekends. Get the waiter to explain the choices rather than rely on the limited English-language menu.

Kweilin

Map 4, F1. 19 Dundas St ℂ0131/557 1875.

Tues–Thurs noon–10.45pm, Fri & Sat noon–11.45pm, Sun 5–10.45pm. Moderate.

A long-running busy Cantonese restaurant that passes the acid test of popularity with the local Chinese community. Large menu with lots of seafood. Three-course dinner for £16.50.

Loon Fung

Map 2, D1. 2 Warriston Place ℂ0131/556 1781.

Mon–Thurs noon–11.30pm, Fri noon–12.30am, Sat 2pm–12.30am, Sun 2–11.30pm. Moderate.

Excellent Cantonese restaurant offering a big spread of dim sum dishes, with plenty of seafood and vegetarian options. Other dishes to go for include squid in black bean sauce, and crispy seaweed.

NEW TOWN: CHINESE

Café St Honoré

Map 4, F4. 34 Thistle St Lane ℗0131/226 2211.
Mon–Fri noon–2pm & 7–10pm, Sat 7–10pm. Expensive.

On a city-centre side street, this popular New Town restaurant
has been done up to look like a Parisian brasserie, serving
French cooking with fashionable influences from points further
east. Tasty bread and scrumptious puddings. Non-smoking.

La Cuisine d'Odile

Map 2, B5. French Institute, 13 Randolph Crescent ℗0131/225
5685.
Tues–Sat noon–2pm, closed Sun & Mon. Closed July. No cards.
Inexpensive.

This highly regarded French café in the basement of the French
Institute in the West End is open lunchtimes only. Sublime
French home cooking is dished up in a relaxed and friendly
atmosphere.

La P'tite Folie

Map 4, E5. 61 Frederick St ℗0131/225 7983.
Mon–Sat noon–3pm & 6–11pm, Sun 6–11pm. Moderate.

Another by-product of the *Pierre Victoire* school of reliable
French cuisine in simple surroundings. Popular and busy. £6
set lunches and à la carte evening menu.

Maison Hector

Map 2, B3. 47 Deanhaugh St ℗0131/332 5328.
Sun–Thurs 11am–midnight, Fri & Sat 11am–1am.
Moderate–expensive.

Trendy Stockbridge postmodernist café. Luxurious seating in
the bar at the front, a more private restaurant to the rear, with
the kitchen visible through a screen. Baguettes and snacks are
available at lunchtime, French/Scottish cuisine at night.

NEW TOWN: FRENCH

Café Royal Oyster Bar
Map 4, K5. 17a West Register St ℗0131/556 4124.
Mon–Sat noon–2pm & 7–10pm, Sun 12.30–2.30pm & 7–10pm.
Expensive.

Now known by everyone as the restaurant featured in *Chariots of Fire*. Look out for the classy stained-glass windows showing various sporting activities, fine wood panelling and marble floor. Oysters from the west of Scotland, and all sorts of fish dishes served in fairly traditional style. On Sundays they do a sumptuous brunch, starting from £12.50, which includes blueberry muffins and a glass of buck's fizz.

Mussel Inn
Map 4, F6. 61–65 Rose St ℗0131/225 5979.
Mon–Thurs noon–3pm & 6–10pm, Fri & Sat 11am–10pm.
Moderate.

The tightly packed tables remind you that the play on words in the name is very apt, and after feasting on a kilo of mussels and a basket of chips for under £10 you'll realize why there's such a demand to get in. It's owned by two west-coast shellfish farmers, which ensures that the time from sea to stomach is minimal.

INDIAN

Indian Cavalry Club
Map 2, A7. 3 Atholl Place ℗0131/228 3282.
Daily noon–2pm & 5.30–11.30pm. Moderate.

Upmarket, but moderately priced West End establishment, with a pseudo-Raj décor. The flavours are rich, but there's nothing too hot. A two-course lunch costs £6.95, while a five-course evening banquet will set you back around £17. There's also a good, reasonably priced wine list.

Lancers

Map 2, C3. 5 Hamilton Place ℂ0131/332 3444.
Daily noon–2.30pm & 5.30–11.30pm. Moderate–expensive.
Upmarket Stockbridge restaurant, offering Bengali and North
Indian cuisine. For a real gourmand experience, the Kurji
lamb, a whole leg of lamb marinated in herbs and barbecued,
costs around £70 for four people. Three-course lunchtime
thalis are available for under £10.

ITALIAN

Cosmo

Map 4, D5. 58a North Castle St ℂ0131/226 6743.
Mon–Fri 12.30–2pm & 7–10.30pm, Sat 7–10pm. Expensive.
Authentic, delicious Italian cuisine, with some notable fish and
meat main courses, at this long-established trattoria. Don't be
put off by the photo parade of famous personalities on the wall
– they come here because it's good.

Est Est Est

Map 4, C6. 135 George St ℂ0131/225 2555.
Daily noon–1am. Moderate.
Pale wood, clever lighting and high ceilings give this popular
modern Italian an irresistibly stylish feel. The big menu mixes
the old favourites with all the designer touches, from squid ink
to flakes of parmesan.

Pizza Express

Map 2, C3. 1 Deanhaugh St, Stockbridge ℂ0131/332 7229.
Daily 11.30am–midnight. Inexpensive–moderate.
The chain, with the winning formula for smart interiors and
decent pizzas. It's combined here with a terrific location in a
clock-tower building overlooking the Water of Leith. Outside
terrace for balmy summer evenings.

NEW TOWN: ITALIAN

MEXICAN

Blue Parrot Cantina
Map 2, C3. 49 St Stephen's St ℗0131/225 2941.
Mon–Fri & Sun 5–10.30pm, Sat 1–10.30pm. Moderate.
Cosy Stockbridge basement restaurant, with a small, frequently changing menu, which dares to deviate from the Mexican clichés, with dishes such as spinach nachos and haddock in lime and coriander sauce.

Tex Mex
Map 4, G5. 47 Hanover St ℗0131/225 1796.
Mon–Sat noon–11pm, Sun 12.30–11pm. Moderate.
Authentic, reasonably priced Mexican burritos and steaks; if you're in between 4 and 7pm ask for the good-value (£12.50) three-course pre-theatre menu.

MOROCCAN

The Marrakech
Map 2, F2. 30 London St ℗0131/556 4444.
Daily 6–9.30pm. Moderate.
The owners are from Rabat, rather than Marrakech, but this is a great little restaurant, housed in the basement of a small hotel. The fare includes Moroccan staples, delicately spiced *tajines* (meat or fish stews), couscous and wholesome *harira* (chickpea broth). There's mouth-melting home-cooked bread, too, and Moroccan pastries. Unlicensed, but no corkage if you bring your own bottle.

SCOTTISH

Duck's at Le Marché Noir
Map 2, E2. 2–4 Eyre Place ℗0131/558 1608.
Mon–Fri noon–2pm & 7–10pm, Sat & Sun 6.30–9.30pm.
Expensive–very expensive.

Scottish cuisine with a considerable French influence – most notably manifest in a huge wine list and some seriously expensive cognacs. Look out for such delicacies as haggis in filo pastry and salmon in pink grapefruit sauce. One non-smoking room.

Martin's
Map 4, C7. 70 Rose St, North Lane ©0131/225 3106.
Tues–Fri noon–2pm, Sat 7–10pm, closed Sun & Mon. Very expensive.

Don't be put off by the lacklustre location: this is a luxurious restaurant, with a great reputation locally. The choice menu features a wealth of organic, unfarmed ingredients, such as salmon, venison and unpasteurized cheeses, as well as game and seafood from the west coast of Scotland.

Stac Polly
Map 4, I2. 29–33 Dublin St ©0131/556 2231.
Mon–Fri noon–1.45pm & 6–10pm, Sat & Sun 6–10pm. Expensive.

Unmistakeably Scottish, but with many original touches. The menu includes good game, fish and meat dishes; try the Scottish lamb in a honey, mustard and herb crumble.

36
Map 4, E1. 36 Great King St ©0131/556 3636.
Sun–Fri noon–2pm & 7–10pm, Sat 7–10pm. Very expensive.

The décor may be minimalist but the top-quality Scottish food is given lavish attention. Meat dishes dominate, surrounded by sculpted vegetables and superb sauces. Good wine list and attentive, if slightly over-formal, service.

SOUTHEAST ASIAN

Siam Erewan
Map 4, E3. 48 Howe St ©0131/226 3675.
Mon–Sat noon–2.30pm & 6–11pm, Sun 6–11pm. Moderate.

NEW TOWN: SOUTHEAST ASIAN

Quality Thai restaurant, with good use of exotic and fresh fruit and vegetables. Specialities include steamed prawns, crispy Thai pancakes and curries of varying degrees of heat. The three-course lunch is £6.95, while evening banquets cost up to £19.95.

Singapura
Map 4, D5. 69 North Castle St ©0131/538 7878.
Mon–Thurs noon–2.30pm & 6–10.30pm, Fri & Sat noon–2.30pm & 6–11pm, Sun 6–10.30pm. Moderate.
Plays up colonial connections with Singapore, with a display of old photographs, pith helmets and trunks. The dishes display influences from all over East Asia, with hot Thai curries, spicy Chinese tofu and a delicious Indonesian gado-gado salad. Wash it down with Tiger Beer from Singapore, or choose from a decent selection of European wines.

Tampopo
Map 4, F5. 25a Thistle St ©0131/220 5254.
Mon noon–3pm, Tues–Sat noon–3pm & 6–9pm. Inexpensive.
Small, plain-décor Japanese noodle shop. This is a fast-food establishment selling filling bowls of noodle soup for around £5; flavours include vegetable and seafood. Not licensed. Also does takeaway.

SPANISH

The Tapas Tree
Map 2, G3. 1 Forth St, Broughton ©0131/556 7118.
Daily 11am–11pm. Moderate.
A fun, authentic tapas bar dishing up all those holiday favourites – *patatas bravas*, squid in batter, aubergines – accompanied by Spanish classical guitar on Wednesday evenings and flamenco on Thursday evenings.

Henderson's Salad Table

Map 4, G4. 94 Hanover St ℂ0131/225 2131.
Mon–Sat 8am–10.45pm. Inexpensive.

Edinburgh's first vegetarian restaurant has been going for thirty years and is still just about the best. There's a daily selection of three or four freshly prepared hot dishes, backed up with a dozen or so salads. Make sure you leave room for the tempting puddings or something off the oozing cheeseboard. It's self-service, however, so don't be surprised to find a long queue. *Henderson's Bistro*, next door at 25 Thistle St (ℂ0131/225 2605) offers equally delicious, moderately priced bistro-style meals, although it's only open in the evenings Thursday–Saturday.

LEITH

The most fashionable place to eat in the city, **Leith** is packed with high-quality restaurants and waterfront brasseries, and is particularly good for seafood. Most places are concentrated along the cobbled edge of the Water of Leith, or grouped around Dock Place. There's also a line of purpose-built restaurant spaces on Commercial Street, opposite the huge new Scottish Office building.

Bar Sirius

Map 1, E4. 10 Dock Place ℂ0131/555 3344.
Mon–Wed 11.30am–midnight, Thurs–Sun 11.30am–1am.
Moderate.

Named after a locally built ship, this is a seriously cool 1990s bar, with low tables and muted colours. There are pasta and salads for lunch, Thai stir-fries or chicken couscous for something more substantial.

Daniel's

Map 1, E4. 88 Commercial St ℂ0131/553 5933.

Daily 10am–10pm. Moderate.

Top-grade bistro in an attractive setting on the ground floor of
a converted warehouse in Leith. The food is from the Alsace
region, and one of the specialities is *tarte flambée*, a sort of
Italian pizza, with a French name and German ingredients.

Malmaison Café Bar

Map 1, E4. 1 Tower Place ℂ0131/555 6969.

Mon–Fri 7–10.30am, noon–2.30pm & 6–10.30pm, Sat & Sun
8–10.30am, noon–2.30pm & 6–10pm. Expensive.

A French-style brasserie, with a pleasant atmosphere, in the
area's most stylish hotel. The small menu features steak frites,
chargrilled chicken and salmon fishcakes with sumptuously
rich potato purée.

CHINESE

Joanna's Cuisine

Map 1, E4. 42 Dalmeny St ℂ0131/554 5833.

Mon–Fri 11.30am–2.30pm & 5–10.30pm, Sat 11.30am–2.30pm &
5–11.30pm. Moderate.

A homely little place on a side street leading east off the middle of
Leith Walk. The menu includes wonderful Pekinese specialities
such as duck, also genuine Chinese tea, served the proper way.

FISH AND SEAFOOD

Marinette

Map 1, E4. 52 Coburg St ℂ0131/555 0922.

Tues–Sat noon–1.30pm & 6–10pm. Expensive.

The light-coloured walls and fishnets provide a Mediterranean
ambience for this well-regarded French seafood restaurant. For
starters, try the bouillabaisse; for the main choose a sauce such

as *meunière*, ginger and coriander or thyme and lemon to go with the fish of the day.

The Shore

Map 1, E4. 3–4 The Shore ℂ0131/553 5080.
Mon–Sat 11am–midnight, Sun 12.30pm–11pm. Moderate.
A non-smoking restaurant, serving good fish dishes and decent wines. For more informal dining, try the adjoining bar where you can eat tapas and sometimes catch live jazz and folk. Both have a pleasant, bohemian atmosphere and there are tables and chairs outside in summer from which to watch the sunsets.

Skipper's

Map 1, E4. 1a Dock Place ℂ0131/554 1018.
Mon–Sat 12.30–2pm & 7–10pm. Expensive.
Opposite The Shore, *Skipper's* has a vaguely nautical atmosphere and a superb – if expensive – fish-oriented menu that changes according to what's fresh.

The Vintner's Rooms

Map 1, E4. The Vaults, 87 Giles St ℂ0131/554 6767.
Mon–Sat noon–2pm & 7–10.30pm. Very expensive.
Luxurious, elegantly decorated restaurant in a former wine warehouse off a cobbled courtyard. Top-class imaginative cooking with intriguing ingredients and combinations such as guinea fowl with lentils.

Waterfront Wine Bar

Map 1, E4. 1c Dock Place ℂ0131/554 7427.
Mon–Thurs noon–11pm, Fri & Sat noon–midnight, Sun 12.30–10.30pm. Moderate.
Housed in the former lock-keeper's cottage, with outdoor seating overlooking the waterfront and an attractive wooden interior, this popular wine bar/restaurant serves moderately priced fish dishes and good wines.

LEITH: FISH AND SEAFOOD

The Raj Restaurant

Map 1, E4. 89–91a Henderson St ✆0131/553 6968.

Mon–Thurs & Sun 5.30–11.30pm, Fri & Sat 5.30pm–midnight.
Moderate.

An excellent ethnic alternative to the waterfront brasseries,
serving quality cooking from Goa and Bangladesh in a large
bright former cinema, with a great view over the Water of
Leith.

ITALIAN

Tinelli

Map 2, K2. 139 Easter Rd ✆0131/652 1932.

Mon–Sat noon–2.30pm & 6–10.30pm. Moderate.

It's worth a detour to an otherwise unlikely part of town for
this very popular restaurant, often said to be Edinburgh's best
Italian. It has a small but interesting menu, including such delicacies as pumpkin-filled pasta. No background music, and
attentive service.

JAPANESE

Daruma-Ya

Map 1, E4. 82 Commercial St ✆0131/554 7660.

Mon 6.30–11pm, Tues–Sat noon–2pm & 6.30–11pm.
Moderate–expensive.

Opposite the new Scottish Office, this restaurant has a
smart, stylish interior, and serves the best sushi and sashimi
in Edinburgh. Staff help you to negotiate the menu; the
wine list is equally intriguing, with Japanese beers and warm
sake.

LEITH: INDIAN, ITALIAN, JAPANESE

SCOTTISH

(Fitz)henry
Map 1, E4. 19 Shore Place ℗0131/555 6625.
Mon–Thurs 12.30–2.30pm & 6.30–10pm, Fri & Sat
12.30–2.30pm & 6.30–10.30pm, closed Sun. Expensive–very
expensive.

Occupying a converted seventeenth-century warehouse, this
individual and stylish contemporary brasserie has already won a
Michelin Red M. The menu is original, defying categoriza-
tion, and can feature anything from sweetbreads to pig's head.
The two-course lunch is good value at £10, while the three-
course set dinner costs £22.

SWISS

Denzlers
Map 1, E4. 121 Constitution St ℗0131/554 3268.
Tues–Fri noon–2pm & 6.30–10pm, Sat 6.30–10pm, closed Sun.
Moderate.

A genuine Central European eating experience, big on meat
and melted cheese, but a high standard is maintained and the
surroundings are attractive, with Scottish art adorning the
walls. The three-course set menu in the evenings costs under
£15.

THE SOUTHSIDE

The **Southside** has plenty of well-priced restaurants
aimed at the local student population, and also has some
of the city's most unusual international eateries. The core
of places are to be found in the area around Nicolson
Street, with a few reliable outposts in Marchmont and
Bruntsfield.

BRASSERIES AND CAFÉS

Brattisani's
Map 1, E5. 85–87 Newington Rd ℭ0131/667 5808.
Daily 9.30am–midnight. Inexpensive.
The capital's oldest Italo-Scottish chippy, with a choice of sit-down or carry-out meals. It ain't glamorous, but you'll get a filling meal and a slice of Edinburgh life.

Café Q
Map 2, I9. 87 Clerk St ℭ0131/668 3456.
Mon–Sat 9.30am–5pm. Inexpensive.
Located in the Queen's Hall, a respected music and arts venue, this café serves well-prepared salads, vegetarian dishes, soups and puddings, as well as some decent wines and beers.

Kaffe Politik
Map 1, D5. 146–148 Marchmont Rd ℭ0131/446 9837.
Daily 10am–10pm. Inexpensive.
Café culture hits the student fiefdom of deepest Marchmont, with a relaxed and stylish venue serving coffees and substantial snacks.

Mango & Stone
Map 1, D5. 165a Bruntsfield Place ℭ0131/229 2987.
Mon–Sat 8am–6pm, Sun 9am–6pm. Inexpensive.
A juice bar serving colourful and wickedly healthy freshly squeezed fruit cocktails. Also does sandwiches and coffee.

Maxies
Map 2, H8. 32b West Nicolson St ℭ0131/667 0845.
Mon–Thurs noon–midnight, Fri & Sat noon–1am. Moderate.
A basement brasserie and wine bar, with regular live music, handily placed for quick pre-show meals and popular with students and University staff. Good-quality French-style seafood,

meat and veggie dishes are washed down with an excellent selection of wine and decent beer.

Metropole

Map 2, H9. 33 Newington Rd ©0131/668 4999.

Daily 9am–10pm. Inexpensive.

A relaxed Art Deco café in a former bank, where you can have a snack and a coffee while you read a newspaper. Food includes soups, sandwiches, quiches and cakes. Non-smoking.

Nicolson's

Map 2, H8. 6a Nicolson St ©0131/557 4567.

Mon–Fri 9am–3pm & 5–11pm, Sat & Sun noon–midnight. Expensive.

Opposite the Festival Theatre, a spacious, unpretentious first-floor restaurant with some classy cuisine. By day, caffeine cures and snacks can be had at the downstairs *Black Medicine* café.

CHINESE

Chinese Home Cooking

Map 2, H9. 34 West Preston St ©0131/668 4946.

Mon–Sat noon–2pm & 5.30–11pm, Sun 5.30–11pm. Inexpensive.

This cheap-and-cheerful BYOB Chinese restaurant is very popular with students. Try the three-course lunch at £4.50 and the daily chef's special in the evening.

FRENCH

La Bonne Mer

Map 1, E5. 113 Buccleuch St ©0131/662 9111.

Tues–Sat noon–2pm & 6–10pm. Moderate.

Easy-going BYOB bistro serving seafood and other Gallic favourites at reasonable prices. The food's nothing startling, but it's good value and popular.

La Bonne Vie

Map 2, H9. 49 Causewayside ℭ0131/667 1110.
Daily noon–2.30pm & 6–10.30pm. Moderate.
Intimate French restaurant specializing in game and fish.
Starters range from duck liver parfait to marinated melon
topped with bacon, while for the main course you can feast on
chargrilled salmon or venison and beef casserole. Three-course
dinner set menu for £15.

INDIAN

Ann Purna

Map 2, H9. 45 St Patrick Square ℭ0131/662 1807.
Mon–Fri noon–2pm & 5.30–11pm, Sat & Sun 5.30–11pm.
Moderate.
Excellent-value restaurant, serving authentic Gujarati and
Southern Indian cuisine. Three-course lunch for £4.95.

Kalpna

Map 2, H9. 2 St Patrick Square ℭ0131/667 9890.
Mon–Fri noon–2pm & 5.30–11pm, Sat 5.30–11pm, closed Sun,
except during Festival. Moderate.
Functional décor, but beautifully cooked food at this outstanding vegetarian restaurant, serving authentic Gujarati dishes. It
offers a good-value eat-as-much-as-you-like lunchtime buffet
for £5, and a gourmet buffet on Wed evenings for £8.95.

Khushi's Lothian Restaurant

Map 2, H7. 16 Drummond St ℭ0131/556 8996.
Mon–Thurs noon–2.30pm & 5–8.30pm, Fri & Sat noon–2.30pm &
5–9pm. No cards. Inexpensive.
Edinburgh's first Indian, and more a café than a restaurant. It's
distinctly unpretentious, and the food is reliable and cheap,
including plenty of vegetarian options. Bring your own drink
or carry in a pint of lager from *Stewart's* bar next door.

Suruchi

Map 2, H8. 14a Nicolson St ©0131/5566583.
Mon–Sat noon–2pm & 5.30–11.30pm, Sun 5.30–11.30pm. Moderate.

A popular establishment serving genuine South Indian cooking;
the other good reason to come is to read (or try to read) the
menu written in broad Scots. The emphasis is on rice and vegetables, with a few splendid poultry dishes and one or two surprises,
such as Tandoori Trout. The set lunches go for £3.50–6.50.

NORTH AFRICAN

Phenecia

Map 2, H8. 55 West Nicolson St ©0131/662 4493.
Mon–Sat noon–2pm & 6–11pm, Sun 6–10pm.
Inexpensive–moderate.

A cheap, eclectic restaurant, serving North African and
Mediterranean dishes. Delicious hummus and couscous.
Three-course lunches cost under £5.

SCOTTISH

Howies

Map 2, H8. 75 St Leonard's St ©0131/668 2917; and 208 Bruntsfield
Place ©0131/221 1777.
St Leonard's St: Mon 6–10pm, Tues–Sun noon–2pm & 6–10pm;
Bruntsfield Place: daily noon–2.30pm & 5–10pm. Moderate.

Dependable brasserie-style Scottish cooking, with some interesting combinations, such as black pudding with walnuts and
chilli. No alcohol served, but you can bring your own bottle.

Kelly's

Map 2, H8. 46b West Richmond St ©0131/668 3847.
Wed–Sat noon–2pm & 7–9.30pm, closed Sun–Tues. Expensive.

This longstanding restaurant enjoys virtual cult status among
Edinburgh foodies, serving modern Scottish food in a calm,

THE SOUTHSIDE: NORTH AFRICAN, SCOTTISH

intimate setting using the best and freshest ingredients. Changing menus, with the possibility of lobster or Barbary duckling, will not disappoint those with a taste for the exotic.

Parrots

Map 1, D5. 3 Viewforth, Bruntsfield ℂ0131/229 3252.
Tue–Sat 6–10.30pm. Inexpensive–moderate.
Rather heavy velvety décor and a bizarre parrot theme, but it's a great place for friendly service and satisfying, old-fashioned food based on stews, curries and stodgy puddings. An antidote to the chargrilled goats cheese and rocket brigade. Non-smoking.

Sweet Melinda's

Map 1, D4. 11 Rosneath St, Marchmont ℂ0131/229 7953.
Tues–Sat noon–2pm & 7–10pm, closed Sun & Mon. Moderate.
Highly regarded, friendly restaurant serving seafood and Scottish fare. On Tuesday nights you pay only what you think the food is worth.

VEGETARIAN

Engine Shed

Map 1, E4. 19 St Leonard's Lane ℂ0131/662 0042.
Daily lunchtimes only. Mon–Fri 10.30am–2.30pm, Sat 10.30am–4pm, Sun 11am–4pm. No cards. Inexpensive.
Worth taking a detour to this excellent vegetarian restaurant near Pollock Halls. The menu features soups, salads, veggie stews and baked potatoes, and there's a wonderful bakery on the premises.

Susie's Diner

Map 2, I9. 51 W Nicolson St ℂ0131/667 8729.
Mon 9am–8pm, Tues–Sat 9am–9pm, Sun noon–7pm. Inexpensive.
A popular unlicensed café serving inventive soups, savouries and puddings, plus a range of vegan food, to crowds of students. Occasional belly-dancing nights.

Drinking

rinking is one of Edinburgh's real pleasures. Many of the city's **pubs**, especially in the Old Town, are hundreds of years old, while others, particularly in the New Town, are unaltered Victorian or Edwardian period pieces that rank among Edinburgh's most outstanding examples of interior design. Add in the plentiful supply of trendy modern bars, and there's a variety of styles and atmospheres to cater for all tastes. The standard licensing hours are 11am–11pm (12.30–11pm on Sundays), but many pubs have extended licensing hours and stay open later. During the Festival, in particular, you'll find no shortage of bars open till at least 1am.

Most of the city's pubs now sell a good selection of "real ale", a dark-coloured, cask-conditioned beer generically called "**heavy**". It comes in various strengths, often described by the amount of duty paid in times past on a barrel of the beer: 60, 70 or 80 shillings. The majority of these are made by Scottish brewing giants Tennant's and Scottish & Newcastle – which produces McEwan's and Younger's ales. It's also worth looking out for the excellent award-winning beers made by the small independent Caledonian Brewery (see box overleaf for details of tours of the brewery), which brews ales using old techniques and equipment. Other independents that produce a range of

Pub and brewery tours

A fun way to expore Edinburgh's pubs is to take the McEwan's 80/- Edinburgh Literary Pub Tour, a pub crawl – with culture – around Old and New Town watering holes. Led by professional actors, the tour takes you to various historic pubs in the city, with stops along the way where the guides act out scenes from the lives of major figures of Scottish literature, including Burns, Scott and MacDiarmid, and recite lines from their work. The tour starts from the *Beehive Inn*, 18–20 Grassmarket (March–May & Oct Thurs–Sun 7.30pm; June–Sept daily 6pm & 8.30pm; Nov–Feb Fri 7.30pm; £7 – not including drinks). You can just turn up, or book ahead by phoning ☏0131/226 6665 or by calling in at the tourist office on Princes Street.

From June to September, the Caledonian Brewery, Slateford Road (☏0131/337 1286), runs tours at 11.30am and 2.30pm Mon–Fri, though it's best to phone ahead before you visit.

very drinkable ales include the Belhaven Brewery in East Lothian and the tiny Rose Street Brewery. Many pubs also serve English **bitter**, a sharper drink than heavy, though you'll have to go to a decent real-ale pub to find a good selection of these. All pubs sell **lager** both on tap and in bottles. The selection of **whisky** is better in some pubs than others, and though a "nip", or measure, of malt whisky will normally cost more than a standard blended whisky, many pubs have lower-priced "malt of the month" specials.

Once upon a time, Edinburgh's main drinking strip was the near-legendary **Rose Street**, a pedestrianized lane of minimal visual appeal tucked between Princes and George streets, and the ultimate Edinburgh pub crawl was to drink a half-pint in each of its dozen or so establishments – plus the two in West Register Street, its eastern continuation. These days the scene is more diverse, with more sophisticated establishments drawing the crowds in. **George Street** is one of the new trendy spots: a number of former banks on this street have received the chain pub makeover, accompanied by the predictable invasion of suits by day and style by night. Most of the **student pubs** are in and around Grassmarket, with a further batch on the Southside, an area overlooked by most tourists. **Leith** has a varied crop of bars, ranging from the roughest type of spit-and-sawdust places to polished pseudo-Victoriana, while two of the city's best and most characterful pubs are further west on the seafront in **Newhaven**.

OLD TOWN

Bannermans
Map 3, H3. 212 Cowgate.
The best pub in the street, formerly a vintner's cellar, with a labyrinthine interior and good beer on tap. On weekdays, tasty veggie lunches are on offer at rock-bottom prices; breakfasts are available at weekends 11am–4pm. Open daily till 1am.

Bar Kohl
Map 3, E4. 54 George IV Bridge.
A trendy vodka bar with a choice of more than two hundred ways to give yourself a fearsome hangover. Open Mon–Sat till 1am. Closed Sun.

Black Bo's
Map 3, H3. 57–61 Blackfriars St.
A small, trendy bar, next to a veggie restaurant of the same name. Mellow during the day, but the music is loud and funky in the evenings, and things can get pretty wild.

OLD TOWN

Bow Bar

Map 3, D4. 80 West Bow.

Old wood-panelled bar that won an award as the best drinkers' pub in Britain a few years back. Choose from among nearly 150 whiskies, an almost equally wide range of other spirits, and a changing selection of first-rate Scottish and English cask beers. Closed Sun afternoons.

City Café

Map 3, G4. 19 Blair St.

Longstanding, trendy bar on the street linking the Royal Mile to clubbers' hub on Cowgate. The American-style bar serves sweets (candies) and wouldn't look out of place on the set of *The Truman Show.*

Doric Tavern

Map 3, F2. 15 Market St.

Favoured watering hole of journalists and arty-types. The downstairs *McGuffie's Tavern* is a traditional Edinburgh howff (pub), while the upstairs *Doric Tavern* has a brasserie, serving highly regarded food, and a cultured wine bar, open till 1am.

EH1

Map 3, G2. 197 High St.

Wrought iron and cool aqua colours dominate in this contemporary Royal Mile bar, popular with a pre-club set. It serves good food throughout the day, and pitchers of vividly coloured cocktails. Open till 1am.

Fiddlers Arms

Map 3, C4. 9–11 Grassmarket.

A traditional bar serving excellent McEwan's 80 Shilling. You can hear fiddlers playing on Monday nights. Open Mon–Thurs till 11.30pm, Fri & Sat 1am.

OLD TOWN

Greyfriars Bobby

Map 3, E5. 34 Candlemaker Row.

Long-established favourite with both students and tourists, with a long bar and a loud jukebox. Named after the statue outside, though happily there's not too much sentimental memorabilia associated with the famously faithful "wee dug". Open till 1am.

Hebrides Bar

Map 3, G2. 17 Market St.

Home from home for Edinburgh's Highland community: ceilidh atmosphere with lots of jigs, strathspeys and reels, but no tartan kitsch.

Iguana

Map 3, F5. 41 Lothian St.

Nineties-style twisted metal stairs and vivid orange walls form the backdrop to this trendy hangout, frequented by a pre-club crowd, with a rota of popular DJs, and videos made by local artists showing on the TVs. All-day food includes a sizeable vegetarian breakfast.

Jolly Judge

Map 3, D8. 7a James Court.

Atmospheric, smoky, low-ceilinged bar in a close just down from the Castle. Cosy in winter and pleasant outside in summer.

Malt Shovel

Map 3, F2. 11–15 Cockburn St.

Dimly lit, comfortable bar just up from Waverley Station, serving an excellent range of cask beers and single malt whiskies, and doling out big portions of chilli and haddock and chips at lunchtime. Open Sun–Thurs 11am–12.30am, Fri & Sat 11am–1am.

OLD TOWN

Sandy Bell's

Map 3, E6. 25 Forrest Rd.

The city's favourite chess-playing pub, as well as a folk music institution, hosting regular impromptu sessions. Stocks an impressive selection of beers and whiskies. Open until 12.30am Mon–Sat.

NEW TOWN

Abbotsford

Map 4, I5. 3 Rose St.

Large-scale pub whose original Victorian décor, complete with wood panelling and "island bar", is among the finest in the city. It does a good range of ales, including a house ale brewed by Broughton Brewery in the Borders. The restaurant upstairs serves hearty Scottish food. Closed Sun.

Baillie Bar

Map 2, C3. 2 St Stephen St.

A traditional basement bar at the corner of Edinburgh's most self-consciously bohemian street. English and Scottish ales are available, including some from the Caledonian Brewery. Open Mon–Thurs till midnight, Fri & Sat till 1am, Sun till 11pm.

The Basement

Map 4, L1. 10a Broughton St.

Packed out, especially at the weekends, with a pre-club crowd, this trendy bar is run by young and enthusiastic staff and serves cheap Mexican food until 10pm every day. Open till 1am.

Bert's Bar

Map 2, B3. 29 William St and 2–4 Raeburn Place.

The former fills up with the office lunchtime crowd, the latter at night with Stockbridge yuppies. Both have excellent beer, good food and strive to be authentic, non-theme-oriented pubs, though the telly rarely misses any sporting action.

Café Royal Circle Bar

Map 4, K5. 17 West Register St.

The pub part of the stylish Victorian restaurant (see p.184), and worth a visit for its décor alone, notably the huge elliptical "island" counter and the tiled portraits of renowned inventors. Thurs open till midnight, Fri & Sat till 1am. Upstairs, the *Café Royal Bistro Bar* is an unlovely rugby-themed affair.

Catwalk Café

Map 2, G3. 2 Picardy Place.

Smart street-side café upstairs, and a cool hangout downstairs, with unadorned white walls and minimalist furniture. It has an unfinished look throughout, with concrete stair slabs and bare plaster walls. It dishes up excellent breakfasts and lunches, as well as coffee, during the day, and is transformed after 6pm into a busy pre-club venue.

Clark's Bar

Map 2, D2. 142 Dundas St.

A traditional no-nonsense Scottish bar at the foot of Dundas Street. There's a big rowdy bar in the front and more secluded "snugs", or ante-rooms, at the back. It's very much a locals' bar, though not at all unfriendly.

Cumberland Bar

Map 2, E3. 1 Cumberland St.

A mellow and much-loved New Town bar, with no jukebox and a wide variety of ales. You can sit out in the garden in summer, and good hearty pub grub is served from noon to 2pm.

The Dome Bar and Grill

Map 4, I5. 14 George St.

An opulent conversion of a massive New Town bank, thronging with minor local celebrities. The stylish side cocktail bar is

NEW TOWN

reminiscent of a 1920s cruise ship, while the main drinking and eating area behind, with its elegant detailing, Grecian columns and a huge glass dome, is probably the most impressive bar interior in Edinburgh. Sun–Thurs open till 11.30pm, Fri & Sat till 1am.

Guildford Arms

Map 4, K5. 1–5 West Register St.

A great city-centre Victorian bar, with an excellent selection of well-kept ales; look out for the Harviestoun brews. Pub grub is served in the gallery, a good place from which to watch the goings-on.

Indigo Yard

Map 4, A7. 7 Charlotte Lane.

Designer chic hits Edinburgh's West End: great for those who like Thai fish cakes with their draught beer. There's a gallery bar for observing besuited bright young things.

Kay's Bar

Map 4, C3. 39 Jamaica St.

Small, civilized one-time wine shop, warmed by a roaring log fire in winter, and serving fine cask ales. Mon–Thurs open till midnight, Fri & Sat till 1am.

Mathers

Map 4, L1. 25 Broughton St.

Relaxed, old-fashioned pub which attracts a mixed crowd and gets noisy during big TV sporting occasions. Open till midnight Mon–Thurs, 12.30am Fri & Sat.

Milne's Bar

Map 4, H6. 35 Hanover St.

Cellar bar once beloved of Edinburgh's literati, including Hugh MacDiarmid, earning it the nickname "The Poets' Pub". It serves a good range of cask beers, including McEwan's 80 Shilling.

Oxford Bar
Map 4, C6. 8 Young St.
Traditional city bar, unpretentious and something of a shrine for rugby fans and off-duty policemen. Good Scottish pub food is available: try the Forfar bridies (similar to Cornish pasties) and mutton pies. Open until 1am.

Po-Na-Na
Map 4, E5. 43b Frederick St.
Is it a pub or a nightclub? Anyway, this trendy "souk" bar will charge you to get in if you arrive after 11pm (Mon–Thurs & Sun £2, Fri & Sat £3) and you still might have to queue. DJs every night. Basic snacks available. Open till 3am nightly.

Rose Street Brewery
Map 4, G6. 55 Rose St.
Edinburgh's only microbrewery, whose equipment can be inspected in the upstairs restaurant; the two beers made here are on tap in the ground-floor bar.

The Standing Order
Map 4, F6. 62–66 George St.
A former bank which has had the chain makeover; it's worth going in for a gawk at the vast central hall or to nestle into a comfy chair in the library. Real ales and good-value meals available. Open till 1am.

THE SOUTHSIDE

Peartree House
Map 2, H8. 36 West Nicolson St.
Fine bar in an eighteenth-century house with a courtyard –

THE SOUTHSIDE

one of central Edinburgh's very few beer gardens; serves decent bar lunches. Open Mon–Wed & Sun until midnight, Thurs–Sat until 1am.

Southsider
Map 2, H8. 3–5 West Richmond St.
Genuine local pub with a superb range of draught and imported bottled beers. Open till midnight Mon–Thurs, 1am Fri & Sat.

Stewart's
Map 2, H7. 14 Drummond St.
A Southside institution since the beginning of the twentieth century, and seemingly little changed since then; popular with lecturers and students. Open till midnight Mon–Sat.

TOLLCROSS

Bennet's Bar
Map 2, D9. 8 Leven St.
Edinburgh's most splendid Edwardian pub, with mahogany-set mirrors and Art Nouveau stained glass. It gets packed in the evenings, particularly when there's a show at the King's Theatre next door. Mon–Sat serves lunch and stays open till midnight.

Blue Blazer
Map 2, D8. 2 Spittal St.
Located between Grassmarket and theatreland, this traditional Edinburgh howff, with oak-clad bar and church pews, serves a good selection of ales. Open till midnight Wed & Thurs, 1am Fri & Sat.

Traverse Bar Café
Map 2, C7. Traverse Theatre, 10 Cambridge St.
Located in the Traverse Theatre, a spacious modern bar, with a

lively, sophisticated crowd. Good food is available in the bar and also at *blue*, the restaurant upstairs.

Carriers Quarters

Map 1, E4. 42 Bernard St.

Dating back to 1775, and still preserved in its original state, this is an intimate pub, with wooden pews and a blazing log fire. Specializes in high-quality cask beers.

Kings Wark

Map 1, E4. 36 The Shore.

Real ale and good food in a restored eighteenth-century pub, with a maritime theme, fronting the Water of Leith.

Malt and Hops

Map 1, E5. 45 The Shore.

Another of Leith's characterful real-ale pubs, offering basic bar snacks. Open till 1am Fri & Sat.

Starbank Inn

Map 1, E4. 64 Laverockbank Rd.

Fine old stone-built pub overlooking the Forth. Has a high reputation for good cask ales and bar food. Open till midnight Thurs–Sat.

Ye Olde Peacock Inn

Map 1, E4. Lindsay Rd; ©0131/552 8707.

Serves cheap, homely food, including the best fish and chips in the city. Advance reservations are advisable for the main bar and restaurant; otherwise try for a table in the small lounge. Don't miss the gallery displaying calotype prints of Newhaven fishwives by the pioneering photographers Hill and Adamson.

Athletic Arms (The Diggers)

Map 1, D4. 1 Angle Park Terrace West.

Out in the western suburbs, near Tynecastle football ground and Murrayfield rugby stadium. Nicknamed after its location near a cemetery, for decades it has had the reputation of being Edinburgh's best pub for serious ale drinkers. Open Mon–Sat till midnight, Sun till 6pm.

Caley Sample Room

Map 1, D4. 58 Angle Park Terrace West.

A large showpiece pub, selling the range of cask ales produced by the Caledonian Brewery, just up the road. Also the place to try cask whiskies. Open Mon–Thurs & Sun till midnight, Fri & Sat till 1am.

Canny Man's (Volunteer Arms)

Map 1, D5. 237 Morningside Rd, Morningside.

Atmospheric and idiosyncratic pub/museum adorned with anything that can be hung on the walls or from the ceiling, ranging from old violins to assorted beer mugs. There's a pleasant beer garden for warm Morningside evenings. Mon–Sat open until midnight.

Hawes Inn

Map 1, B3. Newhalls Rd, South Queensferry; ©0131/319 1120.

Immortalized by Stevenson in *Kidnapped*, a famous old whitewashed tavern virtually under the Forth Rail Bridge. The bar serves a wide range of food and drink, and the rambling complex also includes a hotel and upmarket restaurant.

Sheep Heid

Map 5, G6. 43 The Causeway, Duddingston.

Whether you've walked round Arthur's Seat or jumped on a

bus to get to Duddingston, you shouldn't miss the opportunity to visit this sedate pub. Built in 1670, it's said to be the oldest licensed premises in Scotland. There's an enclosed beer garden out the back and good pub food is served upstairs, including a full roast dinner on Sundays, while the old-fashioned skittle alley next door is popular with student groups.

Temple Hall Hotel
Map 1, E4. 77 Promenade, Portobello.

A seafront bar on Portobello Promenade, with a beer garden for those rare balmy days. Decent beer and friendly staff.

Live music and clubs

Not surprisingly, Edinburgh's **nightlife** is at its best during the Festival (see p.251), which can make the other 49 weeks of the year seem like one long anticlimax. However, when not compared to this misleading yardstick, the city has a lot to offer, especially in the realm of performing arts and **live music**.

You can usually hear live **jazz**, **folk** and **rock** every evening in one or other of the city's hundreds of pubs. Many of the big rock bands miss out Edinburgh altogether, making Glasgow their only Scottish date on a major international tour, but those that do come to Edinburgh perform at venues such as the Castle Esplanade, Murrayfield Stadium and the exhibition halls of the Royal Highland Show at Ingliston – also the site of occasional raves. Touring bands tend to play the city's medium-size clubs.

Edinburgh's top **classical music** venue is the Usher Hall, currently undergoing much-needed renovation, and due to reopen sometime in 2000. Large-scale **opera and ballet** are staged at the Festival Theatre. Smaller ensembles tend to perform at the Queens Hall, which also sees a fair bit of jazz and mellow rock. Choral and organ recitals are held at assorted venues, the best known being the High Kirk of St Giles.

It isn't always easy to get a grip on Edinburgh's **club scene**, partly because it offers an eclectic array of different styles and music, and partly because there aren't that many clubs or venues which have made such an impact that the crowds flock, come rain or shine – as is the case in many other British cities. What you should find, however, is something covering most tastes, from reggae through hip-hop to rock; it's also worth checking out where some of the city's best DJs, such as Eh-wun, Richie Rufftone or TPV, are playing. Look out, too, for the popular Seventies or Eighties nights with the emphasis firmly on fun, dressing up and drinking. In the bigger venues, you may find different clubs taking place on each floor. Most of the city-centre clubs stay **open** till around 3am.

The best way to find out **what's on** is to pick up a copy of *The List*, an excellent fortnightly listings magazine covering both Edinburgh and Glasgow (£1.95). Alternatively, get hold of the *Edinburgh Evening News*, which appears daily except Sunday: its listings column gives details of all performances in the city that day. Information on nightclubs can be found on posters and piles of leaflets distributed to most of the pre-club bars around town. Box offices of individual halls and theatres are likewise liberally supplied with promotional leaflets about forthcoming music and theatre, and some are able to sell tickets for more than one venue.

LIVE MUSIC VENUES

Cas Rock Café
Map 3, B5. 04 West Port ℗0131/229 4341.
Near the art college, a bastion of the Edinburgh pub-rock

scene, the *Cas Rock* is used predominantly by local up-and-coming bands and old-timers like the UK Subs. Also hosts an annual punk festival in the summer, when it fills up with Scandinavian and German mohicans.

Cellar No. 1
Map 3, G4. 1 Chambers St ✆0131/226 7177.
Traditional cellar bar which sways to jazz, salsa or flamenco every night of the week. Open till 1am.

Kulu's Jazz Joint
Map 2, C8. 8 Morrison St, off Lothian Rd ✆0131/221 1288.
Edinburgh's premier jazz and hip-hop venue, with live music every night and regular top performers.

The Liquid Room
Map 3, D4. 9c Victoria St ✆0131/225 2528.
Good-size venue frequented by visiting indie and local R&B bands, while the occasional star act gets queues round the block.

The Queen's Hall
Map 2, H9. 37 Clerk St ✆0131/667 2019.
Converted Southside church seating up to 800, with gigs from African, funk and rock bands on the way up or back down, as well as smaller jazz and folk concerts. Also operates as the home base of both the Scottish Chamber Orchestra and Scottish Ensemble, and hosts occasional comedy nights with well-known comedians.

Royal Oak
Map 2, H7. 1 Infirmary St ✆0131/557 2976.
Friendly, unpretentious folk bar. Music every night with local residencies and visiting artists in upstairs and downstairs bars. Feel free to join in and have a good sing-along.

LIVE MUSIC VENUES

Sandy Bell's

Map 3, E5. 25 Forrest Rd ©0131/225 2751.

A small, friendly bar, with folk music every night of the week. Tends to attract good local musicians.

Tron Ceilidh House

Map 3, F9. 9 Hunter Square ©0131/226 0931.

Busy, huge complex of bars on different levels, with regular jazz and folk nights. Comedy on Friday nights.

The Venue

Map 6, B7. 15 Calton Rd ©0131/557 3073.

Regular stop for up-and-coming indie bands, local and national, and the odd rock'n'roll legend. The dark and dingy setting is just right for raucous guitar-based music.

CLASSICAL MUSIC

Reid Concert Hall

Map 2, G8. Bristo Square ©0131/650 2423.

Owned by Edinburgh University, this hall is used sparingly during the year for classical music concerts. Free lunchtime recitals of organ and piano music.

St Cecilia's Hall

Map 3, G3. Corner of Cowgate and Niddry St ©0131/650 2805.

The oldest purpose-built concert hall in Scotland, now owned by Edinburgh University. The excellent collection of early keyboard instruments is used during the Festival and occasionally at other times. Acoustics are good, but have to compete with a noisy modern city right outside.

Usher Hall

Map 2, C7. Corner of Lothian Rd and Grindlay St ©0131/228 1155.

Large Edwardian concert hall, with a 2500-seating capacity.

CLASSICAL MUSIC

Used for big-scale classical music events and by MOR pop and country giants. Currently undergoing long-overdue renovation after a recent Tony Bennett concert almost brought the roof in. Due to reopen by late 2000.

The Attic
Map 3, H3. Dyers Close, Cowgate ℗0131/225 8382.
In the heart of Edinburgh's clubland, this popular, medium-size venue can hold up to 300 people. It was recently refurbished and now has airconditioning, new toilets and a spanking wooden floor. Try the Transporter Room on Wednesday nights for a hip mixture of live music and DJs.

The Bongo Club
Map 3, I1. 14 New St ℗0131/556 5204.
Great venue above a car park near Waverley Station, attracting some of the most interesting DJs around. Look out for the mighty Messenger Sound System on Saturday nights.

The Cavendish
Map 2, C9. 3 West Tollcross ℗0131/228 3252.
Slightly dingy but still a packed venue for roots, ragga and reggae night on Friday; *The Mambo Club* on Saturday plays African and Latin rhythms. Weekday nights tend to be more studenty. Also used for occasional live shows from Sixties and Seventies stalwarts such as Mungo Jerry and Geno Washington.

Club Mercado
Map 3, F2. 36–39 Market St ℗0131/226 4224.
Queues start forming at 5pm for the cheesy Seventies Kerplunk night on Fridays. Arrive early and dress with style for Saturday nights, which alternate between house and glam. Also see the early evening (7.30–10.30pm) Snog for the under-18s.

Honeycomb

Map 3, G3. 36–38a Blair St ℂ0131/220 4381.

Purpose-built venue opened in 1996, the *Honeycomb* has a
superb sound system, with well-established Friday nights alternating between garage, hip-hop and house. Large enough to
have two separate dance areas; at Saturdays' Groove Theory
you can move between house in the main room and jazz-funk
and disco classics in the back. Sunday's garage and house night
is rated by many as Edinburgh's best night out. Alternatively,
you could try the live jazz sessions from Monday to Wednesday,
including a Coltrane tribute every Tuesday night.

Jaffa Cake

Map 2, C7. 28 King Stables Rd ℂ0131/229 7986.

So called for its three layers with orange in the middle. Normally
a busy student nightclub, with the accent on indie and chart
music. Over the last few years has been at the forefront of the
attempt to bring popular music to the Fringe Festival.

La Belle Angèle

Map 3, G4. 11 Hasties Close ℂ0131/225 2774.

A rotating selection of Latin, soul, hip-hop and jazz.
Edinburgh's best drum'n'bass club on Fridays, while house
rules on Saturdays. Occasionally hosts important touring bands.

The Liquid Room

Map 3, D3. 9c Victoria St ℂ0131/225 2564.

Large, longstanding venue, aiming for the student crowd, with
indie and chart nights and dance music. Big dance floor and a
huge, powerful sound system.

Negociants

Map 3, F5. 45–47 Lothian St ℂ0131/225 6313.

The basement of a very popular bar close to the University,

NIGHTCLUBS

with different clubs every night of the week. Styles cover most forms of modern dance music, house, funk, soul and even some dub. Added attraction of decent beer. Free admission.

The Venue
Map 6, B7. 15 Calton Rd ℗0131/557 3073.

When it's not a seedy rock'n'roll pit, the *Venue* is a stomping nightclub, over three floors, with room for 1000. A string of long-running nights is on offer, the best of which, both fortnightly, are Pure on Friday nights for techno and house, and the Saturday-night Tribal Funktion, which belts out house and garage soul. Other regular events cover a wide-ranging reggae extravaganza and a mixture of disco and funk nights. Attracts a very mixed crowd.

Wilkie House
Map 3, G3. Cowgate ℗0131/225 2935.

Excellent venue capable of taking up to 700 punters, and big enough to contain a handy chill-out room. Friday nights offer Sublime, a hectic trance night, while alternating Saturday nights include Joy, a long-running gay night and Vena, for progressive house.

Theatre, comedy and cinema

Outside the Festival, Edinburgh has a relatively small but thriving **theatre** and **cinema** scene. The Traverse leads the way in original, cutting-edge drama; the Royal Lyceum regularly stages top-quality mainstream plays, often with a Scottish theme; while the huge Festival Theatre presents the biggest and most prestigious touring shows, including opera and ballet. Big London West End successes tend to do runs at the Playhouse, while smaller, more innovative work can be found at places such as the Theatre Workshop and Edinburgh University's Bedlam Theatre. Ticket prices for live theatre vary enormously, ranging from £5 to £25 depending on the venue and the production.

Edinburgh has several multiscreen venues and two excellent repertory **cinemas**, the Cameo and Filmhouse, both of which present a daily choice of art-house and mainstream films. You can expect to pay around £6 for an evening show, less during the day. Check with the venue or read *The List* or *The Scotsman* for details of performances and special offers for previews or reduced tickets for student card-holders.

THEATRE AND COMEDY

Bedlam Theatre
Map 3, E5. 2a Forrest Rd ℗0131/225 9893.
A converted church which operates as the main venue for low-budget but enthusiastic and occasionally notable productions by Edinburgh University students.

W. J. Christie & Son
Map 3, B5. 27–31 West Port ℗0131/228 3765.
Small, intense cellar bar with raw nightly comedy spots and some of the better local acts. Thurs–Sun.

Church Hill Theatre
Map 1, D5. Morningside Rd ℗0131/220 4349.
A converted Victorian church which has been transformed into a rather utilitarian theatre, used mainly by local amateur dramatics groups and visiting festival groups.

Festival Theatre
Map 3, G5. Nicolson St ℗0131/529 6000.
Revamped music-hall theatre, now with a grandiose glass front, where fire claimed the life of a famous illusionist, the Great Lafayette, in 1911. Following renovation it now has the largest stage in Britain, principally used for Scottish Opera's appearances in the capital and other major orchestral performances, but also for everything from the children's show *Singing Kettle* to Engelbert Humperdinck.

King's Theatre
Map 2, D9. 2 Leven St ℗0131/228 5955.
Stately Edwardian civic theatre that offers the most eclectic programme in the city – includes major touring theatre com-

panies, Shakespeare, slap-stick Christmas pantomime and mainstream comedy and music-hall acts.

Netherbow Arts Centre

Map 3, H2. 43 High St ℡0131/556 9579.

Compact Royal Mile venue offering a regular supply of adventurous drama, with storytelling, puppetry, children's theatre and Scots themes prevailing. Has an attractive café.

Playhouse Theatre

Map 2, H3. 18–22 Greenside Place ℡0131/557 2590.

Restored following a serious fire in 1993, the Playhouse is a huge theatre, seating around 3000, and is used most of the year for popular West End musicals such as *Phantom of the Opera* and *Cats*.

Royal Lyceum Theatre

Map 2, C7. 30 Grindlay St ℡0131/229 9697.

Fine Victorian civic theatre with compact auditorium. The city's leading year-round venue for mainstream drama.

St Bride's Centre

Map 2, A8. 10 Orwell Terrace ℡0131/346 1405.

Another converted church that doubles as a busy community centre. Used by school groups and local dramatic societies during the year and for a variety of shows at Festival time.

The Stand Comedy Club

Map 4, J3. 5 York Place ℡0131/558 7272.

The city's top comedy spot, with a different act on every night and some of the UK's top comics headlining at the weekends. The bar itself is a great place to eat and drink, even if the stage is quiet.

THEATRE AND COMEDY

Theatre Workshop

Map 2, C3. 34 Hamilton Place ✆0131/226 5425.

Enticing programmes of international innovative theatre and performance art all year round.

Traverse Theatre

Map 2, C7. 10 Cambridge St ✆0131/228 1404.

A byword in experimental theatrical circles, and unquestionably one of Britain's premier venues for new plays. Going from strength to strength in its new custom-built home beside the Usher Hall, with a great bar downstairs and the inventive *blue* café-bar upstairs.

CINEMAS

ABC Filmcentre

Map 2, C9. 120 Lothian Rd; info line ✆0131/228 1638; credit card bookings ✆0131/229 3030.

One of two older mainstream cinemas in the city centre; shares most of the major releases with the Odeon.

Cameo

Map 2, D9. 38 Home St; info line ✆0131/228 2800, bookings ✆0131/228 4141.

A cultured three-screen venue with a plush main auditorium. Shows new releases of art-house, independent and more challenging mainstream films, as well as a regular selection of cult movies and weekend late-night shows for devotees of the likes of *Betty Blue* and *Reservoir Dogs*, plus interesting Sunday matinées. Tarantino's been here and thinks it's great.

Filmhouse

Map 2, C7. 88 Lothian Rd ✆0131/228 2688.

Eclectic programme of independent, art and classic films in a

CINEMAS

converted church. Main centre for the Edinburgh International Film Festival. Excellent bar/café with monthly film trivia quiz nights. Good facilities for the disabled.

The Lumière

Map 3, F5. Royal Museum of Scotland (enter from Lothian St) ✆0131/247 4219.

Art-house movies grouped into special themes and seasons. Open Fri–Sun only.

Odeon

Map 2, H9. 7 Clerk St ✆0131/667 0971; info and credit card bookings ✆0870/505 0007.

Five-screen cinema showing the latest releases. Huge main auditorium makes it an electric place to watch a newly released blockbuster.

Art galleries

I n addition to Edinburgh's four major art galleries – the National Gallery (see p.76), the Portrait Gallery (see p.84), the Gallery of Modern Art (see p.90) and the Dean Gallery (see p.92) – there are a number of stimulating smaller art galleries around the city, where you can see both traditional Scottish painting, typified by landscapes of beautiful Highlands scenery, and more contemporary works by a new generation of successful young artists.

The places where you're most likely to see important local or touring exhibitions are the **City Art Centre**, an impressive six-storey venue, right beside Waverley Station, or the **Fruitmarket Gallery**, opposite, with its attractive glass-fronted design and art bookshop. Other important shows are exhibited at the **Talbot Rice Gallery** (see p.67) in Edinburgh University's Old College and the **Royal Scottish Academy** (see p.73), beside the National Gallery at the foot of the Mound, notable for its annual show by members and the occasional large Festival retrospective. Complementing these are a raft of commercial galleries, from ritzy upmarket venues, such as the **Scottish Gallery** and the **Ingelby Gallery** in the New Town, to more modern and trendier spaces, like the **Collective Gallery**, which is found in the Old Town. Also in the Old Town are two dynamic photographic galleries, **Portfolio** and **Stills**. You can also stumble on interesting exhibitions at many of the city's arts venues, such as the Filmhouse, Queen's Hall and, particularly, Inverleith House in the Royal Botanic Garden. Check *The List* or *The Scotsman* for details of current shows.

City Art Centre

Map 4, K8. 2 Market St ©0131/529 3993.
Mon–Sat 10am–5pm. Entry charge for some exhibitions.
Big civic venue with six exhibition halls, often used for block-buster exhibitions: notable successes have included *Star Trek* and *Scotland's Art*, mounted in the summer of Parliament's opening. Choice items from the council's own substantial collection of art, including fascinating paintings of Edinburgh in former times and works by notable locals such as Fergusson, McTaggart and Bellany, are also occasionally put on display. There's a pleasant café on the ground floor.

Collective Gallery

Map 4, K8. 22–28 Cockburn St ©0131/220 1260.
Tues–Sat 11am–5pm. Free.
An avant-garde gallery established in the mid-80s by a large group of artists, which shows conventional and mixed-media contemporary art. Changing exhibitions can be a bit hit or miss, but they're ready to tackle taboo subjects, such as drugs and gay sex. The Project Room, a small space off the main room, is used for smaller exhibitions.

Edinburgh College of Art

Map 3, C6. Lauriston Place ©0131/221 6032.
Mon–Fri 10am–4pm, Sat 9am–1pm. Free.
It's always worth checking out the degree show held here in the late spring, and there are regular exhibitions throughout the year, the most interesting often at the time of the Festival.

ART GALLERIES

Edinburgh Printmakers' Workshop
Map 2, H3. 23 Union St ℰ0131/557 2479.
Tues–Sat 10am–6pm. Free.

Bustling working studio used predominantly by local artists, but there's always a couple of rooms displaying some excellent printmaking, and a special show is put on during the Festival. Good place to go to buy reasonably priced screen prints and lithographs. Workshops and courses on offer.

Fruitmarket Gallery
Map 4, K8. 45 Market St ℰ0131/225 2383.
Mon–Sat 11am–6pm, Sun noon–5pm.

Award-winning space behind a giant glass frontage immediately opposite the City Arts Centre, presenting the best in adventurous contemporary and cutting-edge art from Scotland and abroad in a variety of media. Regular exhibitions from high-profile international names. There's an excellent art/architecture bookshop and a popular café (Mon–Fri 11am–3pm, Sat 11am–5.30pm, Sun noon–5pm) serving light lunches and cakes.

Ingelby Gallery
Map 6, I4. 6 Carlton Terrace ℰ0131/556 4441.
Tues–Sat 10am–6pm.

Tiny but impressive gallery located in a family house on one of Edinburgh's grandest terraces on Calton Hill. Displays works by contemporary stars such as Andy Goldsworthy, Callum Innes and Ian Hamilton Finlay.

Open Eye Gallery
Map 4, E1. 75 Cockburn St ℰ0131/557 1020.
Mon–Fri 10am–6pm, Sat 10am–4pm. Free.

Charming commercial gallery at the lower end of the New Town showing many leading Scottish artists and a good range of jewellery, ceramics and crafts. Sister gallery *i2* is immediately opposite.

ART GALLERIES

Portfolio Gallery

Map 3, E4. 43 Candlemaker Row ℂ0131/220 1911.

Tues–Sat noon–5.30pm. Free.

Small photographic gallery near Grassmarket holding consistently interesting and well-presented photographic exhibitions, often on local themes. Produces the lavish *Portfolio* magazine, in which the photos are accompanied by thoughtful essays and criticism.

Scottish Gallery

Map 4, F2. 16 Dundas St ℂ0131/558 1200.

Mon–Fri 10am–6pm, Sat 10am–4pm. Free.

Edinburgh's longest-established fine art dealers in the heart of the commercial gallery district of the New Town. Shows both traditional and contemporary art, with cabinets of jewellery, ceramics or wooden crafts.

Stills Gallery

Map 4, K8. 23 Cockburn St ℂ0131/662 6200.

Tues–Sat 11am–5pm. Free.

An attractive small contemporary space, predominantly showing photography, but an array of exciting contemporary artists can often be found here. Good café on the mezzanine level, and a small bookshop.

Gay Edinburgh

With an estimated homosexual population of around 15,000–20,000, Edinburgh has a dynamic **gay** culture which for years centred round the top of Leith Walk and Broughton Street, an area known as the "Pink Triangle", where the first gay and lesbian centre appeared in the 1970s. The power of the Pink Pound has led to a proliferation of gay enterprises – some transitory, others more durable – and the rate of growth has quickened over the last few years.

Information

Important local **contact numbers** are: Gay Men's Health (Mon–Fri 9am–5pm; ✆0131/558 9444); Lothian Gay & Lesbian Switchboard (daily 7.30–10pm; ✆0131/556 4049); Edinburgh Lesbian Line (Mon & Thurs 7.30–10pm; ✆0131/557 0751). Solas (✆0131/661 0982) is an HIV and AIDS counselling service. Otherwise, the best place for up-to-date information is at the Lesbian, Gay and Bisexual Centre which houses *Nexus Café* (see opposite), or *Blue Moon Café*, just up the road. Useful **Web sites** include: *www.scotsgay.co.uk*, *www.gayscotland.co.uk*, *www.users.global-net.co.uk/~gaymen/*, and *www.pridescotland.org*

The annual Pride Scotland march takes place in June and alternates between Edinburgh and Glasgow. For further information on gay life in Edinburgh, check out *The List*, *Gay Scotland*, a monthly publication, or *Scotsgay*, a bi-monthly magazine available in most pubs and clubs.

CAFÉS

Blue Moon Café
Map 4, K1. 1 Barony St (off Broughton St) ☏0131/557 0911.
Mon–Thurs 11am–midnight, Fri & Sat 9am–1am, Sun 9am–midnight.
Blue Moon Café has a relaxed, friendly vibe that's popular with many sections of Broughton's arty establishment, not just the gay crowd. Serves snacks, drinks and coffees through the day, with main meals at night, including a couple of decent vegetarian dishes. Good place to come to read up about the gay scene and watch the world go by over a coffee.

Nexus Café Bar
Map 2, G3. 60 Broughton St ☏0131/478 7069.
Daily 11am–11pm.
Pleasant and bright licensed café at the back of Edinburgh's long-running Lesbian, Gay and Bisexual Centre, with a striking ceiling mural titled "We are one!" All-day breakfasts and light meals of soups and bacon rolls, along with snacks and coffees, with larger meals available in the evening. Full of useful information on all aspects of gay life in Scotland's capital, and has a PC with Internet access.

Solas Café
Map 2, K4. 2/4 Abbeymount ☏0131/661 0982.
Mon, Tues, Thurs & Fri 11am–4pm, Wed 5–9pm.
Vegetarian home cooking on weekday lunchtimes and

CAFÉS

Wednesday evenings at the local HIV information centre for those living with HIV.

CLUBS AND BARS

CC Bloom's
Map 2, H3. 23 Greenside Place, Leith Walk ℂ0131/556 9331.
Mon–Sat 6pm–3am, Sun 4pm–3am. Free.
The only gay/lesbian bar in town to have a disco every night, playing non-stop, sweaty dance music from 10.30pm to 3am. Consistently Edinburgh's liveliest gay bar, with a friendly, welcoming crowd. Karaoke nights on Thursdays and Sundays, male dancers on Sunday afternoons.

French Connection
Map 4, F6. 87 Rose St Lane North ℂ0131/226 7651.
Mon–Sat noon–1am, Sun 1pm–1am.
Well away from the rest of Edinburgh's gay bars and a much calmer atmosphere apart from karaoke nights on Tuesdays and Fridays. Small and cosy bar with a bunch of almost totally male friendly regulars looked after by the bar's owner, Babs.

Newtown Bar
Map 4, I2. 26a Dublin St ℂ0131/538 7775.
Daily noon–1am.
Still very near to the Broughton Triangle, but more of a New Town feel to this smart, men-only bar, which attracts a high number of professionals. Downstairs, the aptly named Intense music night plays from Wednesday to Sunday.

Planet Out
Map 2, H3. 6 Baxter's Place, Leith Walk ℂ0131/556 5991.
Mon–Fri 5pm–1am, Sat & Sun 12.30pm–1am.

Another venue beside the Playhouse, this is an easy-going, friendly bar, with tacky décor. Tends to attract a younger gay crowd, though it's also popular at weekends as a warm-up for *CC Bloom's* up the road.

Apart from the pubs listed here, the most popular gay club nights in Edinburgh are weekly or monthly slots in the city's main nightclubs. Look out for *Joy* at *Wilkie House* in the Cowgate (Sat 10.30pm–3am; monthly), Scotland's biggest gay club and always lively; *Taste* at the *Honeycomb* on Blair Street (Sun 11pm–3am; weekly), playing house and garage; and *Tackno* at *Club Mercado* (Sun 11pm–4am; weekly), with wall-to-wall cheesy classics. Check *The List* (see p.6) or posters in gay venues for forthcoming dates.

SHOPS

Atomix
Map 2, G3. 60 Broughton St ℗0131/558 8174.
Mon–Sat noon–7pm, Sun noon–5pm.
Part of the same complex as the Lesbian, Gay and Bisexual Centre and *Nexus Café*, a shamelessly outrageous gay stockist with a broad-ranging selection from clothing to knick-knacks, watches, magazines, cards and posters.

Out of the Blue
Map 4, K1. 1 Barony St (off Broughton St) ℗0131/478 7048.
Daily noon–7pm.
Scotland's largest gay and lesbian shop, and the capital's prime gay sex shop, situated at the heart of the Pink Triangle in the basement below *Blue Moon Café*.

SHOPS

ACCOMMODATION

Garlands Guest House
Map 2, I1. 48 Pilrig St ℭ0131/554 4205.

Neat gay and straight-friendly guest house, with six en-suite rooms, located half-way down Leith Walk. Non-smoking. ③.

Mansfield House
Map 4, I2. 57 Dublin St ℭ0131/556 7980.

Large, popular New Town guest house opposite the *New Town Bar*, so handy for the Broughton Street scene. Five rooms, including two en-suite. ③.

Kids' Edinburgh

The dramatic visual impact of Edinburgh and its plethora of fascinating historic buildings make it a place children are likely to enjoy and remember. Older children especially will appreciate many of the city's attractions covered in other parts of this book, especially **Edinburgh Castle**, with its battlements, winding staircases and dungeons. Other places which children are likely to connect with are the **Camera Obscura** (see p.22) on the Royal Mile, **Greyfriars Bobby** (see p.56), on George IV Bridge, and the **Scott Monument** (see p.72) on Princes Street, with its tight spiral staircase winding for ever up into the Edinburgh stratosphere. Also covered elsewhere in the guide, and popular with children, are the **Brass Rubbing Centre** in Trinity Apse (see p.35), the **Museum of Childhood** (see p.35) and **Our Dynamic Earth** (see p.47). It's also worth remembering how close open areas such as **Holyrood Park** and **Calton Hill** are for running around and letting off steam.

The attractions we've listed below are either directly targeted at younger children or have dedicated child-friendly sections. **Edinburgh Zoo** and **Gorgie City Farm** offer contrasting choices of wild and tame animals, while the extremely popular **Deep Sea World** is an imaginatively mounted display of all kinds of sea creatures, including conger eels and sharks. For animal-life on a smaller scale, try **Edinburgh Butterfly and Insect World**. There are a number of places which successfully make the historical aspect of Edinburgh more relevant to children, including the **National Museum of Scotland** and **Scotland's Black Diamonds**, a mining museum a little way out of town. Meanwhile, there's plenty of good clean fun to be had at the city's two best swimming centres, **Leith Waterworld** and the **Royal Commonwealth Pool**, both of which have flumes and baby pools. If you're planning to visit more than a couple of these places during your stay in Edinburgh, it's worth getting hold of the tourist board's *Essential Guide to Edinburgh and Lothians* (£1), available at the Tourist Office, which has a centre pull-out with various **discounts** and offers, many relating to family attractions.

Look out also for child-friendly events in the **Edinburgh International Science Festival** (see p.272) in April, while the **Puppet and Animation Festival** in March (see p.272) and the **Children's Festival** (see p.273) give kids (and parents) a taste of the wall-to-wall entertainment of the grown-up Festival. During the grown-up Festival itself, in August, a separate programme, entitled *Festival for Kids*, gives details of children's shows, though you'll also find children's listings in the regular Fringe programme and the daily *What's On* guide. A particularly strong programme of events for children is put on by the **Book Festival** (see p.263) in Charlotte Square, with various famous children's authors, including JK Rowling, making appearances, along with other entertainers and participation events. Both during the Festival and at other times of year, the **Netherbow Theatre** and the **Theatre Workshop** frequently put on children's shows (see the "Theatre, Comedy and Cinema" chapter for details).

Deep Sea World

Map 1, B3. North Queensferry, Fife; 24-hour customer info line ©0930/100300.

April–Oct daily 10am–6pm; Nov–March Mon–Fri 11am–5pm, Sat & Sun 10am–6pm; £6.25, children £3.95, family tickets from £16.95.

The most visited modern attraction in Scotland, this is a well-thought-out and well-run high-tech aquarium showcasing all kinds of sea creatures. The highlight, suitable for all but the youngest children, is a walk along a transparent acrylic tunnel surrounded by conger eels and sharks. Knowledgeable staff are on hand to allow the inquisitive to touch some of the gentler fish in the rockpool. The centre was involved in the attempted rescue of Moby, a whale that strayed up the Firth of Forth and eventually died on mudflats. One of the more recent attractions is a piranha tank. The nearest railway station is North Queensferry. By car, cross the Forth Road Bridge, leave the M90 at Junction 1 and follow signs. At the busiest times, you will have to use a free park-and-ride service operating from the road into North Queensferry.

Edinburgh Butterfly and Insect World

Map 1, F6. Melville Nursery, Lasswade, Midlothian ©0131/663 4932.

Daily: April–Oct 9.30am–5.30pm; Nov–March 10am–5pm; £3.95, children £2.85, family tickets from £12.

Hundreds of brightly coloured butterflies and moths inside a large glasshouse. Streams and a bubbling mud pool add to the excitement, and at the back is a "Nocturnal World", with bee hives, scorpions, snakes and ants.

Edinburgh Zoo

Map 1, D4. Costorphine Rd ©0131/334 9171.

Daily: April–Sept 9am–6pm; Oct & March 9am–5pm; Nov–Feb 9am–4.30pm; £6.80, children £3.80, family ticket from £19.

Edinburgh's zoo, two miles west of the city centre on the main Glasgow road, is built on an eighty-acre site stretching up the side of Costorphine Hill. The zoo has over a thousand animals, including a number of endangered species such as white rhinos, red pandas, pygmy hippos and Madagascar tree boas. The highlight for children, however, is the famous penguin parade (daily at 2pm from April to Sept, and on sunny March and Oct days), which attracts large crowds; other delights for young children include polar bears, sea lions and plenty of cheeky monkeys. The new African Plains Experience and a Lion Enclosure have viewing platforms over the animals, while other popular new additions include the Magic Forest, showcasing smaller primates, and a water-filled Evolution Maze – it's great fun, though fastidious parents should be warned that few children emerge with their clothes dry. The zoo is well served by a number of buses (#2, #26, #31, #36, #69, #85, #86).

Gorgie City Farm

Map 1, D4. 51 Gorgie Rd, Tynecastle Lane ℘0131/337 4202.
Daily: March–Oct 9.30am–4.30pm, Nov–Feb 9.30am–4pm; free.
Lots of cute animals, including sheep, hens, ducks and rabbits, on a 2.5-acre site in the west of the city. There's an old tractor for clambering and a good picnic and play area. The adjacent *Farm Café* is well-prepared for children. Some organic produce for sale.

Leith Waterworld

Map 1, E4. 377 Easter Rd, Leith ℘0131/555 6000.
During school term Wed & Thurs 10am–1pm, Fri–Sun 10am–5pm, closed Mon & Tues; during school holidays daily 10am–5pm; adults £2.05, children 5–17yrs £1.45, family ticket £6.
Big new swimming complex in Leith with a main pool, flumes, a "learner lagoon" and a sloping "beach", suitable for babies. Also has a crèche and café.

National Museum of Scotland

Map 3, F5. Chambers St ℘0131/225 7534.
Mon & Wed–Sat 10am–5pm, Tues 10am–8pm, Sun noon–5pm;

adults £3, £5 for one-year season ticket, free Tues 4.30–8pm; children of school age free.

A great place for children of most ages, with plenty of objects on display to capture the imagination and tell some of Scotland's story. When setting up the museum, selecting the objects to be displayed and writing the captions displayed beside them, the curators paid close attention to the comments of the NMS Junior Board, made up of schoolchildren of different ages from across Scotland. In addition to the displays, occasional interactive screens, the see-through lift and even the museum's unusual layout with tiny balconies and spiral staircases, are all big hits with children, while there are also audio guides in plain English, special Themed Pathways around the museum with objects to hunt out and puzzles to complete, and various books about the museum aimed at children available in the shop. A particular highlight is the Discovery Centre on the third floor, which is specially aimed at 5–14-year-olds, with an assortment of puzzles, games, storyboards, computer challenges and dressing-up clothes related to both the themes and actual objects found in the musuem. See p.59 for a fuller account of the museum.

Royal Commonwealth Pool

Map 5, B7. 21 Dalkeith Rd, Newington ©0131/667 7211. Mon, Tues, Thurs & Fri 9am–9pm; Wed 10am–9pm, Sat & Sun (summer) 8am–7pm (winter) 10am–4pm; £1.80 (swim), £2.35 (swim + flume).

A complex built for the 1970 Commonwealth Games, now slightly tatty round the edges, but still a good venue with a large pool, a separate diving pool, a baby pool, play area for under 8s, and flumes.

Scotland's Black Diamonds

Map 1, F6. Lady Victoria Colliery, Newtongrange, Midlothian ©0131/663 7519. Mon–Sat 10am–5pm; adults £4, children £2.20, family ticket £10.

One of Scotland's best industrial heritage experiences for kids, this mining museum is on the site of one of the country's most important old collieries. A brand-new visitors' centre helps bring the mine and the local community to life, helped by some entertaining innovations, including "magic helmets", with which you can experience a virtual reality tour of life below ground.

FOOD

The problems of taking young children out for a meal in Edinburgh are the same as anywhere in Britain, with many establishments unsuitable for children under the age of 10. The restaurants below have been chosen for their child-friendliness and the acceptable quality of the food for both adults and children. Apart from this selection, the **Royal Museum** on Chambers Street, adjoining the National Museum, and the **National Gallery of Modern Art** both have child-friendly cafés.

Fat Sam's
Map 2, C8. 56–58 Fountainbridge, near Tollcross ℗0131/228 3111.
Sun–Thurs noon–midnight, Fri & Sat noon–1am. Moderate.
Large fun-loving American-style eatery, themed on the Chicago gangsters of the 1920s. In a typical evening, the entertainment comes thick and fast, from the huge fish tank with piranhas and sharks to the puppet jazz band and large screen for birthday greetings and other messages. The staff are great with children and the menu is fun and filling.

Giuliano's on the Shore
Map 1, E4. 1 Commercial St ℗0131/554 5272.
Daily noon–10.30pm. Moderate.
Children can assemble their own pizzas and check out the electronic board displaying birthday messages. There's also a good range of seafood dishes.

Harry Ramsden's
Map 1, D4. 5 Newhaven Place ©0131/551 5566.
Daily noon–10pm. Inexpensive.

Big, slick, well-run fish'n'chips emporium next door to the
Newhaven fishing museum. A perennial winner with kids,
grandparents and big groups, you'll find everything you need
for children, from special menus to high chairs and an in-house
entertainer at weekends. There's also a big play ship outside and
a play area inside for rainy days.

Terrace Café
Map 2, C1. Royal Botanic Garden ©0131/552 0616.
Daily: April–Sept 10am–5pm; Oct–March 10am–2.30pm.
Inexpensive.

Scones, cakes and juices, soup, baked spuds and coffee. The
food's not stunning but the setting is. If you're lucky, the
weather will be mild enough for you to be able to sit outside
and enjoy the fantastic view across to the Old Town, while the
children gambol in the gardens.

TGI Friday
Map 4, D7. 22–26 Castle St ©0131/552 0616.
Mon–Sat noon–11pm, Sun noon–10.30pm. Moderate.

A good bet in the city centre, with child-friendly waiters and
waitresses. The special children's menu includes soft-drink refills
and the chance for kids to help make their own pud. Around early
evening it tends to get packed with fast-drinking office escapees.

Umberto's
Map 1, E4. 2 Bonnington Rd Lane ©0131/554 1314.
Mon–Sat noon–2.30pm & 5–10pm, Sun noon–6pm. Moderate.

This is the best bet for anyone hoping to have a decent meal while
the children are happy, with play areas both outside in the enclosed
garden and inside. Pasta dishes start from about £6, and there are
decent, realistic portions from about £2 for the young ones.

FOOD

239

Shopping

Despite the relentless advance of the big chains, central Edinburgh remains an enticing place for **shopping**, with many of its streets having their own individual character. **Princes Street** retains one or two distinctive emporia, including Jenners, the "Harrods of the North". Parallel to Princes Street, pedestrianized Rose Street and grand George Street both contain a number of more glamorous and upmarket boutiques, including designer clothes shops and large bookshops. At the eastern end of Princes Street is the underground **Princes Mall**, a glossy centre of specialist shops, while **Cockburn Street**, leading up from Waverley Bridge, is a hub for trendy clothes and record shops. On the **Royal Mile** there are several distinctly off-beat places among the tacky souvenir sellers, and down **Victoria Street** and in and around **Grassmarket** you'll find an eclectic range of antique and arts and crafts shops, plus some antiquarian booksellers. The main concentration of general, academic and remainder bookshops is in the area stretching from **South Bridge** to **George IV Bridge**. The best areas for antique shops are **St Stephen Street** in Stockbridge and **Causewayside** in Southside. Thursday night is **late-night shopping**, with many of the larger shops open till around 8pm.

BOOKS AND MAPS

Edinburgh's **book** scene is dominated by just two names, the Scottish company James Thin and the national group Waterstones, each with a number of well-stocked, efficiently run branches, open late most nights. Check the individual shops and the local press for details of regular promotional readings. Edinburgh also has numerous secondhand bookshops, many of which are to be found in the Grassmarket area. Some of the best are listed below.

Bauermeisters

Map 3, E4. 19 George IV Bridge ℂ0131/226 5561.
Mon–Fri 9am–8pm, Sat 9am–5.30pm.
A row of bookshops between the Royal Mile and the University, selling a slightly limited but conventional range of general and academic books, music, stationery and paperbacks.

Carson Clark

Map 3, J2. 181–183 Canongate ℂ0131/556 4710.
Mon–Fri 10am–5pm, Sat 10.30am–5.30pm.
Small but fascinating Royal Mile shop selling antique maps, charts and globes.

The Cooks' Bookshop

Map 3, D4. 118 West Bow ℂ0131/226 4445.
Mon–Fri 10am–5.30pm, Sat 10.30am–5.30pm.
Owned by Clarissa Dickson Wright, of TV's *Two Fat Ladies* fame, this bright shop has an attractive uncluttered display of new and secondhand books on every imaginable branch of cooking and type of food.

James Thin

53–59 South Bridge ℂ0131/556 6743 (**Map 3, G4**); and 57 George St ℂ0131/225 4495 (**Map 4, G5**).

Mon–Fri 9am–10pm, Sat 9am–5.30pm, Sun 11am–5pm.
One of Edinburgh's best general bookstores, this is a long-established local institution. The main South Bridge branch caters for university courses, but also has good sections of broader interest, with big travel and Scottish departments. The George Street branch covers most areas, with a good variety of Scottish titles and a particularly wide range of magazines, while there's a famous if rather old-fashioned café on the first floor.

McNaughtan's Bookshop

Map 2, H2. 3a–4a Haddington Place ✆0131/556 5897.
Tues–Sat 9.30am–5.30pm.
A big shop covering all the main areas of the art and literary world. Sections include history, travel, classics and an excellent choice of Scottish titles and antiquarian books. Searches are undertaken for that elusive long-lost work. A great place to browse, but not cheap.

Peter Bell

Map 3, C5. 68 West Port ✆0131/229 0562.
Mon–Sat 10am–5pm.
Wide selection of quality secondhand books, concentrating on the academic end of the market. Philosophy, science, literature and history are all well represented, with a healthy display of recent first editions.

Second Edition

Map 2, E1. 9 Howard Place ✆0131/556 9403.
Mon–Fri noon–5.30pm, Sat 9.30am–5.30pm.
A great location for an Edinburgh bookshop, opposite the house where Robert Louis Stevenson was born (8 Howard Place). It has a large collection of all sorts of secondhand books, said to number up to 20,000. The owner's choice of jazz makes this a pleasant place to while away an afternoon.

Waterstones

128 Princes St ✆0131/226 2666 (**Map 4, D7**); 13–14 Princes St
✆0131/556 3034 (**Map 4, K6**); and 83 George St ✆0131/225 3436
(**Map 4, E6**).
Daily: varying hours.

The customary tasteful Waterstones recipe of browser-friendly
shops. Huge range in most subjects, and particularly good for
Scottish books, both fiction and non-fiction. *Starbucks Coffee*
have a café around the first-floor bay window of the branch at
128 Princes St.

Word Power

Map 2, H8. 43 West Nicolson St ✆0131/662 9112.
Mon–Fri 10am–6pm, Sat 10.30am–6pm.

Small, well laid-out radical bookshop close to the University,
with books on feminism, gay and lesbian studies, ecology, politics and black studies. Good general literature section, with a
healthy input from small independent publishers.

CLOTHES

Scottish **tartans** and **woollens** are available from the standard chain stores on Princes Street, the St James Centre and
the Gyle, a huge retail park on the western fringe of the
city near the airport. There are also a number of smaller
specialist outlets, reviewed below. You should be able to
find anything from ball gowns to kitsch-wear for that
Seventies disco in one of Edinburgh's many secondhand
clothes shops, the best of which are to be found in the
Grassmarket/Cowgate area.

Wm Armstrong

313 Cowgate ✆0131/556 6521 (**Map 3, H3**); 85 Grassmarket
✆0131/220 5557 (**Map 3, D4**); and 64 Clerk St ✆0131/667 3056
(**Map 2, H9**).

CLOTHES

Mon–Fri 10am–5.30pm, Sat 10am–6pm, Sun noon–6pm.
The biggest of Edinburgh's secondhand clothes shops, selling a vast range of garb, of both refined and dubious taste. Take your pick from velvet or leather coats and jackets, denim shirts, jackets and trousers, and just about any other style and cut of the last fifty years.

Byzantium
Map 3, E3. 9a Victoria St ©0131/225 1768.
Mon–Sat 10am–5.30pm.
Located in one of Edinburgh's many converted churches, Byzantium has the air of a Sixties-style emporium with a massive range of goods for sale under the one roof. Browse through boutiques selling antiques, clothes from home and abroad, books and prints, all of widely varying quality, before going up to the airy mezzanine café.

Elaine's
Map 2, C3. 55 St Stephen St.
Mon–Sat 1–6pm.
From the sublime (Thirties ball gowns and cocktail dresses) to the ridiculous (Seventies tank tops and flares) in one small Stockbridge shop.

Geoffrey (Tailor)
Map 3, G2. 57–59 High St ©0131/557 0256.
Mon–Sat 9am–5.30pm, Sun 10am–5pm.
One of the best of the Royal Mile Highland outfitters, and the place to go if you need to hire or buy a kilt. Tweed and tartan wear made on the premises for men and women. Various Scottish gifts also on offer.

Jenners
Map 4, I6. 48 Princes St ©0131/225 2442.
Mon, Wed, Fri & Sat 9am–5.30pm, Tues 9.30am–5.30pm, Thurs

9am–7.30pm, closed Sun.

Edinburgh's most prestigious department store is stocked with luxury items of every shape and size. There's a fantastic food hall and a sumptuous selection of toys, gifts and racks of men's and women's designer-label fashions.

Kinloch Anderson

Map 1, E4. Corner of Commercial and Dock sts, Leith ©0131/555 1390.

Mon–Sat 9am–5.30pm.

One of the best suppliers for made-to-measure Highland wear, including kilts and full dress outfits, in a large warehouse in Leith. Also hires out Highland dress for formal wear.

Paddy Barrass

Map 3, C4. 15 Grassmarket ©0131/226 3087.

Mon–Fri noon–6pm, Sat 10.30am–5.30pm.

Small establishment selling vintage items. Clothing from the Victorian and later eras, including nightshirts, kilts and dinner jackets. Also small linen and lace items, many of which are displayed on the walls for inspection.

Tiso

Map 4, E6. 115–123 Rose St ©0131/225 9486.

Mon, Wed, Fri & Sat 9.30am–5.30pm, Tues 10am–7.30pm, Thurs 9.30am–7.30pm, Sun noon–5pm.

Biggest city-centre selection of good-quality outdoor gear, including waterproof jackets, boots, and more gadgets than a team of sherpas could carry. Also stocks maps, outdoor books and ski-wear.

MUSIC

A wide range of mainstream music is available at branches of the **Virgin Megastore** at 131 Princes St and **HMV** in the St James Centre. For something more unusual try one of the shops listed below.

Avalanche

17 West Nicolson St ✆0131/668 2374 (**Map 2, H8**); 63 Cockburn St ✆0131/225 3939 (**Map 3, F2**); and 28 Lady Lawson St ✆0131/228 1939 (**Map 3, A5**).

Mon–Sat 10am–6pm, Sun (West Nicolson St only) noon–6pm.

Three busy shops traditionally specializing in indie stuff, but nowadays also moving into the massive dance market. New and secondhand, with lots of bargains, especially in the West Nicolson Street branch, for anyone prepared to spend some time digging around.

Backbeat

Map 2, H8. 31 East Crosscauseway ✆0131/668 2666.

Mon–Sat 10am–5.30pm, Sun 12.30–5.30pm.

New and secondhand Southside shop with a huge choice in all formats. For many years, Backbeat has been strong on all forms of black music, with a particularly tasty selection of Northern Soul in the back room. Now also selling interesting rock records.

Bauermeister Records

Map 3, E4. 19 George IV Bridge ✆0131/226 5561.

Mon–Sat 9am–6pm.

Large selection of classical music, tastefully presented and carefully tied in with visiting performers. Limited jazz and Scottish folk sections.

Coda

Map 3, E3. 12 Bank St ✆0131/622 7246.

Mon–Sat 9.30am–5.30pm, Sun noon–4pm.

Good selection of contemporary Scottish folk and roots music, with helpful staff.

Fopp
Map 3, F2. 55 Cockburn St ℂ0131/220 0133.
Mon–Sat 9.30am–7pm, Sun 11am–6pm.
Good, broad range of cutting-edge and mainstream sounds, in rather more hip surroundings than the vast highstreet stores.

Professor Plastics Vinyl Frontier
Map 2, H8. 15a West Richmond St ℂ0131/622 7168.
Mon–Sat 11am–6pm.
Another great place to dig out some long-lost vinyl. Good for used and new funk, jazz and soundtracks.

Underground Solu'shun
Map 3, F2. 9 Cockburn St ℂ0131/226 2242.
Mon–Sat 10am–6pm, Sun 1–5pm.
On the city's best street for offbeat record shops, a great place for house, garage, techno and drum'n'bass vinyl, as well as info about the hottest clubbing venues in town.

Vinyl Villains
Map 2, I3. 5 Elm Row ℂ0131/558 1170.
Mon–Fri 10.15am–6pm, Sat 10.15am–5.30pm, Sun noon–4pm.
Sizeable secondhand store still stubbornly clinging on to a selection of secondhand records, but now moving with the times and selling CDs and all sorts of odd memorabilia. The choice is dominated by rock music, with a good range of old punk singles.

FOOD AND DRINK

On hot summer days, there are a number of places to pick up tasty sandwiches and snacks for an impromptu picnic in one of the city's many open spaces. Two premier addresses for souvenir hunters in search of Scotland's best-known specialities, haggis and whisky, are also given below.

Charles MacSween & Co

Map 1, E6. Dryden Rd, Bilston Glen, Loanhead ✆0131/440 2555.
Mon–Fri 9am–5pm.

Makers of the finest local haggis, Scotland's national dish and something of an acquired taste, though undoubtedly worth sampling. There's even a passable vegetarian version with kidney beans and lentils instead of meat. You can buy it from the factory in the southeastern suburbs of Edinburgh or look for the brand name in various outlets around Edinburgh, such as the Food Hall in Jenners at 48 Princes St, or Peckhams, 155–159 Bruntsfield Place.

Charlie McNair's Deli and Sandwich Bar

Map 3, F5. 30 Forrest Rd ✆0131/226 6434.
Mon–Fri 9am–5.45pm, Sat 9am–4.30pm.

Small takeaway near the main hospital and the Meadows, purveying great sandwiches and rolls with exotic flavours like spicy bean paté and delicious hummus. Wine, coffee and pastries also available. Big queues at lunchtime, but always a pleasant atmosphere. Look out for Charlie in his other incarnation as a stalwart of the local jazz scene.

Iain Mellis

30 Victoria St ✆0131/226 6215 (**Map 3, D3**); and 205 Bruntsfield
Place (**Map 1, D5**).
Mon–Sat 9.30am–6pm.

Wooden shelves and fridges piled high with rounds and wedges of delicious fresh cheeses from all over Britain and Ireland, plus Italian Parmesan, the only foreign cheese they stock. The smells alone are wonderful, and the taste will make you swear off plastic supermarket cheese for ever.

Lupe Pintos

Map 2, D9. 24 Leven St ✆0131/228 6241.
Mon–Sat 10am–6pm.

FOOD AND DRINK

Fabulous shop offering Spanish and Mexican delicacies and mouth-stinging chilli with everything. Buy a sandwich filled with Spanish cheese or guacamole and some Mexican beer and chill out on Bruntsfield Links just round the corner. If you're really thirsty, you could choose from the big selection of tequila, with prices ranging from £13 to £35.

Nature's Gate
Map 2, I9. 83 Clerk St ℭ0131/668 2067.
Mon–Sat 10am–7pm, Sun noon–4pm.
Vegetarian and vegan delights next to the Queen's Hall and close to the Meadows. Organic wines and beers, a big range of Japanese macrobiotic food and all sorts of goodies for anyone on a special diet, whether sugar-, salt- or gluten-free. Plenty of choice also for lunches and snacks. *Isabel's café* in the basement serves similarly tasty food.

Real Foods
37 Broughton St ℭ0131/557 1911 (**Map 4, L1**); and 8 Brougham St ℭ0131/228 1201 (**Map 2, D9**).
Mon–Fri 9am–6pm, Sat 9am–5.30pm, Sun 11am–5pm.
The place to stock up on dried fruits, cereals, spices and a good selection of organic fruit and veg. For more immediate pleasures, sandwiches, snacks and all kinds of refreshing drinks are available, including organic beers and wines. Also sells numerous health products. Don't miss the notice board for an insight into alternative Edinburgh.

Royal Mile Whiskies
Map 3, E8. 379–381 High St ℭ0131/225 3383.
Mon–Sat 10am–6pm.
Solve all your present problems in this specialist shop opposite St Giles, with everything the whisky enthusiast could ever need. Recent and vintage malt and blended whisky in bottles and miniatures. Smoked salmon and haggis also on offer.

FOOD AND DRINK

Valvona and Crolla

Map 2, H2. 19 Elm Row, Leith Walk ✆0131/556 6066.
Mon–Wed & Sat 8.30am–6pm, Thurs & Fri 8.30am–7pm.

The finest Scottish Italian deli anywhere, now ninety years
old, is full of wallet-emptying Italian wonders: fresh bread,
oozing cheeses, pasta sauces and a huge selection of wine.
The wonderful choice has been further enhanced by the
arrival of quality vegetables, fresh from the Italian markets.
Regular wine tastings and cookery demonstrations, as well as
a café at the back.

The Edinburgh
Festival

F or three weeks in August, Scotland's capital is transformed by the **Edinburgh Festival**. Every available
performance space – from the city's grandest concert
halls to pub courtyards – plays host to a packed programme
of cultural entertainment, ranging from high drama to base
comedy; the streets fill with buskers, hustlers, circus acts
and craft stalls; the capital's population swells to twice its
normal size, as tourists, celebrities, performers, media types
and festival-goers throng the streets; pubs and restaurants
stay open later; posters plaster every vertical space; and the
atmosphere of the centre of town takes on a slightly surreal,
vital buzz.

The Edinburgh Festival is actually an umbrella term
which encompasses different festivals taking place at around
the same time in the city, principally the **Edinburgh
International Festival** and the much larger **Edinburgh
Festival Fringe**, but also **Film**, **Book**, **Jazz and Blues**
and **Television** festivals, the **Military Tattoo** on the Castle
Esplanade, and the **Edinburgh Mela**, a Southeast Asian
festival held over the first weekend in September.

The Edinburgh Festival began in 1947, when, driven by a desire for postwar reconciliation and escape from austerity, the Viennese-born former manager of the Glyndebourne Opera, Rudolf Bing, brought together a host of distinguished musicians from the war-ravaged countries of central Europe. At the same time, eight theatre groups turned up in Edinburgh, uninvited, performing in an unlikely variety of local venues; the next year a critic dubbed their enterprise "the fringe of the official festival drama", and the name and the spirit of the Fringe was born. Nowadays, the Festival is by some margin the largest arts festival in the world, and remains one of Edinburgh's biggest draws.

For the visitor the sheer volume of the Festival's output can be mind-boggling: virtually every branch of arts and entertainment is represented somewhere, and world-famous stars mix with pub singers in the daily line-up. It can be a struggle to find accommodation, get hold of the tickets you want, book a table in a restaurant or simply get from one side of town to another; you can end up seeing something truly dire, or something mind-blowing; you'll inevitably try to do too much, or stay out too late, or spend too much money – but then again, most Festival veterans will tell you that if you don't experience most of these things then you haven't really done the Festival.

Note that dates, venues, names, star acts, happening bars and burning issues in the Festival change from one year to the next. The **unpredictable nature** of the Edinburgh Festival is one of it's greatest charms, however, so while the information given in this chapter will help you get to grips with many aspects of the Edinburgh Festival, always be prepared for – indeed, enjoy – the unexpected.

EDINBURGH INTERNATIONAL FESTIVAL

The legacy of Rudolf Bing's Glyndebourne connections ensured that, for many years, the **Edinburgh**

International Festival (sometimes called the "Official Festival") was dominated by opera. Although in the 1980s, a broader cultural mix of international theatre, ballet, dance and classical music was introduced, it's still very much a highbrow event, and forays into populist territory remain rare. The Festival responds to the inevitable charges of cultural elitism by pointing to healthy box-office returns.

The International Festival attracts truly international stars, such as actress Vanessa Redgrave and conductor Simon Rattle, along with some of the world's finest orchestras and opera, theatre and ballet companies. Performances commonly take place at the city's larger venues, such as the Usher Hall and the Festival Theatre, and while ticket prices at the top end balloon over £35, it is possible to see shows for £10 or less. The most popular events, however, are frequently sold out only a few days after tickets are released.

Since 1999, the International Festival's headquarters have been located at **The Hub** (see p.23), just down from Edinburgh Castle at the junction of the Royal Mile and Johnston Terrace. An imaginatively converted Pugin church, The Hub, open year-round, houses an information centre and ticket office for the International Festival and various other events throughout the year. You can contact them for further **information**, including the annual programme – released in April – at The Hub, Edinburgh's Festival Centre, Castlehill, Royal Mile, Edinburgh EH1 2NE (℗0131/473 2000, *www.eif.co.uk/thehub/*).

The useful web site *www.edinburghfestivals.co.uk* has links to the home pages of most of Edinburgh's main festivals, including those that take place outside August.

EDINBURGH INTERNATIONAL FESTIVAL

EDINBURGH FESTIVAL FRINGE

Even standing alone from its sister festivals, the **Edinburgh Festival Fringe** is easily the world's largest arts gathering. Each year sees over 15,000 performances from over 600 companies, with more than 10,000 participants from all over the world. There are something in the region of 1500 shows every day, round the clock, in 200 venues around the city. While the headlining names at the International Festival reinforce the Festival's cultural credibility, it is the Fringe which dominates Edinburgh every August, giving the city its unique buzz.

For the first three decades of its existence, the Fringe was a fairly intimate affair, dominated by drama, and peopled largely by graduating Oxbridge students and talent-spotting producers (often Oxbridge graduates themselves). The burgeoning of the Fringe began in earnest in the late 1970s as other forms of entertainment established themselves, notably new comedy, which over the next quarter of a century became almost synonymous with the Edinburgh Fringe. Nowadays, the Fringe is *the* place where artists of every conceivable description come to get discovered or re-launched, and audiences can expect to see glimpses of the household names of today and tomorrow.

The **first Fringe Programme** appeared in 1951, the bright idea of a local printer. A single sheet of paper then, it's now a fat magazine crammed with information on most, though not all, participating shows. In 1959, the **Fringe Society** was founded by participants to provide basic marketing and co-ordination between events. Crucially, no artistic control was imposed on those who wanted to produce a show, a defining element of the Fringe which continues to this day – anyone who can afford the registration fee can take part. This means that the shows range from the inspired to the diabolical, and ensures a highly competitive atmosphere, in which one bad review in a prominent publication means box-office disaster. Many unknowns rely on self-publicity, taking to the streets to perform highlights from their show, or pressing leaflets into the hands of every passer-by. Performances go on round the clock: if so inclined, you could sit through twenty shows in a day.

The full Fringe **programme** is usually available in June from the Festival Fringe Office, Box YQ, 180 High St, EH1 1QS (©0131/226 5257, *www.edfringe.com*). Postal and telephone (©0131/226 5138) **bookings** for shows can be made immediately afterwards, while during the Festival, tickets are sold at the Fringe office (daily 10am–7pm), the venue itself, or at various locations around the city (in recent years, James Thin Booksellers at 53–59 Southbridge, Waterstones bookshop at 83 George St and HMV, 93 Princes St).

Ticket prices for most Fringe shows start at £5, and average from £8 to £10 at the main venues, with the better-known acts going for even more. Although some theatre and music acts can be longer, most performances are scheduled to run for an hour, which means that you can easily spend £40–50 on admission alone in the course of a hard day's festivalling.

The International Festival and the Fringe don't quite coincide: the former tends to run over the last two weeks of August and the first week of September, whereas the latter starts a week earlier, culminating on the last weekend in August, traditionally an English (but, confusingly, not a Scottish) Bank Holiday weekend.

THEATRE

Comedy grabs more headlines, but **theatre** still makes up the bulk of the Fringe. Right from the start, innovative, controversial, wonderful and sometimes downright ghastly productions have characterized the Fringe's drama content. In the late 1970s, director Ken Campbell's 22-hour epic *The Warp* was the toast of the town, while the play *Rooting* at the Traverse Theatre featured several pigs in its cast, and a six-hour Cambridge-student production called *The Burning Of Carthage* was hailed as the worst play in the Fringe's history. More recently, a trilogy of plays called *Glad*, *Mad* and *Bad*, involving local homeless men, won awards; and in 1998, *Soldiers*, featuring real-life fighters, was cancelled after one of the cast was recalled to active service in Bosnia. Content ranges from Molière to Berkoff, from Shakespeare to Beckett (someone, somewhere, always puts on *Krapp's Last Tape*). There are numerous student productions, as well as the appearance of Scottish favourites, such as playwright Liz Lochhead or actor Russell Hunter. Unusual venues add spice to some productions: Inchcolm Island in the Firth of Forth has been used to stage *Macbeth*, *2001: A Space Odyssey* was performed to an audience sitting in a Hillman Avenger, while current favourite venues include the back-room café at Valvona and Crolla's Italian delicatessen on Elm Row, and the Royal Botanic Garden in Inverleith.

One way of saving money on tickets is to look out for two-for-one ticket offers, usually advertised at venue box offices or in newspapers.

COMEDY

Comedy is the Fringe's success story. Until the 1970s the Festival was a rite of passage from the Cambridge Footlights or Oxford Revue to the BBC or the London stage, with teams such as Beyond the Fringe and Monty Python appearing in Edinburgh before making their big break on TV. Although this still happens, the arena opened out in the

Making it big at the Festival

There's hardly a serious entertainer worth their salt who hasn't played the Edinburgh Festival at some time. Best known are the satirists of *Beyond the Fringe*, the 1960 Edinburgh revue which launched the careers of Peter Cook, Jonathan Miller, Alan Bennett and Dudley Moore. Miller and Cook had come fresh from the Cambridge Footlights; other Footlighters have included the entire casts of *Monty Python* and *The Goodies*, David Frost, Germaine Greer, Richard Harris, Douglas Adams, Clive James, Griff Rhys-Jones, Stephen Fry and Emma Thompson. From Oxford came Rowan Atkinson and Mel Smith, while Manchester University graduates Ben Elton, Rik Mayall and Adrian Edmondson were first seen in Edinburgh in a revue called *Twentieth Century Coyote*. They teamed up with a duo called The Outer Limits (Nigel Planer and Peter Richardson) to form *The Young Ones*.

Comedian Arthur Smith first attracted attention in the student revue *Hamalongayorick*, while his bogus historical tours shepherding unsuspecting tourists down the Royal Mile became the stuff of legend. Actor Robbie Coltrane was seen in the Traverse's original *Slab Boys Trilogy* long before fame struck, while Billy Connolly's serious play *The Red Runner*, part of the International Festival, was panned by the critics, but a hit with the crowds. Other celebs who got their break at the Fringe include Paul Merton, Jo Brand, Steve Coogan, Frank Skinner and drag queen Lily Savage, while various soap stars have arrived in Edinburgh to reinvent themselves, including Nigel Pivaro (*Coronation Street*), Tom Watt (*Eastenders*), Dannii Minogue (*Home and Away*) and the most successful of the lot, Mark Little (*Neighbours*).

1980s with an explosion of talent and opportunities for selling it, and the Fringe became a hot-house for a generation of new comics once known as "alternative" and now mostly working for the BBC or Channel 4: performers such as Stephen Fry, Jeremy Hardy, Steve Coogan and Eddie Izzard all arrived with shows, and saw their careers take off shortly afterwards. At the same time, the success of the Perrier Award for new comedy heralded a symbiosis between commercial sponsors and performers which had previously only been seen in sport.

Aside from a few variety artists, the entire UK comedy scene – plus many international acts – can be found in Edinburgh at some point during the Fringe season. Artists range from household names to wannabes, who stand in line for their chance to tell a few shaggy dog stories at smaller stages and open mic slots around town. The bigger names are booked by the Assembly Rooms, Pleasance or Gilded Balloon, while Edinburgh's own comedy club, The Stand, has become an increasingly viable alternative. Look out for "Best of the Fest" shows, held at the main venues, featuring a selection of the year's big names, or live recordings of BBC radio shows such as *Loose Ends* at the Pleasance.

MUSIC

While **classical music** fans will no doubt find something to drool over in the International Festival programme, the Fringe offers a wealth of reasonably priced recitals and other concerts to choose from. Near-professional standards are reached by the Rehearsal Orchestra, which performs a two-week season of classical music concerts – possibly the oldest Fringe music event, running since 1956. Established for top amateur musicians and aspirant top-grade orchestral performers, the orchestra often plays the same pieces that are being performed in the International Festival – hence the name "Rehearsal" Orchestra. The annual Festival of Youth Orchestras at Tollcross, featuring orchestras from around the world, also sets high standards, and music-lovers with a sense of humour should check to see if there's an appearance by the Really Terrible Orchestra, a recent Fringe sensation which brings together music-loving amateur players – often lawyers and doctors – who are given the chance to live out their dream of playing in an orchestra. Despite their best efforts (and they do rehearse), the result is, well, really terrible.

Fans of **folk**, **roots**, **world** and **alternative** music should keep a close eye on the line-up at Adam House at 5 Chambers St (previously The Famous Grouse House), which opened in the late 1990s as a venue for Scots and international folk and roots music; Café Graffiti has an unblemished twenty-year track record in unearthing winning and exotic musical treats, although at the time of going to press it was without a home and its existence is under threat. As a travelling venue, the Famous Spiegeltent (a wooden Victorian circus tent) faces regular headaches finding somewhere to park for the Festival, but when present it hosts gigs in an inspiring mix of genres, from serious instrumentalists to light-hearted, banjo-strumming duos, with a slight bias towards Australian acts.

Standing out in the lists of **rock** and **pop** events, relative newcomer the Flux Festival Flux, with a rock'n'roll theme, has brought serious credibility to the Fringe music scene, with artists like Pulp, Nick Cave, Ivor Cutler, Howard Marks, The Fall, Orbital and Ken Kesey. The Fringe has also witnessed the rise of the independent non-folk-singing **songwriter** as a performing force, with the success of performances by established artists such as Tom Robinson, Ray Davies, John Otway and Paul Kelly.

While the greatest concentration of **jazz and blues** takes place in early August (see p.266), late greats like Rory Gallagher and British blues' founding father Alexis Korner stormed the Fringe in their day, while the hardiest perennial of all is gruff-voiced Scots bluesman and Hollywood character actor Tam White, whose stomping shows with the Celtic Groove Connection are the most sought-after tickets in town.

DANCE AND PHYSICAL THEATRE

Ranging from easy-watching box-office smashes like *Tap Dogs*, *Gumboots* and Harlem blues-tapper Will Gaines, through cutting-edge companies such as The Kosh or, in years gone by, Dancers Anonymous, to full-on participation shows such as The Jiving Lindyhoppers, **dance** shows make up a small but entertaining section of the Fringe programme. Companies like Trestle Theatre or Jim Rose's Circus sideshow blur the line between physical theatre, drama, circus and comedy. The 1999 Fringe saw a clever marriage between dance and food with the Bangladesh Festival of Food and Culture at Leith's *Raj* restaurant; meanwhile, Scottish dancing is never hard to find, with a fine selection of ceilidhs on and beyond the Fringe.

ART

When the entire capital is already a canvas it's sometimes hard for **visual artists** to get themselves noticed. Fortunately, Fringe art has an honorable tradition of providing respite from the frenetic festival atmosphere. Special festival exhibitions are mounted at many of the city's leading galleries, while visitors such as the Glasgow Printmakers Workshop literally set up shop in whatever vacant premises they can find in central Edinburgh. New technology has inspired some exciting interactive shows, and multimedia multi-arts are alive and well - most successfully in recent years at the Bongo Club in New Street.

CHILDREN'S SHOWS

Children's shows at the Fringe range from those performed by people who want to (and sometimes do) work

The Fringe –
a brief guide to where it happens

The three **main Fringe venues** are The Assembly Rooms, The Pleasance and The Gilded Balloon. If you're new to the Fringe, these aren't a bad place to start, as there's a high chance you'll see something good, starring well-known names.

The atmosphere at the **Pleasance** (map 3, I4) is usually less frenetic than at the other venues, with classy drama and whimsical appearances by media stars, such as Miles Kington, Radio 4's *Just A Minute* team and Channel 4 icon Richard Whiteley, sitting easily alongside the wackier acts. The **Assembly Rooms** (map 4, G6) provides a grand setting for top-of-the-range drama by companies such as the RSC and big-name music and comedy acts. The Fringe's premier comedy venue **The Gilded Balloon** (map 3, G4) hosts the "Late and Live" show, crammed with TV performers and wannabes competing to be noticed.

The best-kept secret among the mid-size venues is **The Southside** at 117 Nicolson St (map 2, H8), a community venue with a tradition of nurturing talent. Nearby, **The Queen's Hall** (map 2, H9) puts on high-quality jazz, blues and classical concerts, while **Adam House**, on Chambers Street (map 3, G3), has long been the heart of the folk, roots and Celtic section of the Fringe.

The **Traverse Theatre** (map 2, C7), long champion of new drama, combines avant-garde and slick presentation both in the theatre itself and its bar. Less glam, but with an excellent line-up of thought-provoking drama is the **Theatre Workshop** (map 2, C3). **Café Graffiti**, always a hotbed of off-the-wall acts and good vibes, is househunting at the time of going to press, but in its twenty-odd years on the Fringe has always found interesting locations and no doubt will again. Similarly nomadic is **The Famous Spiegeltent**, where, during the day, alternative therapies and soothing music contrast happily with the evening's energy.

in children's television, to those which make their young audience members want to run away and join the theatre. The best of the latter are the memorable, award-winning musicals put on by the National Youth Music Theatre. Children's shows also take in puppetry, clowns, pantomime, magic and straightforward drama, and are staged mostly in the mornings.

OTHER EVENTS

In addition to all the Fringe performances, there is also a host of other activities – numerous daytime workshops, masterclasses, meetings, trade fairs, talks and guided tours; there are debates on drama, courses in theatre administration, poetry readings and discussion forums, including the Fringe Society's Annual General Meeting, plus a broad selection of fare for mind, body and spirit, from meditation sessions to complementary therapies.

Two free Fringe events

The Festival annually stages **two major free events** which regularly attract huge crowds of townspeople and visitors. Held in Holyrood Park on the first Sunday of the Fringe, **Fringe Sunday** is a one-day roadshow-style carnival, which gives festivalgoers a chance to browse snippets of many different shows. The second of these events is the dramatic **Fireworks Concert**, held late at night on the final Saturday of the International Festival: the Scottish Chamber Orchestra belts out pop classics from the Ross Bandstand in Princes Street Gardens, accompanied by a spectacular fireworks display high up above the ramparts of the Castle. Hundreds of thousands view the display from various vantage points throughout the city, the prime spots being Calton Hill or Inverleith Park in Stockbridge.

EDINBURGH INTERNATIONAL FILM FESTIVAL

The **Edinburgh International Film Festival** runs for the last two weeks of August, normally finishing at around the same time as the Fringe. It's the longest continually running film festival in the world, having begun, like the International Festival and Fringe, in 1947. It can also claim a distinguished history at the cutting edge of cinema, premiering American blockbusters from directors like Stephen Spielberg and Woody Allen, discovering low-budget smashes such as *My Beautiful Laundrette* and *Strictly Ballroom*, and introducing serious contenders such as *Mrs Brown* and the *Blair Witch Project*.

The Film Festival is a chance to see some of the year's big cinema hits before they go on general release, along with a varied and exciting bill of reissued or reworked movies. For those in the industry, it is also a vital talking shop, with debates, seminars and workshops, spiced up by the attendance of Hollywood stars at the succession of glittering parties which accompany the launches. Most of the action takes place at the Filmhouse, the ABC and the *Sheraton Hotel* on Lothian Road and the Cameo, in Home Street. A charming antidote to the large-scale business of the Film Festival is the presence of La Cinerama – one of the smallest cinemas in the world, based in the back of a truck, which parks itself as close to the action as possible.

Tickets and information are available from the main venue, the Filmhouse, 88 Lothian Rd, EH3 9BZ (©0131/228 2688, *www.edfilmfest.org.uk*). The programme usually comes out in late June.

EDINBURGH INTERNATIONAL BOOK FESTIVAL

Begun in 1983, the annual two-week **Edinburgh International Book Festival**, which takes place in the last two weeks of August, is the largest celebration of the written word worldwide. A model plugfest, it's held in a tented village in the douce setting of Charlotte Square, and offers talks, readings and signings by a star-studded line-up of visiting authors, as well as panel discussions and workshops on as many subjects as there are books. Well-known local authors such as Iain Banks, Ian Rankin and AE Kennedy are good for an appearance most years, while visitors from further afield have included Doris Lessing, Louis de Bernières, Ben Okri, John Updike and Vikram Seth. In addition, there are cook-ups by celebrity chefs promoting their latest tomes, late-night musical events with a literary flavour and numerous children's activities. An on-site café and, of course, a bookshop, ensure that all the participants' needs are met.

For further **information**, contact the Scottish Book Centre, 137 Dundee St, EH11 1BG (©0131/228 5444, *www.edbookfest.co.uk*).

EDINBURGH INTERNATIONAL TELEVISION FESTIVAL

The **Edinburgh International Television Festival** is essentially a closed conference and is a chance for the British TV industry to do an annual stocktake. A packed schedule of lectures, seminars and parties takes place over the peak Festival Bank Holiday weekend. A formal agenda is set by the prestigious McTaggart Lecture, delivered each year by a senior personality in the television world. However, the real business is done in the bar of the *George Hotel*, as producers, schedulers, performers and Fringe participants who want to get in on the act network and hustle like crazy. The Television Festival's presence in Edinburgh at this time adds focus and urgency to the Fringe's sub-plot

Finding out what's on

In addition to each festival's programme, there are various useful publications containing information about what's on day by day during the Festival. Every day the Fringe Office publishes *The Guide*, giving a chronological listing of virtually every Fringe show scheduled for that day. It's available free from the Office and hundreds of other spots around Edinburgh. Of the local newspapers, the best coverage is in *The Scotsman*, which issues an excellent daily Festival supplement. Their star-rating system and controversial *Page of Shame* – a weekly round-up of their critics' least favourite shows – carry a lot of weight. *The Herald*, published in Glasgow, also has good coverage. Most London-based newspapers print daily festival news and reviews, notably *The Guardian,* which publishes a daily Festival supplement, available only in Edinburgh. Many of the broadsheets sponsor at least one major event, venue or award. For a local view, the *Edinburgh Evening News* provides a no-nonsense round-up of news and festival issues.

Of the weeklies, *The List* gives the most sensible and comprehensive coverage, while *The Stage* and *Time Out* can be useful. For music, *The Gig Guide* can be picked up in most pubs – published monthly, it also includes local, non-Festival events.

There's also coverage of the Festival on radio and TV. **Radio Forth** (97.3FM), Edinburgh's independent local radio station, broadcasts up-to-the-minute news on ticket offers and the traffic situation, plus reviews and interviews with participants. **BBC Radio Scotland** (94.3FM and 810MW) and **BBC2 TV** cover the shiny end of the Festival spectrum. **Festival Revue**, live for twelve hours a day from Prince's Street Gardens, transmits over the Internet (*www.festivalrevue.com*), on cable TV and, sometimes, via satellite link-up with locations outside Edinburgh, including a big screen in London's Covent Garden.

as an employment showcase – in fact the event has such a direct bearing on subsequent viewing schedules that it has been said that if a bomb dropped on George Street over the Television Festival weekend, all the TV screens in Britain would probably go dark within a few weeks.

For **further details** contact the Guardian Edinburgh International Television Festival, 2nd Floor, 24 Neal St, London WC2 9PS (℡0207/379 4519, *www.arena-digital.co.uk/geitf-welcome.htm*).

EDINBURGH INTERNATIONAL JAZZ AND BLUES FESTIVAL

The **Edinburgh International Jazz and Blues Festival**, which used to run concurrently with the other festivals, now runs immediately prior to the Fringe in the first week in August, easing the city into the festival spirit with a full programme of gigs in many different locations. Just like all the other festivals, this one has grown over the years from a concentrated international summer camp to a bigger, more modern affair, reflecting the panoply of generations and styles which appear under the banner of jazz and blues. Scotland's own varied and vibrant jazz scene is always fully represented, and late-night clubs with atmosphere complement major concerts given by international stars. Past visitors have included BB King, Bill Wyman, Dizzy Gillespie, Dave Brubeck, Van Morrison, Carol Kidd, the Blues Band and many more. Highlights include Jazz On A Summer's Day, a musical extravaganza in Princes Street Gardens; and a colourful New Orleans–style street parade.

The **programme** is available at the end of May from the office at 29 St Stephen's St, EH3 5AN (℡0131/225 2202, *www.jazzmusic.co.uk*).

THE MILITARY TATTOO

Staged in the spectacular stadium setting of the Edinburgh Castle Esplanade, the **Military Tattoo** is the Festival showpiece most instantly recognized by tourists. An unashamed display of pomp and military pride, the Tattoo's programme of choreographed drills, massed pipe bands, historical tableaux, energetic battle re-enactments, national dancing and pyrotechnics has held audiences spellbound every year since it began over fifty years ago. The emotional climax is provided by a lone piper on the Castle battlements. Followed by a quick firework display (longer and more splendid on Sat), it's a successful formula barely tampered with over the years.

   Tickets need to be booked well in advance, and it's advisable to take a cushion and protective rainwear. Tickets and information are available from The Tattoo Office, 32 Market St, EH1 1QB (©0131/225 1188, *www.edintattoo.co.uk*).

THE EDINBURGH MELA

A festival within a festival, the **Edinburgh Mela** is held at Meadowbank Stadium, off London Road, just to the north of Holyrood Park, over the first weekend in September, coinciding with the finale of the International Festival. Truly a people's event, it was introduced to Edinburgh in the mid-1990s by the capital's Southeast Asian community. The word "Mela" is a Sanskrit term meaning "gathering", and is used to describe many different community events and festivals on the Asian subcontinent. In Edinburgh, the Mela is about cultural diversity, and the family-oriented programme is designed to celebrate the many different cultures resident in the city. Music, dance, foods, carnivals, fashion shows, sports, children's events, crafts and a two-day

A few Festival survival tips

1. Everyone else is completely bewildered too. Trust your judgement and ride your luck.

2. Accept that you're not going to see everything that sounds, or looks, or other people say is, good. Go and see something rather than spending two hours frozen by indecision. It's part of the Festival experience to sit through a complete turkey of a show while the one you nearly went to gets rave reviews, is sold out for three weeks, goes on national tour and spawns a hilarious, ground-breaking series on TV.

3. Don't try and see too much. Sometimes the best show is watching the world go by, and Edinburgh has plenty of non-Festival attractions, some of them free, such as climbing up Arthur's Seat and looking down on the madness below.

4. August weather in Edinburgh is notoriously fickle. Be prepared for both rain and sunshine.

5. Set a budget in advance and try to stick to it. Allow for outrageous temptations, because there will be plenty, and some of them will be worth it.

6. Don't give yourself a stiff neck starspotting – if they're that famous you'll see them on TV, and there are plenty more interesting people and places to look at.

7. Don't bother going to see anything with "searing" in the blurb. It will be ghastly.

8. Don't take front row seats in comedy shows unless you don't mind being material from the act.

9. Try to sleep at some point, even if it's during the day. The Festival works on LA time: if you try and stay on British Summertime you'll miss half the fun.

10. All sorts of people will offer you advice, recommendations, 10 survival tips, that sort of thing. Ignore them all and remember tip no. 1.

careers fair for school-leavers combine in a hectic programme of events designed to see the festival season out
with a bang rather than a whimper. Further **details** from
The Edinburgh Mela, 14 Forth St (✆0131/557 1400,
www.edinburgh-mela.co.uk).

Calendar of events

Though the Edinburgh Festival is a cultural binge of massive proportions, it doesn't quite leave Edinburgh spent for the other eleven months of the year. In addition to the regular diet of arts and entertainment, there are a variety of special **annual events**, including a famously riotous Hogmanay (New Year's Eve) party, international sporting events, as well as festivals of folk music, science and beer-drinking.

JANUARY

Hogmanay

A week-long series of events, culminating at midnight on 31st December, **Edinburgh's Hogmanay** (tickets and information from The Hub; ©0131/473 2000) is one of *the* places to see in the New Year. In the lead-up to the big day, look out for a Central Park-style outdoor ice rink in Princes Street Gardens, a Carnival on Waterloo Place, a torchlit procession along Princes Street and numerous late-night gigs and ceilidhs. On the night itself, most of the city-centre streets are closed to traffic, as big-name bands entertain the 200,000 strong crowds from various stages and the revels build up to a massive midnight climax, when a huge fireworks display is set off above the Castle.

Hogmanay in Edinburgh

In Scotland, much more than in other parts of Britain, **Hogmanay** has always furnished an excuse for some seriously uproarious revelling. This tradition has its roots in the sixteenth century, when the Protestant fathers of the Kirk discouraged the observance of Christmas, because of its associations with the pagan winter solstice celebrations; even up until the 1950s, many shops in Scotland remained open on Christmas Day. New Year's Eve provided an alternative for an annual national letting-off of steam, and it seems oddly apt that the celebrations have reached their apotheosis in Edinburgh, where the zealous Protestant reformer John Knox proselytized.

Edinburgh's New Year street parties were initially impromptu, the first official Hogmanay bash being organized in 1993, when 50,000 people turned out for three days of celebrations. Through word of mouth, the event grew to legendary proportions, with 300,000 people attending in 1995/6. Overcrowding, especially on the great thoroughfare of Princes Street, became a serious problem, and in 1996/7 the authorities instituted a system of free passes which limited the number of people in the city centre to 180,000. While this was a necessary step, it seems to have gone hand-in-hand with a tendency to commercialize the whole experience: the prospect of the "Bank of Scotland Torchlight Procession" may not exactly set your pulse racing. However, there's always enough going on in different parts of the city centre that Hogmanay in Edinburgh can feel like an Italian *passeggiata*, with crowds of people roaming the streets, looking for the action. The evening culminates in mass inebriated emotion when the bells finally sound and the celebratory fireworks are let off into the night sky above the Castle.

Turner Watercolours

January (when the light is weakest) is the only month of the year when you can see the splendid collection of **Turner watercolours** owned by the National Gallery on the Mound (see p.80). Entrance is free.

Rugby Internationals

Scotland's **rugby union** team plays in the annual Six Nations competition against England, France, Ireland, Italy and Wales. In any given year, matches against at least two of these countries are held at Murrayfield Stadium in the west of the city. The ground holds around 65,000 spectators, and has a terrific atmosphere when full. Tickets for all games sell out extremely quickly; contact the Scottish Rugby Union, 7–9 Roseburn St (℃0131/346 5000).

Puppet and Animation Festival

Shows are put on across central Scotland, in March. The main venue in Edinburgh is the Netherbow Theatre.

Edinburgh International Science Festival

Edinburgh has important connections with the world of science: the city is the home of John Napier, inventor of logarithms, James Clerk Maxwell, the "father of electronics", and James Hutton, founder of modern geology, as well as being the birthplace of Alexander Graham Bell, inventor of the telephone. These links helped inspire the establishment in the mid-1980s of the increasingly respected **Edinburgh International Science Festival** (℃0131/530 2001), which incorporates serious lectures on ground-breaking topics as well as hands-on children's events.

Shoots and Roots

A long-weekend folk festival with sessions in both April and November (℡0131/557 1050), drawing local and international performers. Plays at venues large and small around the city.

Beltane Fire Festival

Beltane is the name of the old **Celtic Festival** at the beginning of May, celebrating the arrival of spring. There's a New Agey feel to this festival, held on Calton Hill on the night of April 30 and May 1, the dominant images being fire-lighting and faces covered in woad. More conventionally, locals wash their faces in the dew on Arthur's Seat at dawn on May Day.

Scottish International Children's Festival

The **Children's Festival** (℡0131/225 8050) is a sort of mini-Edinburgh Festival for mini folk, with a lively line-up of book readings, magic shows, mime and puppetry in venues across the city.

Beer Festival

The **Beer Festival** is held at the Caledonian Brewery, 42 Slateford Rd, one of Scotland's finest independent beer-makers. Look out for their excellent 80 Shilling and award-winning IPA (India Pale Ale), pitted against a leg-wobbling line-up of real ales from around Britain.

Gay Film Festival

Celebration of **gay cinema** from around the world at the Filmhouse (℡0131/228 2688).

Royal Highland Show

Vast **agricultural fair** held at Ingliston, near the airport. Prize livestock and all sorts of agricultural machinery are on show, plus displays of everything from butter-making to show-jumping. There are green wellies and Range Rovers galore, but also flat caps and shepherd's crooks (©0131/335 6200).

AUGUST

The Edinburgh Festival

See the previous chapter for details of Edinburgh's world-famous three-week long festival.

SEPTEMBER

Open Doors Day

A great opportunity to visit a number of historically and architecturally interesting buildings, most of which are otherwise closed to the public. In recent years, these have included private homes in the New Town, disused churches, the Central Mosque and the marvellous Signet Library. Normally held over one of the last two weekends in September – look out for leaflets in public buildings or contact the Cockburn Association (©0131/557 8686) for details.

NOVEMBER

French Film Festival

A choice selection of old favourites and new work from **French cinema**, held at the Filmhouse (©0131/228 2688).

Shoots and Roots

Autumnal outing for this lively folk festival (see April, overleaf).

Directory

AIRLINES British Airways, 32 Frederick St (℡0345/ 222111); British Midland, Edinburgh Airport (℡0131/344 5600); easyJet (booking line ℡0870/600 0000); Ryanair (℡0541/569569).

AMERICAN EXPRESS 139 Princes St (Mon–Fri 9am–5.30pm, Sat 9am–4pm; ℡0131/225 9179).

BANKS Bank of Scotland, The Mound (head office), 38 St Andrew Square, 103 George St; Barclays, 1 St Andrew Square; Clydesdale, 20 Hanover St; Lloyds, 113–115 George St; HSBC, 76 Hanover St; NatWest, 80 George St; Royal Bank of Scotland, 36 St Andrew Square; TSB, 109 George St.

CAR RENTAL Arnold Clark, Lochrin Place (℡0131/228 4747); Avis, 100 Dalry Rd (℡0131/337 6363); Budget, 111 Glasgow Rd (℡0845/606 6669); Carnies, 46 Westfield Rd (℡0131/346 4155); Europcar, 24 East London St (℡0131/557 3456); Hertz, Waverley Station (℡0131/557 5272); Mitchells, 32 Torphichen St (℡0131/229 5384); Thrifty Car Rental, 24 Haymarket Terrace (℡0131/313 1613).

CONSULATES Australia, 37 George St (℡0131/624 3333); Canada, 30 Lothian Rd (℡0131/220 4333); Denmark, 4 Royal Terrace (℡0131/556 4263); France, 11 Randolph Crescent (℡0131/225 7954); Germany, 16 Eglinton Crescent (℡0131/337 2323); Italy, 32 Melville

St (℗0131/226 3631); Netherlands, 53 George St (℗0131/220 3226); Norway, 86 George St (℗0131/226 5701); Poland, 2 Kinnear Rd (℗0131/552 0301); Spain, 63 North Castle St (℗0131/220 1843); Sweden, 22 Hanover St (℗0131/220 6050); Switzerland, 66 Hanover Place (℗0131/226 5660); USA, 3 Regent Terrace (℗0131/556 8315).

DENTIST The National Health Service Line ℗0800/224488 will tell you where your nearest surgery is. For emergencies go to Edinburgh Dental Institute, Lauriston Place (℗0131/556 4913) or the Western General Hospital, Crewe Rd South (℗0131/537 1338).

EXCHANGE Thomas Cook, 28 Frederick St (Mon–Sat 9am–5.30pm; ℗0131/465 7600); currency exchange bureaux in the main tourist office (Mon–Wed 9am–5pm, Thurs–Sat 9am–6pm, Sun 10am–5pm) and beside platform 1 at Waverley Station (July–Aug Mon–Sat 7am–10pm, Sun 8am–10pm; Sept–June Mon–Sat 7.30pm–9pm, Sun 8.30pm–9pm). To change money after hours, try one of the upmarket hotels – but expect to pay a hefty commission charge.

FOOTBALL Edinburgh has two Scottish Premier Division teams, who are at home on alternate Sat. Heart of Midlothian (or Hearts) play at Tynecastle Stadium, Gorgie Rd, a couple of miles west of the centre; Hibernian (or Hibs) play at Easter Road Stadium, a similar distance east of the centre. Between them, the two clubs dominated Scottish football in the 1950s, but neither has won more than the odd trophy since, though one or the other periodically threatens to make a major breakthrough. Tickets from £12.

GENEALOGICAL RESEARCH Scots Ancestry Research Society, 29a Albany St (℗0131/556 4220); Scottish Genealogy Society, 15 Victoria Terrace (℗0131/220 3677); Scottish Roots, 16 Forth St (℗0131/477 8214).

GOLF Apart from several prestigious private golf courses in Edinburgh, there are also good public courses, the best being the pair on the Braid Hills (℗0131/447 6666); others are Carrick Knowe (℗0131/337 1096), Craigentinny (℗0131/554 7501), Silverknowes

(℡0131/336 3843) and Portobello, Stanley St (nine-hole; ℡0131/669 4361).

HOSPITAL Royal Infirmary, 1 Lauriston Place (℡0131/536 1000), has a 24hr casualty department.

LAUNDRY Capital Launderette, 208 Dalkeith Rd, Newington; Sundial Launderette at 7–9 East London St, Broughton; Tarvit Launderette, 7–9 Tarvit St, Tollcross.

LEFT LUGGAGE Lockers available at Waverley Station (Mon–Sat 7am–11pm, Sun 8am–11pm) and St Andrew Square bus station (Mon–Sat 6.35am–10pm, Sun 8am–10pm).

LIBRARIES Central Library, George IV Bridge (Mon–Thurs 10am–8pm, Fri 10am–5pm, Sat 9am–1pm; ℡0131/225 5584). In addition to the usual departments, there's a separate Scottish section, plus an Edinburgh Room which is a mine of information on the city. The National Library of Scotland, George IV Bridge (Mon–Fri 9.30am–8.30pm, Sat 9.30am–1pm; ℡0131/226 4531), a magnificent copyright library, is for research purposes only, although accreditation is necessary to use the facilities. There is freer access to an annex which contains the Map Room, 33 Salisbury Place (Mon–Fri 9.30am–5pm, Sat 9.30am–1pm).

LOST PROPERTY Edinburgh Airport (℡0131/333 1000); Edinburgh Police HQ (℡0131/311 3141); Lothian Regional Transport (℡0131/554 4492); Scotrail (℡0141/332 9811).

NEWSPAPERS *The Scotsman* is the city's quality daily paper with sound coverage of national and international news, and is strong on the arts. Its sister paper, the tabloid *Evening News*, hits the streets around midday and covers local Edinburgh news, while the sensationalist *Daily Record* is Scotland's most widely read tabloid. On Sundays, the pick of the wide range of heavies is the *Scotland on Sunday*, from the same stable as the *Scotsman*, though it's stronger on the arts and features than political round-ups.

PHARMACY Boots, 48 Shandwick Place (Mon–Fri 8am–9pm, Sat 8am–7pm, Sun 10am–5pm; ✆0131/225 6757) has the longest opening hours.

POLICE STATION In an emergency call 999. Otherwise contact Lothian and Borders Police HQ, Fettes Ave (✆0131/311 3131); or local police station at Queen Charlotte St, Leith (✆0131/554 9350); St Leonard's St, Southside (✆0131/662 500); or Torphichen Place, West End (✆0131/229 2323).

POST OFFICE 8–10 St James Centre (Mon 9am–5.30pm, Tues–Fri 8.30am–5.30pm, Sat 8.30am–6pm; ✆0345/223344).

RAPE CRISIS CENTRE ✆0131/556 9437.

RUGBY Scotland's international fixtures are played at Murrayfield Stadium, a couple of miles west of the city centre. Phone the stadium on ✆0131/346 5000 for advice on ticket sales, but be warned that tickets can be very hard to come by for the big games.

SPORTS STADIUM Meadowbank Sports Centre and Stadium, 139 London Rd (✆0131/661 5351), is Edinburgh's main venue for most spectator and participatory sports. Facilities include an athletics track, a velodrome and indoor halls.

SWIMMING POOLS The city has one Olympic-standard modern pool, the Royal Commonwealth Pool, 21 Dalkeith Rd (✆0131/667 7211), and a number of considerably older pools at Caledonian Crescent (✆0131/313 3964), Glenogle Rd (✆0131/343 6376), 15 Bellfield St, Portobello (✆0131/669 6888), and 6 Thirlestane Rd (✆0131/447 0052).

TRAVEL AGENTS USIT/Campus Travel (student and youth specialist), 53 Forrest Rd (✆0131/225 6111) and 5 Nicolson Square (✆0131/668 3303); Edinburgh Travel Centre (student and youth specialist), 196 Rose St (✆0131/226 2019) and 3 Bristo Square (✆0131/668 2221). For three- and six-day coach trips to the Highlands, try Haggis Backpackers, 11 Blackfriars St (✆0131/558 1177) or MacBackpackers, 105 High St (✆0131/558 9900).

CONTEXTS

History

Early settlement and the Middle Ages

The site of Edinburgh has been inhabited since the **Stone Age**; hunters and fishermen first came to the area around 5000 BC, followed two millennia later by farmers and shepherds. They in turn were succeeded by immigrant Beaker people from the continent, who introduced metalworking. In later periods of tribal warfare, forts were constructed on the extinct volcanic hills, notably **Castle Rock**. The rock's self-evident strategic value was of crucial importance in the subsequent rise of the city. This makes it seem all the more anomalous that the Romans, whose Imperial frontier lay just to the north, chose to build their fort close to the seashore at Cramond.

The name of Edinburgh – in its early forms of Dunedin or Din Eidyn ("Fort of Edin") – seems to have originated with the local tribes of the sixth century, rather than, as was long supposed, King Edwin of Northumbria, whose reign predated the **Northumbrian conquest** of the Lothians in 638 AD. Edinburgh subsequently remained under the control of English-speaking Anglo-Saxons until the middle of the tenth century, when it was abandoned to the army of King Indulf of Scotland.

Castle Rock served as the nation's **southernmost border post** until 1018, when King Malcolm I's victory over the Northumbrians established the River Tweed as the permanent frontier with England. Half a century later, under King Malcolm III and his queen Margaret, who replaced the indigenous Celtic church with Roman Catholicism, the castle became one of the main seats of the Scottish court. It was probably also around this time that a town, which was immediately given the privileged status of a **royal burgh**, first began to grow up on the sloping ridge immediately to the east of the castle.

Edinburgh's status grew further during the reign of Malcolm's and Margaret's son, David I, who established Holyrood Abbey at the foot of the slope in 1128, and shortly afterwards granted its monks permission to found a separate burgh, known as **Canongate**. David also founded a church in honour of St Giles on the present site of the High Kirk of St Giles, and built a chapel dedicated to his mother at the highest point of Castle Rock – where it stands to this day.

The Wars of Independence (1286–1371) were a turbulent time for Edinburgh, with the castle a prime target for any army invading from the south. During this period it was captured in turn by the armies of English kings Henry II, Edward I, Edward II and Edward III, and each time either relinquished as part of a treaty or retaken by the Scots. King Robert the Bruce's victory at Bannockburn in 1314, however, won Scotland a degree of security it had seldom enjoyed before, and trade with the continent began to prosper. Bruce granted Edinburgh a new charter in 1329, whereby the entire municipality, rather than its individual burgesses, was regarded as a vassal of the crown. He also gave it jurisdiction over the port of Leith, which was developed to take the place of the strategically vulnerable burgh of Berwick-upon-Tweed: the latter fell under English control four years later, and thereafter regularly passed backwards and forwards between the two countries. The prosperity brought by foreign trade enabled the newly fortified Edinburgh to establish itself as the undisputed capital of Scotland during the following century, with a fixed royal residence, central administration and law courts replacing the previous peripatetic setup.

Renaissance and Reformation

Under King James IV, the city enjoyed a short but brilliant **Renaissance era**. This saw not only the construction of a new residential palace alongside Holyrood Abbey, but also the granting of a royal charter to the College of Surgeons (the first of the city's long line of academic and professional bodies), and the establishment of the first printing press, which presaged an equally distinguished literary and publishing tradition.

This golden period came to an abrupt end in 1513 with the calamitous defeat of the Scots by the English at the Battle of Flodden, which led to several decades of political instability. Panicked by the prospect of the English army marching north from Flodden, the citizens of Edinburgh hurriedly began building a defensive wall around the town. The English didn't advance, however, and the wall was only completed in 1560, but this "**Flodden Wall**" was to serve as the city boundary for the next two centuries, in which time the population rose from 10,000 to 30,000, forcing the tenement houses higher and higher.

In 1542, the Scots suffered another punishing defeat at the hands of the English at the battle of **Solway Moss**. News of the defeat crushed the dying king, James V, and even the news of the birth of a daughter could not revive his spirit. He died on December 14, 1542, leaving his three-week-old daughter Mary as Queen of Scots. Quick to see an opportunity, King Henry VIII of England attempted to force a royal union (the so-called "Rough Wooing") by having his son Edward pledged in marriage to the infant Mary, which prompted the Scots to turn to France for help: French troops arrived to defend the city, while the young queen was despatched to Paris as the promised bride of the Dauphin.

Although the French occupiers succeeded in removing the English threat, they themselves antagonized the local citizenry, which had increasingly become sympathetic to the ideals of the **Reformation**. When the great preacher John Knox was allowed to return from exile in 1555, he became minister of Edinburgh's parish church, the High Kirk of St Giles, and quickly won the city over to his radical Calvinist message. A Protestant league, the Lords of the Congregation, appealed to Queen Elizabeth I of England for help, and in 1560, the French were driven out and Scotland proclaimed a Protestant nation.

The unions with England

Mary returned from France in 1561, but her fervent Catholicism was instrumental in dooming her reign to the status of a melodramatic interlude, and she was deposed in favour of her son, James VI. His rule saw the foundation of the University of Edinburgh in 1582 – giving Scotland its fourth institution of higher learning, a total England did not match until well into the nineteenth century. However, James's dynastic ambitions, resulting in his nomination as heir to the English throne, were to prove fateful for the city. Following the Union of the Crowns in 1603, when James succeeded Elizabeth to become James I of England, Edinburgh found itself totally upstaged by London: although the king promised to visit his northern capital every three years, it was not until 1617 that he made his one and only return trip.

In 1633, his son Charles I came to Edinburgh to be crowned, but soon afterwards precipitated a crisis by introducing episcopacy to the Church of Scotland, in the process making Edinburgh a bishopric for the first time in its history, with St Giles as its cathedral. This prompted a number of leading figures in Scotland to draw up a National Covenant in support of Presbyterianism. It was signed by thousands of townsfolk as well as important nobles in Greyfriars churchyard in 1638. An army dedicated to upholding the Covenant was sent to fight on the royalist side in the English Civil War. Cromwell's army arrived in Edinburgh in 1650, laying waste to many buildings, including Holyroodhouse, the High School and Greyfriars. Following the restoration of the monarchy, the brother of Charles II, James, Duke of York, moved into the rebuilt Holyroodhouse, but when he succeded to the English throne as James II of England (and James VII of Scotland), his overt Catholicism proved too much even for the Scots' loyalty to a Stewart monarch, and the English-nominated Dutch Protestant William III was reluctantly accepted as king north of the border as well as south, as James fled to France in 1689.

Despite these vicissitudes, Edinburgh expanded throughout the seventeenth century, with a virtual tripling of its population to 57,000. The capital was proving itself an important catalyst for significant developments in many fields. In 1674, the Advocates' Library in Parliament Square was founded as a focal point for the legal profession, to be followed in 1681 by Lord Stair's *Institutions of the Law of Scotland*, a tome still regarded as the definitive bedrock of Scots Law. In the same year the Royal College of Physicians was established in Edinburgh, while in 1695, William Paterson, who had founded the Bank of England the previous year, set up the Bank of Scotland. This was to be the first major step in Edinburgh's development as an international financial centre.

The much-debated **Union of the Parliaments** of 1707 dealt a further blow to Edinburgh's political prestige, though the guaranteed preservation of the national church, the distinctive legal and educational systems, and the special status of the royal burghs, ensured that it was never relegated to a purely provincial role.

The Enlightenment

Paradoxical as it may seem following the internal struggles within Scotland and the loss of political power to London, it was in the second half of the eighteenth century that

Edinburgh achieved the height of its influence, becoming a leading centre of the European **Enlightenment**. Internationally celebrated as, in the words of eighteenth-century novelist Tobias Smollett, "a hotbed of genius", it was home to a host of intellectual luminaries, including the philosopher and historian David Hume, the scientist James Hutton (founder of modern geology), and Adam Smith, father figure of the new discipline of political economy. Inspired by the ideals of the Age of Reason, and under the leadership of a dynamic Lord Provost, George Drummond, the city belatedly began to expand beyond its cramped medieval boundaries. Following a public competition, a plan by James Craig was accepted in 1766 as the basis for the laying out of a **New Town** on a gridiron plan to the north of Castle Ridge. The result, one of the masterpieces of the European Neoclassical style, was so successful that separate northern, western and eastern extensions were made in the early nineteenth century.

Edinburgh's lofty intellectual reputation was maintained until well into the new century, and the city's greatest artist, Sir Henry Raeburn, immortalized the features of most of its leading figures in a magnificent series of portraits. The dominant figure of the era's last phase was the novelist and poet **Sir Walter Scott**, whose influence is almost impossible to exaggerate: his highly individual, extremely romantic vision of Scotland and its history inspired many of the greatest European writers, artists and composers of the nineteenth century, and (for good or ill) became implanted on popular imagination throughout the world.

The expansion of the city

Nineteenth-century **industrialization** affected Edinburgh less than any other major city in the British Isles, and it never lost its predominantly professional character. The industries which took a hold, such as brewing, distilling, confectionery and glass manufacturing, caused relatively little damage to the environment, and even the railway lines were concealed by the city's topography. Edinburgh lost its longstanding position as Scotland's largest city to Glasgow, which mushroomed into one of the industrial strongholds of the British Empire. Ever since then an intense rivalry has characterized relations between these two geographically close and mutually dependent (yet quite different) cities. Nonetheless, Edinburgh's status as capital was never threatened, and it became the automatic choice as headquarters for the national institutions which were founded in the course of the century.

The city underwent an enormous **urban expansion** in the nineteenth century. The old burghs of Canongate, Calton and Portsburgh were incorporated into Edinburgh in 1856; the seaside resort of Portobello was added forty years later, and various new residential suburbs sprang up. In the meantime, the Old Town, which had become notorious for its overcrowding and disease, was revitalized through the initiatives of the crusading conservationist and town planner, Patrick Geddes.

In 1920, the city boundaries were extended once again, reaching to Cramond in the west and the Pentland Hills in the south. Despite considerable local opposition, the port of Leith – which just over a century before had gained full municipal independence and thereafter developed into one of Scotland's largest towns – was annexed as well. Another important development was the **administrative devolution** granted just before World War II, whereby the Scottish Office was established in Edinburgh, replacing several UK ministries in the day-to-day running of the nation's internal affairs.

The postwar city

Edinburgh came through the war unscathed, and received another major fillip in 1947 when it was chosen as the permanent home for the great **International Festival** of music and drama which was established as a symbol of the new peaceful European order. Despite some hiccups, this has flourished ever since, in the process helping to make tourism one of the mainstays of the local economy. The **Fringe**, originally set up as an adjunct to the main event, now ranks as the world's largest arts event in its own right, and several specialist festivals, which run concurrently, have likewise become established annual events.

Edinburgh has also been fortunate enough to escape the worst effects of the postwar **planning** policies which blighted so many British cities. There have been some unfortunate losses, notably much of George Square, which was torn down to make way for the tower blocks required by the fast-expanding University, and many fine shop fronts on the north side of Princes Street, sacrificed to chain-store uniformity. At the east end of the latter, the hideous St James Centre and New St Andrew House are blots on the magnificent cityscape, though things would have been much worse had plans for an inner-city ring road come to fruition. In 1975, Edinburgh carried out its latest territorial expansion, moving its boundaries westwards as far as the old burgh of South Queensferry and the Forth Bridges.

Four years later, with Scottish Nationalism in the ascendant, the Labour government proposed a scheme for **political devolution**, whereby the activities of the Scottish Office would be subject to an elected assembly in Edinburgh. This was put to a referendum, but, although the scheme narrowly won a majority of votes cast, it failed to gain the required support of forty percent of the electorate. The Conservative government which took office later the same year was implacably opposed to the idea of devolution – a hardline stance which eventually had the reverse of its desired effect. As the Tories kept winning election after election in England, so their support in Scotland dwindled, and the opposition parties became united in their determination to introduce some form of home rule. In May 1997, Edinburgh, along with the rest of Scotland, voted out its remaining Conservative MPs, as the Labour Party swept to power and Tony Blair, who had attended Fettes College boarding school in Edinburgh, became Prime Minister. In the referendum held in September of the same year there was a large majority in favour of the government's proposal to establish a parliament in Edinburgh.

Elections were held in May 1999, with Edinburgh voting in among its representatives David Steel, a former leader of the British Liberal Party who was subsequently chosen as Presiding Officer (or Speaker) of the Parliament; and the first Green Party candidate to be elected to a national parliament in Britain. On July 1 of the same year, on a day which saw crowds lining the streets of Edinburgh and fireworks bursting above the Castle after a night of city-centre parties, the Queen officially opened the parliament, Scotland's first in nearly three hundred years. Initially, the parliament is meeting in the General Assembly Hall of the Church of Scotland, just off the Lawnmarket, while the construction of a purpose-built parliament chamber and offices takes place at the foot of the Royal Mile opposite Holyroodhouse. The new building is eagerly awaited, not simply for the importance it will have as the heart of political life in Scotland, but also in the anticipation that its design and impact will admit it to the ranks of highly regarded public buildings which have come to Edinburgh in recent years and which include the National Museum of Scotland on Chambers Street and the vast Scottish Office complex at Commercial Quay in Leith. Meanwhile, the presence of Scotland's decision-makers on the streets of the capital, together with the media attention they inevitably draw, the international importance of many

THE POSTWAR CITY

Edinburgh-based banks and financial institutions, the continued success of the Festival and the high profile being enjoyed by a number of actors, authors and politicians with Edinburgh connections, all combine to give the city a vitality and sense of importance it has arguably not seen since the days of Sir Walter Scott.

Film

In spite of the city's photogenic qualities, surprisingly few **films** have been made entirely in Edinburgh. The city has been used more often to provide an elegant setting for isolated scenes: the *Café Royal* and Arthur's Seat were used in the Oscar-winning *Chariots of Fire*; the 1995 film *Jude* featured Parliament Square, used in place of the too-modern-looking Oxford; and the Royal Mile appeared in *Mary Reilly*, a disastrous version of *Jekyll & Hyde* starring John Malkovich and Julia Roberts. The huge success of *Trainspotting,* however, has led to a rack of Edinburgh-made films in recent years, including *Complicity*, based on an Iain Banks novel, and *The Acid House*, a rather less successful adaptation of another Irvine Welsh novel. The following are the pick of the movies with an Edinburgh setting.

Waverley Steps (John Eldridge, 1947). A hangover from World War II propaganda, this "Lets-all-get-on-together" documentary shows postwar life in the capital, social differences and all, through the eyes of a visiting Danish sailor.

Happy Go Lovely (Bruce Humberstone, 1950). Millionaire David Niven and chorus girl Vera Ellen get together during the Edinburgh Festival.

Battle of the Sexes (Charles Crichton, 1959). Ealing-style comedy, based on a short story by James Thurber, in which a mild-mannered Peter Sellers seeks to disrupt an efficiency drive at an Edinburgh tweed factory led by Constance Cummings.

Greyfriars Bobby (Don Chaffey, 1960). No prizes for guessing which American company, well-known for classic anthropomorphic cartoons, made this version of Edinburgh's most sentimental tale, previously filmed in 1949 as *Challenge to Lassie*. Although there were too many TV aerials in the environs of Greyfriars Kirk to allow filming, local actors were used, including Donald Crisp as the dog's owner and Andrew Cruickshank as the city's Lord Provost.

The Prime of Miss Jean Brodie (Ronald Neame, 1969). Maggie Smith won an Oscar for her portrayal of the eccentric teacher in this well-regarded version of Muriel Spark's classic tale of life in an Edinburgh girls' school.

My Childhood, **My Ain Folk** and **My Way Home** (Bill Douglas, 1972–78). Powerful, moving and unremittingly bleak trilogy of films on growing up in the mining town of Newcraighall, on the eastern tip of the city. Sadly, Douglas died in 1991 never having filmed his screenplay of James Hogg's *Confessions of a Justified Sinner*.

Restless Natives (Michael Hoffman, 1985). Comic tale of a couple of young lads from an Edinburgh housing scheme who hold up American tourists and become celebrities.

Tickets to the Zoo (Brian Crumlish, 1994). A look at the problems caused by youth unemployment in the Eighties, set in Costorphine and Leith.

Shallow Grave (Danny Boyle, 1995). Three Edinburgh yuppies get lucky then squabble over the proceeds in a patchy film noir. The exciting opening sequence shows a car racing through the New Town.

Trainspotting (Danny Boyle, 1996). This hugely successful film version of Irvine Welsh's best-selling novel of Edinburgh lowlife kicks off with a great chase along Princes Street.

Complicity (Gavin Millar, 1999). A thriller based on one of the novels of South Queensferry's Iain Banks, starring Jonny Lee Miller as a journalist on an Edinburgh newspaper.

Women Talking Dirty (Coky Giedroyc, 1999). Set in Edinburgh suburbia, the funny and poignant soul-baring of two women who become fast friends over a bottle of vodka and detailed post-match analysis. Stars Helena Bonham Carter.

FILM

Books

Many of the **books** listed below are in print and in paper-back – those that are out of print (o/p) should be easy to track down in secondhand bookshops. Publishers follow each title; first the UK publisher, then the US. Only one publisher is listed if the UK and US publishers are the same. Where books are published in only one of these countries, UK or US comes after the publisher's name.

Fiction

Iain Banks, *Complicity* (Abacus; Bantam). Typically lurid tale by Scotland's best contemporary author, dealing with a journalist on *The Caledonian* (a barely disguised *Scotsman*) himself caught up in paranoia and misdeeds. Also look out for *The Bridge* (Abacus; Bantam), centring on the Forth Rail Bridge and Banks' home town, South Queensferry.

Pat Barker, *Regeneration* (Penguin; NAL Dutton). First part of the prize-winning trilogy based on the real-life meeting of Siegfried Sassoon and Wilfred Owen in Edinburgh's Craiglockhart Hospital, where the two try to come to terms with the horrors they have witnessed in the trenches.

Christopher Brookmyre, *Quite Ugly One Morning* (Abacus, UK). Cynical investigative journalist, Jack Parlabane, sorts out skullduggery in an Edinburgh NHS trust hospital in a hard-boiled post-Irvine Welsh novel.

Isla Dewar, *Women Talking Dirty* (Headline Review, UK). Two women, both recognizable Edinburgh stereotypes, but unlikely friends, indulge in some gently amusing reflections on their lives, loves and relationships.

James Hogg, *Confessions of a Justified Sinner* (Penguin). First published in 1824, a scary tale of the inner torments of the human psyche; an inspiration for much later Scottish fiction.

Paul Johnston, *Body Politic* (New English Library, UK). Blues fanatic private investigator Quentin Dalrymple handles a series of grisly murders in the brave new world of 2020 AD when Edinburgh, the only stable city in the British Isles, exists largely to serve a massive tourist industry.

Eric Linklater, *Magnus Merriman* (Canongate). Vivid descriptions of Edinburgh landmarks in this humorous satire of the Scottish literary and political world of the 1930s.

Ian Rankin, *Knots and Crosses* (Coronet o/p; St Martin's Press), *Hide and Seek* (Coronet o/p; Simon & Schuster). Jazz-loving copper John Rebus trawls through Edinburgh lowlife.

Sir Walter Scott, *The Waverley Novels* (Penguin). The books that did much to create the romanticized version of Scottish life and history.

Muriel Spark, *The Prime of Miss Jean Brodie* (Penguin/NAL Dutton). One of the most famous Edinburgh novels of the twentieth century, superbly evoking the world of middle-class Edinburgh inhabited by strict schoolteacher Jean Brodie.

Robert Louis Stevenson, *The Scottish Stories and Essays* (Edinburgh University Press); *Dr Jekyll & Mr Hyde* (Penguin). The former includes "The Misadventures of John Nicholson", an entertaining account of an innocent's escapades, and the grisly "The Body Snatchers". Though nominally set in London, Stevenson's classic, and still resonant, horror story of Jekyll and Hyde is generally considered to be based on the author's misspent youth in the bowels of Edinburgh's Old Town.

Alan Warner, *The Sopranos* (Jonathan Cape, UK). Riotous account of the arrival of a group of girls from a convent school in the West Highlands for a choir competition in Edinburgh, and their determined efforts to find out what the big city has to offer in the way of sex, drugs, rock'n'roll and shopping.

Irvine Welsh, *Trainspotting* (Minerva; Heinemann). No-holds-barred account of Nineties Edinburgh lowlife; sordid and guttural. *Marabou Stork Nightmares* (Vintage; Norton) is similarly gross but has more of a plot. *Ecstasy* (Vintage; Norton), a collection of three novellas published in 1996 at the height of *Trainspotting* fever, covered the same ground and suggested either a rushed job or that Welsh was beginning to run out of ideas.

History and biography

Robert Chambers, *Traditions of Edinburgh 1824* (Chambers). An
extraordinary collection of lively tales, many of which would today
count as urban myths, about the Old Town streets and closes.

David Daiches, *Two Worlds* (Canongate, UK); *Edinburgh*
(Constable, UK). The first is a very dry account of growing up in
Edinburgh in the 1920s as the son of the city's chief rabbi.
Glimpses of a lost world with its own hybrid language, Scottish
Yiddish, now long vanished. A single-volume history full of
entertaining material, *Edinburgh* is especially strong on the city's
literary history.

Charles McKean, *Edinburgh: Portrait of a City* (Century o/p, UK). A
short, elegantly written account of the city's history.

Eileen Miller, *The Edinburgh International Festival 1947–1996*.
(Scolar Press). Dry account of the history of the Festival; includes
cast lists for every major production over the period.

Sandy Mullay, *The Edinburgh Encyclopedia* (Mainstream, UK). For
the completist, a huge amount of detail about every corner of
Edinburgh's history, from the colours of school rugby shirts to
listings of all the city's MPs.

Tim Niel and Allan Campbell (eds), *A Life in Pieces – Reflections
on Alexander Trocchi* (Canongate, UK). Biographical essays,
interviews and stories about Edinburgh's controversial, drug-
fuelled Beat writer of the 1960s.

Sir Walter Scott, *Journal* (Canongate, UK). A hefty but incredibly
eloquent and honest diary set mainly in Edinburgh and the
Borders, covering the years from the height of the great novelist's
success through to his debt- and illness-ridden final years.

Art and architecture

John Gifford, Colin McWilliam and David Walker, *The Buildings of
Scotland: Edinburgh* (Penguin, UK). Scholarly architectural
account of the city's buildings. Critical where necessary, but full of
praise for the great monuments of the Old and New Towns.

Duncan Macmillan, *Scottish Art 1460-1990* (Mainstream).
Authoritative and up-to-date guide through the history of Scottish
art, with all the big names receiving due attention.

Charles McKean, *Edinburgh: An Illustrated Architectural Guide*
(RIAS Publications). A beautifully produced, slim guide to
Edinburgh's buildings, full of pertinent and judicious comments
and quotations.

Robert Louis Stevenson, *Edinburgh: Picturesque Notes* (Barnes &
Noble). This collection of beautifully crafted vignettes couched in
hyper-refined prose is considered by most experts to be the finest
book ever written about Edinburgh.

A.J. Youngson, *The Making of Classical Edinburgh* (Edinburgh
University Press; Colorado University Press). Full account, with
wonderful illustrations, of the creation of the New Town.

INDEX

T

U

V

W

Z

Stay in touch with us!

ROUGH*NEWS* is Rough Guides' free newsletter.
In four issues a year we give you news, travel issues, music reviews, readers' letters and the latest dispatches from authors on the road.

I would like to receive ROUGH*NEWS*: please put me on your free mailing list.

NAME . . . .

ADDRESS . . . .

Please clip or photocopy and send to: Rough Guides, 62-70 Shorts Gardens, London WC2H 9AB, England

or Rough Guides, 375 Hudson Street, New York, NY 10014, USA.

ROUGH GUIDES: Travel

ROUGH GUIDES:
Reference and Music CDs

REFERENCE
Classical Music
Classical:
   100 Essential CDs
Drum'n'bass
House Music

World Music:
   100 Essential CDs
English Football
European Football
Internet
Millennium

**ROUGH GUIDE
MUSIC CDs**
Music of the Andes
Australian
   Aboriginal
Brazilian Music
Cajun & Zydeco
Classic Jazz
Music of Colombia
Cuban Music
Eastern Europe
Music of Egypt
English Roots
   Music
Flamenco
India & Pakistan
Irish Music
Music of Japan
Kenya & Tanzania
Native American
North African
Music of Portugal

Jazz
Music USA
Opera
Opera:
   100 Essential CDs
Reggae
Rock
Rock:
   100 Essential CDs
Techno
World Music

Reggae
Salsa
Scottish Music
South African
   Music
Music of Spain
Tango
Tex-Mex
West African Music
World Music
World Music Vol 2
Music of Zimbabwe

AVAILABLE AT ALL GOOD BOOKSHOPS

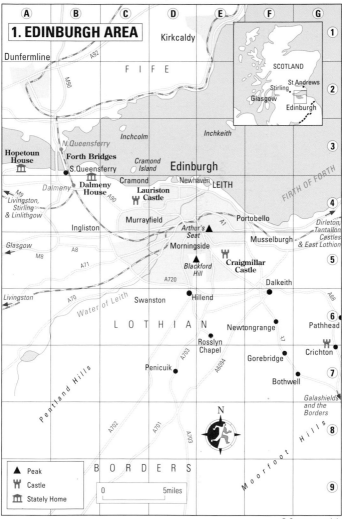

1. EDINBURGH AREA

Kirkcaldy

Dunfermline

FIFE

SCOTLAND

St Andrews

Stirling

Glasgow

Edinburgh

Inchcolm

Inchkeith

N.Queensferry

Hopetoun House

Forth Bridges

S.Queensferry

Cramond Island

Edinburgh

Dalmeny

Cramond

Newhaven

LEITH

FIRTH OF FORTH

Dalmeny House

Lauriston Castle

Livingston, Stirling & Linlithgow

Ingliston

Murrayfield

Arthur's Seat

Portobello

Dirleton, Tantallon Castles & East Lothian

Glasgow

Morningside

Musselburgh

Blackford Hill

Craigmillar Castle

Dalkeith

Livingston

Water of Leith

Swanston

Hillend

LOTHIAN

Newtongrange

Pathhead

Rosslyn Chapel

Gorebridge

Crichton

Penicuik

Bothwell

Galashields and the Borders

Pentland Hills

N

Moorfoot Hills

BORDERS

▲	Peak
♜	Castle
🏛	Stately Home

0   5miles

© Crown copyright

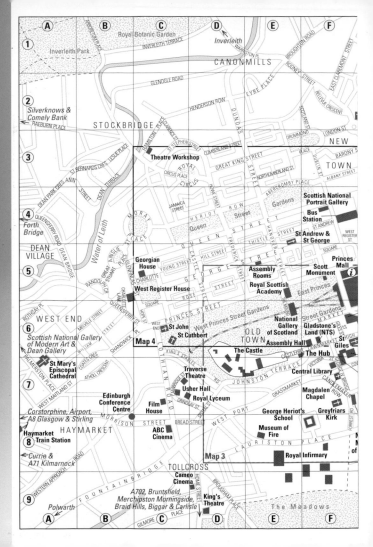

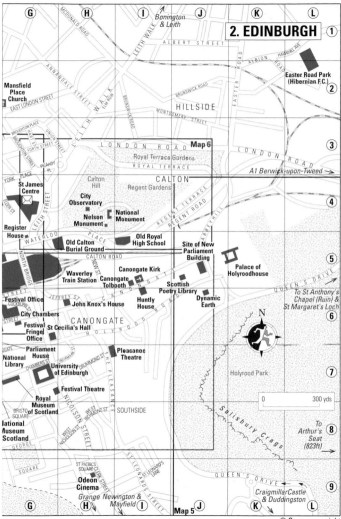

Bonington & Leith

MCDONALD ROAD

ALBERT STREET

ALBION ROAD

HAWKHILL AVE.

Easter Road Park (Hibernian F.C.)

EASTER ROAD

LEITH WALK

ANNANDALE STREET

BRUNSWICK ROAD

BRUNSWICK ROAD

MONTGOMERY STREET

HILLSIDE

Mansfield Place Church

EAST LONDON STREET

ELM ROW

BROUGHTON PLACE

NORTH STREET

UNION STREET

LONDON ROAD

Map 6

LONDON ROAD

BROUGHTON STREET

PICARDY PL.

Royal Terrace Gardens

ROYAL TERRACE

A1 Berwick-upon-Tweed →

YORK PLACE

Calton Hill

CALTON

Regent Gardens

REGENT TERRACE

St James Centre

LEITH STREET

City Observatory

National Monument

REGENT ROAD

Register House

WATERLOO PLACE

Nelson Monument

ABBEY HILL

NORTH BRIDGE

Old Calton Burial Ground

CALTON ROAD

Old Royal High School

Site of New Parliament Building

Palace of Holyroodhouse

QUEEN'S DRIVE

Waverley Train Station

Canongate Kirk

Canongate Tolbooth

Scottish Poetry Library

To St Anthony's Chapel (Ruin) & St Margaret's Loch →

JEFFREY ST.

CANONGATE

HOLYROOD ROAD

Festival Office

COCKBURN ST.

John Knox's House

Huntly House

Dynamic Earth

City Chambers

Festival Fringe Office

St Cecilia's Hall

N

Parliament House

Pleasance Theatre

THE PLEASANCE

CANONGATE

National Library

University of Edinburgh

DRUMMOND ST.

Holyrood Park

Festival Theatre

Royal Museum of Scotland

NICOLSON STREET

WEST RICHMOND ST.

SOUTHSIDE

0   300 yds

National Museum Scotland

GEORGE SQUARE

Salisbury Crags

To Arthur's Seat (823ft)

ST PATRICK SQUARE

ST LEONARD'S LANE

ST LEONARD'S STREET

QUEEN'S DRIVE

Odeon Cinema

Grange Newington & Mayfield

WEST NICOLSON STREET

CraigmillarCastle & Duddingston

Map 5

© Crown copyright

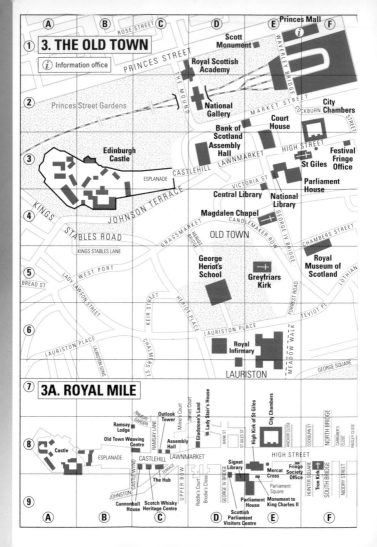

3. THE OLD TOWN

ⓘ Information office

A **B** ROSE STREET **C** **D** **E** Princes Mall **F**

1

Scott Monument

PRINCES STREET

Royal Scottish Academy

THE MOUND

WAVERLEY BRIDGE

2

Princes Street Gardens

MARKET STREET

COCKBURN STREET

National Gallery

City Chambers

Bank of Scotland Assembly Hall

Court House

3

Edinburgh Castle

CASTLEHILL

LAWNMARKET

HIGH STREET

St Giles

Festival Fringe Office

Parliament House

ESPLANADE

VICTORIA ST

GEORGE IV BRIDGE

4

KINGS

STABLES ROAD

JOHNSON TERRACE

Central Library

National Library

Magdalen Chapel

CANDLEMAKER ROW

KINGS STABLES LANE

GRASSMARKET

MERCHANT BRIDGE

OLD TOWN

CHAMBERS STREET

5

BREAD ST

WEST PORT

LADY LAWSON STREET

KEIR STREET

HERIOT PLACE

George Heriot's School

Greyfriars Kirk

FORREST ROAD

Royal Museum of Scotland

LOTHIAN

TEVIOT PL

6

LAURISTON PLACE

LAURISTON GDNS

CHALMERS ST

LAURISTON PLACE

Royal Infirmary

MEADOW WALK

GEORGE SQUARE

LAURISTON

7 # 3A. ROYAL MILE

8

Castle

RAMSAY GARDEN

Ramsay Lodge

Outlook Tower

Old Town Weaving Centre

Assembly Hall

Milne's Court

James Court

Gladstone's Land

Lady Stair's House

BANK ST

ST GILES ST

High Kirk of St Giles

City Chambers

ANCHOR CLOSE

COCKBURN ST

NORTH BRIDGE

CARRUBER'S CLOSE

PAISLEY CLOSE

ESPLANADE

CASTLEHILL

LAWNMARKET

HIGH STREET

RAMSAY LANE

TERRACE

CASTLEWYND

UPPER BOW

9

JOHNSTON

Cannonball House

The Hub

Scotch Whisky Heritage Centre

Riddle's Court

Brodie's Close

GEORGE IV BRIDGE

Scottish Parliament Visitors Centre

Signet Library

Parliament House

Mercat Cross

Parliament Square

Monument to King Charles II

Fringe Society Office

HUNTER SQUARE

Tron Kirk

SOUTH BRIDGE

NIDDRIE STREET

A **B** **C** **D** **E** **F**

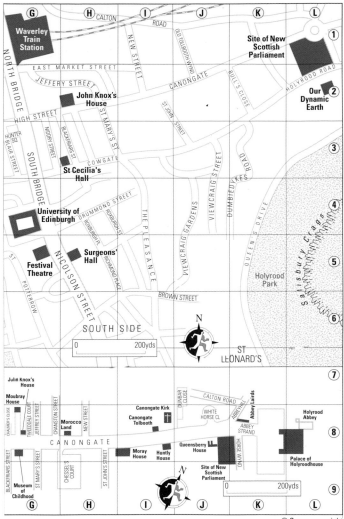

© Crown copyright

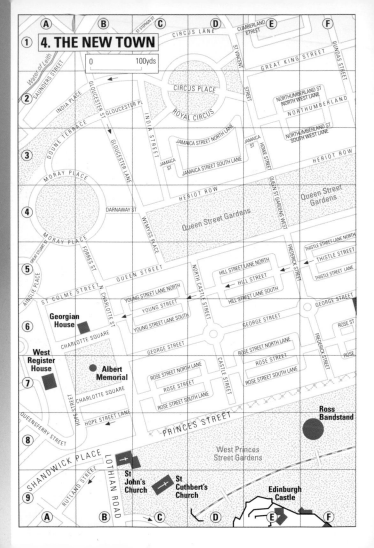

4. THE NEW TOWN

0   100yds

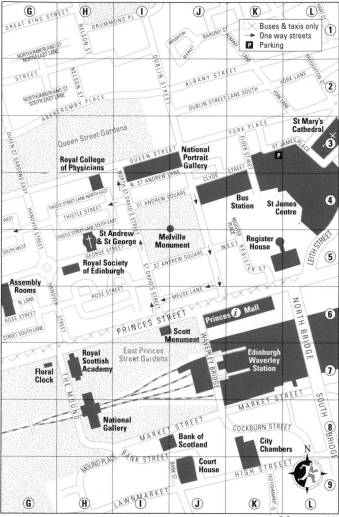

© Crown copyright

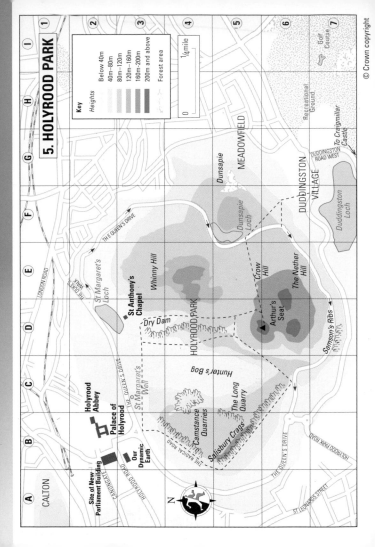

5. HOLYROOD PARK

Key

Heights
- Below 40m
- 40m–80m
- 80m–120m
- 120m–160m
- 160m–200m
- 200m and above
- Forest area

0   ¼ mile

© Crown copyright

CALTON

Site of New Parliament Building

Holyrood Abbey

Palace of Holyrood

Our Dynamic Earth

HOLYROOD ROAD

CANONGATE

LONDON ROAD

THE DUKE'S WALK

St Margaret's Loch

THE QUEEN'S DRIVE

St Margaret's Well

St Anthony's Chapel

Whinny Hill

Dry Dam

HOLYROOD PARK

Hunter's Bog

Camstance Quarries

The Long Quarry

THE RADICAL ROAD

Salisbury Crags

Samson's Ribs

Arthur's Seat

Crow Hill

The Nether Hill

Dunsapie

Dunsapie Loch

MEADOWFIELD

DUDDINGSTON

DUDDINGSTON VILLAGE

DUDDINGSTON ROAD WEST

Duddingston Loch

To Craigmillar Castle

Recreational Ground

Golf Course

THE QUEEN'S DRIVE

HOLYROOD PARK ROAD

ST LEONARD'S STREET

N

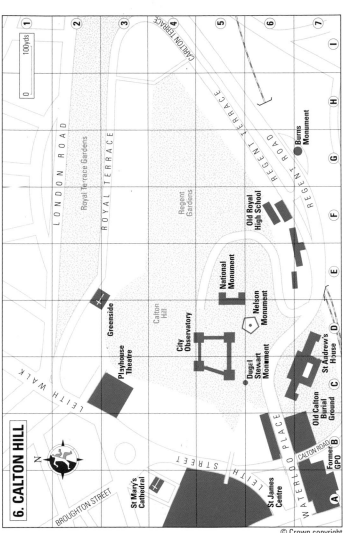

6. CALTON HILL

N

0 100yds

LEITH WALK

BROUGHTON STREET

St Mary's Cathedral

Playhouse Theatre

Greenside

LONDON ROAD

Royal Terrace Gardens

ROYAL TERRACE

Regent Gardens

CARLTON TERRACE

Calton Hill

City Observatory

National Monument

Dugald Stewart Monument

Nelson Monument

Old Royal High School

REGENT TERRACE

REGENT ROAD

Burns Monument

St Andrew's House

LEITH STREET

St James Centre

WATERLOO PLACE

Old Calton Burial Ground

CALTON ROAD

Former GPO

© Crown copyright

A   B   C   D   E   F   G   H   I

1   2   3   4   5   6   7

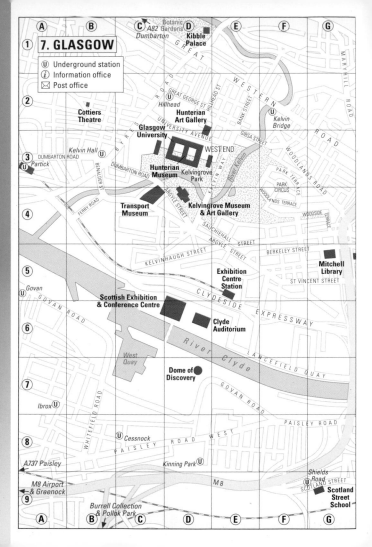

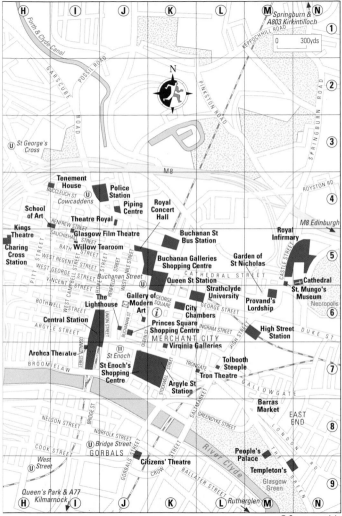

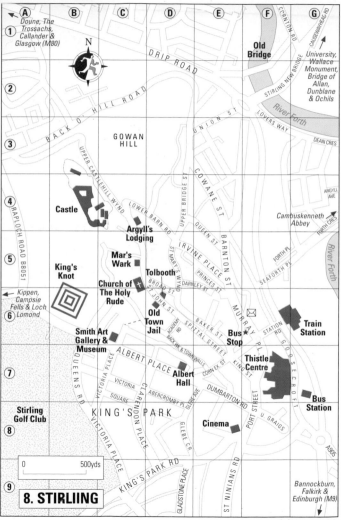

8. STIRLING